D1568312

FOREIGN INVESTMENT LAW

IN A NUTSHELL®

RALPH H. FOLSOM
Professor of Law
University of San Diego School of Law

WEST
ACADEMIC
PUBLISHING

The publisher is not engaged in rendering legal or other professional advice, and this publication is not a substitute for the advice of an attorney. If you require legal or other expert advice, you should seek the services of a competent attorney or other professional.

Nutshell Series, In a Nutshell and the Nutshell Logo are trademarks registered in the U.S. Patent and Trademark Office.

© 2016 LEG, Inc. d/b/a West Academic
    444 Cedar Street, Suite 700
    St. Paul, MN 55101
    1-877-888-1330

West, West Academic Publishing, and West Academic are trademarks of West Publishing Corporation, used under license.

Printed in the United States of America

ISBN: 978-1-63460-283-9

PREFACE

Foreign investment is commonplace around the globe. Inbound and outbound foreign investment flows are massive, with home country investors merging or acquiring existing host nation businesses or establishing new companies abroad. Foreign investors also purchase stocks and bonds on numerous exchanges, and sometimes foreign sovereign debt. The sums involved are staggering.

Foreign Investment Law in a Nutshell examines the law, practice, regulation and dispute settlement of foreign investment. Unlike international trade law, which is governed significantly by the World Trade Organization, no uniform body of foreign investment law exists. There is no "World Investment Organization". Hence foreign investment law is predominantly national in character and varies considerably.

After introducing entry and operational control patterns found primarily in the developing world, and expropriation risks and insurance, this Nutshell focuses on investing in China, Europe and North America as "case studies". It also explores the multitude of foreign investment treaties (BITs) and the dynamic law of NAFTA on foreign investment. Controversial BIT and NAFTA foreign investor-host state arbitration systems for disputes are closely examined.

Following the Nutshell tradition, citations are minimized. This creates a book that reads easily and is suitable for law, business and undergraduate studies. Students and professors who enjoy this Nutshell may wish to know that West has published a course book of which I am a co-author, *International Business Transactions: Foreign Investment Law*.

It has been a genuine pleasure to prepare this Nutshell on Foreign Investment Law. I am indebted to Professor Michael Gordon, Emeritus of the University of Florida Law School, for his prior work on some of the materials appearing in the Nutshell. I hope that students, academics, lawyers, government officials and people in business will find it a useful introduction. Your comments and suggestions are most welcome.

RALPH H. FOLSOM
RFOLSOM@SANDIEGO.EDU

San Diego, 2016

ABOUT THE AUTHOR

Ralph H. Folsom has been a Professor at the University of San Diego School of Law since 1975. A graduate of Princeton University, Yale Law School and the London School of Economics (LLM), Professor Folsom teaches, writes and consults extensively in the field of international business law.

Folsom has been a Senior Fulbright resident scholar in Singapore and a Visiting Professor at the University of Hong Kong, University of Aix-Marseille, University of Brest, University of Paris, University of Toulouse, University of Puerto Rico, Monash University in Australia and Tecnológico de Monterrey in México.

Professor Folsom has authored or co-authored a range of books with West Academic Publishing. These include course books on: *International Business Transactions; IBT: International Trade and Economic Relations; IBT: Foreign Investment Law; IBT: Contracting Across Borders.*

He is the author of other West Academic Nutshells, including the Nutshells on *International Business Transactions* (co-authored), *International Trade and Economic Relations, NAFTA—Free Trade and Foreign Investment in the Americas,* and *European Union Law.*

Professor Folsom has also written more extensively than Nutshells permit in the West

Concise Hornbook Series: *Principles of International Litigation and Arbitration, Principles of European Union Law, Principles of International Trade Law, and Principles of International Business Transactions* (co-authored).

Ralph Folsom is married to Pixie Haughwout, an avid sailor and author of *Canal Cruising in the South of France: The Romantic Canal du Midi* and *Well-Favored Passage: The Magic of Lake Huron's North Channel*. See www.SeaFeverCruisingGuides. com.

OUTLINE

TABLE OF CASES

References are to Pages

FOREIGN INVESTMENT LAW

IN A NUTSHELL®

INTRODUCTION

The World Trade Organization (WTO), covered in my Nutshell on International Trade Law, has generated substantial harmony among roughly 165 member-nations. In contrast, there is no "World Investment Organization". Hence the law governing foreign investment varies considerably around the globe among the approximately 200 countries and other jurisdictions (such as the European Union and NAFTA). Put another way, the law of foreign investment is seriously chaotic. The level of this chaos escalates when both home and host countries decide to regulate foreign investment transactions.

For purposes of this Nutshell, "host-nation" is used to identify the nation in which the investment is made. "Home-nation" is used to designate the nation from which the investment capital, technology and the like comes, often the nation in which a multinational parent is incorporated and has its management center. Whatever the motivation, foreign investment will almost always encounter laws in the host nation that differ from the laws regulating investment in the home nation.

TYPES OF FOREIGN INVESTMENT

This Nutshell will attempt to bring some understanding to the chaos of foreign investment law. There are distinctions, trends and patterns that repeat. One of the most essential is the difference between direct and indirect foreign investment. Direct investment, often referred to as "greenfields investment", typically involves starting from scratch in a host country. Direct investors may be engaged in manufacturing, infrastructure projects, sales and distribution of goods or services, or franchising.

Lower labor and regulatory costs, expanding consumer markets, and access to natural resources, are often major incentives to invest abroad. These incentives may vary over time. In recent years, for example, China's seemingly endless supply of labor has faded and wages have risen causing a considerable exodus of assembly plant investments to move to Southeast Asia.

Classic "concession agreements" for development of natural resources generally involved ownership by foreigners for extended time periods. In 1901, for example, the Shah of Persia granted 500,000 square miles of exclusive oil rights to a foreign investor for 60 years (the D'Arcy Concession). Gradually, particularly since the end of the colonial era, developing nations have repudiated, renegotiated or expropriated natural resource concessions, often favoring instead "production sharing" and service contracts with multinational businesses.

Services are the most rapidly growing foreign investment sector, with branches and subsidiaries of banks, insurance companies, brokerage houses, utilities, E-commerce, transport and telecoms are leading the way, facilitated in many instances by market openings under the WTO General

Agreement on Trade in Services (GATS). See my *International Trade and Economic Relations Nutshell*. Multinational legal, accounting and other service firms have been multiplying, often using a Swiss association called a "Verain", which separates the liability of each independent office from the others.

Foreign goods, capital, technology, machinery, know-how, components, and often management personnel are exported, often from one part of the developed world into another. Since 2012, foreign direct investment in developing nations has surpassed investment in developed nations. But this pattern is changing. China and India, for example, longstanding recipients of direct foreign investment, are increasingly exporters thereof. China alone now has over $100 billion invested abroad, including numerous companies in the United States employing nearly 100,000 Americans as well as trophy properties like the Waldorf Astoria Hotel. Amidst economic uncertainty, it is reported that over $700 billion left China in 2015, much of it headed into foreign investments. U.S. scrutiny of Chinese investments on "national security" grounds is on the rise. See Chapter 6.

A variation on the theme of direct investment is the purchase of an existing business in the host country. In other words, mergers and acquisitions . . . which avoid the labor intensive nature of a greenfields investment. Trillions of dollars of cross-border mergers and acquisitions occur yearly. Most jurisdictions have M & A controls that must be navigated. See Chapters 4, 5 and 6. The privatization of state-owned companies by formerly nonmarket economies (for example, the Soviet Union and its satellites) also creates acquisition opportunities. "Tax inversion" mergers and acquisitions are currently the rage, with U.S. companies commonly "taken over" by European or Canadian competitors generating substantial tax savings. The United States has the highest overall corporate tax rate of any of the OECD industrial nations.

Indirect investment involves buying securities, normally stocks or bonds, in existing host country businesses. Any student of securities law will appreciate the regulated nature of such markets. For example, until 2015 foreigners were not allowed to purchase shares on the Saudi Arabia stock market. Foreign access to China's fledgling stock exchanges has been significantly controlled. When "foreigners" are the buyers, legal scrutiny likely will increase, particularly say if the buyers are speculators (hello hedge funds). Special issues may arise when sovereign bonds or other debt are involved, notably the risk of default, as has been prominently the case with Argentina and Greece.

Lastly, there is a growing foreign investment trend driven by individuals and their families seeking permanent residency or citizenship in stable societies. In the Caribbean, for example, citizenship can be bought for as little as a $200,000 investment in Dominica. Malta and Cyprus proffer residency rights and EU-wide visa-free travel for roughly the same amount. The United States "million dollar" green card, frequently discounted to $500,000 (see Chapter 6), is very popular with Chinese investors.

RISKS IN FOREIGN INVESTMENT

There are risks, and usually restrictions, involved with every investment. Risks are threats to the investment that may cause a loss of part or all of the invested capital and technology. Restrictions are rules of the host nation applicable to foreign investment. For example, there is a risk of expropriation (see Chapter 3), and there may be restrictions that limit foreign investment to a minority equity position, the familiar joint venture (see Chapter 1). Rule of law risks can be major in many parts of the world, particularly concerning piracy of intellectual property and corrupt legal systems.

There is also a risk of failure due to a lack of understanding of different cultures, although perhaps that is more a challenge than a risk. For example, Venezuela as an investment location may be a risk if democratization is not successful and the nation continues to nationalize foreign businesses. India may impose too many restrictions in the form of mandatory joint ventures or local content requirements. Nigeria may have a corrupt government whose officials constantly demand bribes. Brazil may be unable to control inflation and periodically establish exchange controls which prohibit repatriation of profits. Thus, Poland, Thailand, and Kenya may be better from the viewpoint of fewer risks and fewer restrictions on the formation and operation of the investment, even though they may be less favorable when only business issues are evaluated, such as the demographics of the market.

Many such risks can be avoided by investing in a developed nation such as within the European Union (see Chapter 5). While risks and restrictions also exist with respect to developed nations, they tend to be more similar to the risks and restrictions in the United States (see Chapter 6), and they tend to be less severe than in developing or nonmarket economy nations in transition.

Some risks at a foreign plant are easily covered by insurance, such as fire or theft, just as they would be in the United States. Risks of injuries to employees may be covered by a state or national plan similar to workman's compensation, but liability insurance for injuries to visitors and other individuals may be less expensive because of lower court awards. Some risks of investing abroad are for the most part unique to foreign investment, such as convertibility of currency, or expropriation of the company's property, or damage due to war, revolution or insurrection. Special insurance, such as that written by the U.S. Overseas Private Investment Corporation (OPIC), the World Bank's Multilateral Investment Guarantee Agency (MIGA), or private insurers may cover those risks (see Chapter 3).

THE ROLE OF LAWYERS IN FOREIGN INVESTMENT TRANSACTIONS

Where, why and how to invest abroad is a complex business decision. Expectations of profitability are a dominant factor. Other issues may influence where and why decisions related to foreign investment. Lawyers tend to be involved in advising on taxation, regulatory rules, political stability, technology and IP issues, rule of law and the like. U.S. lawyers often play a leading role in foreign investment counseling and negotiation, quite frequently with foreign as well as American clients, and are generally thought to have expertise in the area. In Asia, and elsewhere, lawyers play a more subsidiary role in foreign investment, perhaps limited to drafting documents for a transaction that business leaders have already negotiated.

Chapters 4, 5 and 6 explore investing in China, Europe and North America respectively. These jurisdictions provide a representative sampling of legal issues impacting the where, why and how of foreign investment decisions and the role of lawyers therein.

CHAPTER 1
ENTRY CONTROLS OVER FOREIGN INVESTMENT

Home and Host Nation Regulation   Entry Controls

Technology Transfers   Performance Requirements

The OECD   MAI   TRIMs   GATS

Mergers and Acquisitions   Investment Securities

Sovereign Debt   Franchising Investments

Individuals and multinationals have many reasons to invest abroad. It may be part of an initial overall plan to produce goods or provide services worldwide. It may be the next progression considered after a home market is saturated. Foreign investment abroad often occurs subsequent to less extensive contact with the host country in the form of trading goods or transferring production technology

A further step, increasingly undertaken by United States and European Union firms, is to move the state of incorporation to another country where the organizational, tax and regulatory laws are more favorable. This is not an action without critics, especially in the country the corporation is departing. But the reality is that bad hosts cause guests to depart. For example, what if Bank of

America moved its place of incorporation and management center to Zurich, Switzerland, in reality to benefit from more favorable executive compensation laws, but for the publicly stated reason that the company's business was increasingly centered in Europe? The generally accepted rule that the law of the state of incorporation applies to internal affairs may encourage such moves.

Whether to invest abroad is a complex, multi-faceted decision. A business of one country may remain, even when some significant advantages suggest incorporation elsewhere. The corporation may not wish to risk disturbing its market share at home, even though its sales are increasingly abroad in countries where labor costs are lower. Avoiding high tariffs may be a factor in deciding whether to stay or move. So may be a perception that the host country is moving away from remaining a market economy. A move might be considered when a licensee abroad is creating problems, and the company believes it can make a better product or provide a better service on its own. Poor-quality products or services by licensees, or disappointment with partners, is often a reason for assuming control of production abroad. In China, for example, many foreign investors that commenced as joint venture partners with local companies (frequently state-owned), are now becoming wholly foreign owned enterprises, known as WFOEs. See Chapter 4.

Foreign investment involves ownership and control of the enterprise abroad, whether branch or subsidiary in form. Enterprises which undertake foreign investment are referred to by several names, multinational corporations (MNCs) or enterprises (MNEs), or transnational corporations (TNCs) or enterprises (TNEs). More important than what they are called are the percentages of ownership, and control by the home-nation individual or entity. Share ownership discloses whether or not the enterprise is a joint venture involving two countries, and which country is likely to assert authority over it. Both the governments of the home nation (place of incorporation) and the foreign host nation (place of the productive part of the business) may attempt to assert such authority, leading to intergovernmental conflicts.

Foreign investment is a major part of the business of many companies chartered in developed nations. Especially since the early 1980s, multinational enterprises have moved toward global supply chains, production and division of labor. As a result, global foreign direct investment rose to over $2 trillion by the opening of this century. Intra-regional foreign investment is another aspect of this development. The creation in 1957 of the European Economic Community (now European Union) and the adoption of the North American Free Trade Agreement in 1994 stimulated increased foreign investment within these trading areas. The completion of the Uruguay GATT Round in 1995 added new WTO investment opportunities and rules (TRIMs and GATS), discussed below. These rules have encouraged even more foreign investment.

The composition of the rules which should govern foreign investment has been a subject of frequent debate among developed and developing countries. The North-South dialogue split developed countries in the northern hemisphere from less developed countries generally in the southern hemisphere. The North-South dialogue led in the 1970s to both restrictive United Nations General Assembly Resolutions, and restrictive foreign investment laws in many developing nations. The less developed countries argued that they were poor because the developed countries were rich, and that the development gap was increasing.

The less developed countries made demands that were largely aspirational, and invariably unrealistic. They wanted transfers of the most advanced technology at little or no cost, increased investment capital in companies with majority local control and ownership, and both forgiveness of old debt and assurances of new borrowing with few restrictions as to use. The dialogue was most active in the late 1960s and through the 1970s. It unraveled with sovereign debt defaults in the early 1980s, and the election of more market oriented leaders in many developing nations who realized that development lay more in local effort than foreign largesse.

Subsequent election of governments more determined to join the developed world than to lead the third world removed impediments to foreign investment. Nationalizations in the 1960s and 1970s gave way to privatizations in the 1980s and

1990s. Investment restrictions gave way to investment incentives as nations that had rejected foreign investment welcomed it. Legal requirements mandating joint ventures were changed to voluntary joint ventures. But even though this liberalization has provided investors with significant opportunities in many foreign nations, obstacles to foreign investment remain, and old ones may be exhumed as governments change.

GOVERNANCE BY HOME NATIONS

Governance of multinational enterprises may be divided into three spheres: Governance by the home nation, by the host nation, or by multi-nation organizations. One might also wish to add a fourth, governance by international law. Although the latter might constitute an ideal method in an ideal world, international legal norms that govern multinational enterprises are few in number and contested in status.

The regulation of a U.S. multinational abroad by the home nation is essentially a matter of U.S. federal law. See Chapter 6. These laws tend to fall into one of two classes. First are those laws enacted to deal with domestic issues without serious consideration of their impact on foreign activities of American firms. Examples are the federal securities and antitrust laws. Both can have extraterritorial application, although their potential impact abroad was not seriously debated when these laws were enacted. Second are laws that address specific foreign policy issues and are intended to achieve

what are largely political goals. Examples are the
Foreign Corrupt Practices Act (FCPA) and U.S.
boycott and anti-boycott laws. See R. Folsom,
*International Trade and Economic Relations in a
Nutshell.*

There are other U.S. laws that affect
multinationals' actions abroad, such as tax laws
that may encourage investment in friendly nations,
customs provisions allowing assembly of U.S. made
parts with duties applied only to the value added
abroad when the products re-enter the United
States, and the Generalized System of Preferences
(GSP) that is intended to assist development.
Foreign nations should understand that home
nations in which multinationals are registered and
usually "seated" tend only to enact laws that are in
the best interests of their nations, usually without
serious regard for any special interests of the
various possible host nations. Thus, as discussed
below, it is only the host nations' laws that may
effectively regulate multinational activity in that
country.

GOVERNANCE BY DEVELOPING AND
TRANSITION HOST NATIONS

The laws enacted in the 1970s by developing
nations, notably in Latin America, to govern foreign
investment tended to be very restrictive. In addition
to restrictions based on the desire to have host
nation nationals participate in equity and
management, restrictions were often imposed when
foreign investment was believed to infringe upon

national sovereignty, contrary to a development plan, unbalanced in favor of the foreign party, environmentally damaging, or violated host nation law. Mandatory joint ventures were a key element in developing nation restraints on foreign investment during the 1970s. In theory, and on paper, laws of this nature were mandatory, but as Professor Michael Gordon ably demonstrated, foreign investors were sometimes able to avoid such restrictions under an "operational code" or unwritten law that allowed much needed foreign investment.

Developing nation laws of the 1970s that governed foreign investment tended to evolve from two quite different perspectives. One group which enacted restrictive laws mandating joint ventures included nations which already had considerable foreign investment, such as India, Mexico, and Nigeria. These nations viewed the new laws as a way to gain greater control over foreign multinationals and to allow their nationals to participate in the equity and management of the means of production in the nation. At the same time nonmarket economy nations were beginning to adopt joint venture laws that were used to admit for the first time in decades some limited foreign equity. The reason was usually that the nation needed technology that would not be transferred unless it accompanied an equity investment. Nations adopting such laws included several in Eastern Europe, plus China and Cuba.

Governance by host nations has been a dynamic process. By the early 1990s the restrictiveness of the earlier laws had largely been replaced by laws encouraging foreign investment. Written incentives to invest have been replacing unwritten policy-based disincentives. Host nations often strongly promote foreign investment and offer diverse incentives to foreign investors. States or provinces within nations may offer incentives, possibly diverging with federal policy. These changes were both internally induced after the financial crises of the early 1980s when foreign national debts could not be paid, and externally induced in order to participate in regional pacts and the GATT/WTO. The decade of the 1990s was clearly one of marketization and privatization, rather than nationalization, with some notable exceptions in Latin America, which has remained true through and beyond the first decade of the new century. That said, many developing nations continue to restrict foreign investment. Indonesia, for example, has of late notably expanded its list of no foreign entry industries. In addition to legislation governing foreign investment, there may be constitutional provisions that affect investment. These may reserve areas for national ownership. For example, until recently the Mexican Constitution reserved basic oil and gas rights and production to the nation by vesting ownership in PEMEX, a state-owned monopoly. Mexico retains most subsurface rights when surface ownership is sold. Other constitutions allocate regulation to or among specific government agencies, such as the Indian Constitution which outlines government involvement in investment, including the ability to exclude private participation. Still other constitutions outline the form of economy the nation has adopted, often reserving in nonmarket economies the means of production and distribution to the state. When China initially welcomed foreign investment with the adoption of a law on joint ventures in 1979, it first amended the Constitution of 1978 to sanction foreign investment. If a foreign investment law is inconsistent with the nation's constitution, but is not questioned by the current government, problems may arise for the foreign investor with a later government not inclined to view the investment law as liberally.

RESTRICTIONS UPON ENTRY

The United States is almost unique in not having a general foreign investment control commission. Except for national security and other limited circumstances (see Chapter 6), U.S. policy on foreign investment is wide open and welcoming. Most of the rest of the world is not so inclined. Canada, for example, scrutinizes mergers and acquisitions of existing Canadian firms in the "national interest." This control system continues to operate under NAFTA, though with somewhat more relaxed criteria for U.S. and Mexican investors. See Chapter 8.

At what point in the investment process government regulation or law takes effect presents another key distinction. Some nations make *entry* very difficult by mandatory review of proposed investments, requirements of joint ventures or exemptions gained only after long negotiation and concessions, restrictions on acquisitions, and numerous levels of permission from various ministries and agencies. Mexico, until the late 1980s, possessed in its legal structure an example of each such restriction. But by 1994 it had removed many of these restrictions for U.S. and Canadian investors, a negotiated change for Mexico to participate in NAFTA. See Chapter 6. Comparable removals of investment restraints were subsequently granted EU and Japanese investors under their free trade agreements with Mexico.

Restrictions upon entry tend to assume one of two forms. Nations which recognize the corporate form sometimes restrict the maximum foreign equity allowed. Additional rules may also limit the foreign management or control to a minority interest. The enterprises resulting from these restrictions are referred to as equity joint ventures. Those few nonmarket economies that remain do not usually allow private ownership of the means of production and distribution, and may not have corporation laws. The manner of control over permitted foreign investment has typically been by contract. The foreign investor's rights are detailed in what is referred to as a contractual joint venture. The foreign party receives a percentage of the profits and is granted certain management rights.

As nonmarket nations have converted to market economies, they have adopted corporation laws and shifted from the use of contractual to equity joint ventures. Many have also shifted from mandatory to voluntary joint ventures. In some cases the shift has involved a change from contractual joint ventures directly to permitting wholly foreign owned corporate entities (WFOEs), without an intermediate stage of mandating equity joint ventures. China made this leap early on, allowing contractual and equity joint ventures as well as WFOEs. See Chapter 4.

PROHIBITIONS AND LIMITATIONS ON FOREIGN OWNERSHIP

Although foreign investor ownership restrictions may assume a seemingly infinite number of alternatives, there are several forms that continue to appear in the laws of various nations.

Total Prohibition in Certain Sectors

Almost every nation prohibits foreign investment in certain sectors. Both developed and developing nations limit investment where national security is threatened. Aeronautics, high-tech, petroleum, and iron and steel industries also rank high among the key sectors protected by European nations, even those with generally open investment policies, such as Germany. But developing nations sometimes increase the scope of prohibited investment to a degree that may suggest the nation is really a nonmarket economy—it mandates state ownership of most of the means of production and distribution.

Foreign investment is most often prohibited in the exploitation of the nation's most important natural resources. Until recently, Mexico, for example, has long prohibited nearly all foreign investment in the petroleum industry. Canada's early foreign investment regulations discouraged foreign investment in railroads by limiting ownership of railroads receiving government aid to British subjects. Canada also restricted natural resources, limiting oil and gas leases, mining, and exploration assistance grants to Canadian companies, or foreign companies having at least 50 percent Canadian ownership or being listed on the Canadian stock exchange.

Outside of the North American hemisphere, similar restrictions on foreign investment have been imposed by many nations. For example, India reserved some industries to its public sector in its Industrial Policy Resolution of 1948. In the 1970s India took such a strong position about limiting foreign investment that it attempted to force foreign-owned corporations in India to reduce ownership to less than 50 percent. IBM and Coca-Cola withdrew. Additionally, some sectoral barriers through legislation and national monopolies remain impediments to "foreign" (meaning non-EU) investment in the European Union. Transportation, telecommunications, and utilities offer examples, but again intra-EU investors have much less trouble than non-EU investors within the region.

Reservation of Investment to Domestic Private Investors

A second group of industries may be permitted as private rather than national ownership, but the private owners must be host-nation nationals. These are industries where the nation believes that public national ownership is not necessary, but the country prefers to reserve the areas for their own nationals. The reasons may be no greater than protectionism and the power of lobbying efforts of domestic industry, which does not wish to compete with foreign owned investment.

If the nation admits private ownership in a specific industry, it may have difficulty reserving that industry for its own nationals if it is a member of the GATT/WTO. The current trend under the concept of national treatment is to require that the host nation offer the same investment opportunities to foreigners that it offers to its own nationals. This could cause nations to move these industries not to ownership by nationals or foreigners, but exclusively to state ownership.

Foreign Investment Allowed But . . .

Industries not included in the protected classes mentioned above may have foreign ownership participation. But that foreign private ownership may be limited to joint ventures, and possibly only minority interests. In some joint venture laws, it appears at first that all areas are open to foreign investment, because the law does not reserve any spheres of activity for the state or its nationals. This was true of the Cuban joint venture law of 1982, but it was clear that foreign investment was to be directed to restoring Cuba's tourist industry, which would help obtain foreign currency. The Tanzanian law specifically prohibited foreign participation only in petroleum and minerals, but the Investment Promotion Centre could refuse investments in other areas, particularly if they were not joint ventures. The Namibian law referred only to "eligible investment", without defining what areas were open or closed to foreign investment. Notices regarding areas reserved for Namibians were issued broadly defining "services or the production of goods which can be provided or produced adequately by Namibians."

Outright bans on foreign investment appear less frequent than equity limitations, but such laws present the first question a foreigner looking to invest abroad must consider—Is the industry in which I am interested open to me? If the industry is one which is historically sensitive, such as natural resources and transportation, the answer may remain—no, it is not open to foreign investment. Where foreign investment is limited to minority participation in joint ventures in all industries not subject to even greater restrictions, the country is not a very receptive location for foreign investment.

Equity Percentage Limitations, Mandatory Joint Ventures

The equity percentages allowed to foreign investors have varied with the type of industry and the host nation's goal in applying the restriction. The reason for equity percentage limitations may be to allow the amount to depend on what the investment is perceived to offer the nation, such as needed technology, or an economic/social philosophy that foreign investment is inherently evil and to be prohibited. The former may be overcome by the foreign investor, the latter often may not. For years the nonmarket economy nations adopted the latter view, but moved to the former when it was apparent that their development levels had remained at best static.

When nations adopt mandatory joint venture rules, they often limit foreign ownership to a minority share, usually 49 percent. The reason is stated to be a preference to keep a majority of the ownership and control in the hands of nationals. If the nation decides to allow majority control to be owned by foreign investors, it often takes the additional step and allows the investment to be *wholly* foreign owned. If there is one certain characteristic of equity percentage limitations, it is that they are neither likely to remain static over a number of years, nor likely to be enforced absolutely. The host nation may often waive restrictive equity limitations. Mexico, for example, waived its mandatory joint venture rule to facilitate an early computer plant investment in Guadalajara by IBM, subsequently sold to Lenovo of China. Several reasons for such waivers are commonly found in exception provisions in written investment laws, or in the unwritten "operational code" of the government.

Waivers of mandatory joint venture rules and equity percentage limits have been characteristically granted for the following reasons:

Technology. Some companies with high technology, such as IBM, have been able to avoid joint venture mandates and retain total ownership. Contrastingly, IBM withdrew from India in the late 1970s when India demanded that IBM convert its wholly foreign parent owned investment in India to a joint venture. Minority shares would be owned by the parent, with the majority owned by Indian nationals. What form of technology will gain such a waiver is likely to vary from one nation to another. Where there is a transfer of technology law, it is likely to state several reasons allowing registration of a technology agreement. These reasons include technology that assists import substitution, the most up-to-date technology, high priority areas such as computers, technology intended to enhance job opportunities, and technology viewed as reasonable in cost.

Plant Location. The willingness to locate a production facility away from already saturated areas, such as the most populated cities, will increase chances of gaining a mandatory joint venture waiver. Some countries specify areas that the nation feels are already sufficiently industrialized, other specify areas that they have designated for industrial development, or simply mention "less developed" areas.

Education. The willingness to establish training centers in the host nation, especially centers that will teach jobs to function with new technology, is a method of gaining a waiver.

Research and Development. A major criticism of many nations is that multinationals only export their technology while undertaking all the research to develop that technology in their home nation. Being willing to undertake some research and development in a host nation may gain a waiver of maximum equity participation requirements.

Balance Imports with Exports. Because of chronic shortages of hard currencies, many host nations grant waivers of investment restrictions where the investment will require little demand on the host nation's scarce hard currency reserves. Thus, exporting part of the production to earn sufficient hard currency to pay for imports and cover profit and royalty payments may be decisive. The host nation's appreciation will increase as the export earnings continue to exceed the import demand. China initially placed great emphasis on exports; it was often the key to obtaining permission to establish a wholly owned foreign investment.

Sourcing Capital from Abroad. In addition to shortages of foreign currency, some nations have shortages of domestic currency to lend to companies. They often wish to reserve that lending capacity for locally owned business. Thus, commencing an investment with capital from outside the host nation is another possible key to gaining a mandatory joint venture waiver.

Reasons for Accepting Equity Restrictions

Foreign investors generally prefer to have total ownership of their foreign investments. Why would a foreign investor agree to limit participation to a minority interest?

An investment in place at the time of enactment of a government demand to either convert to a joint venture or withdraw from the nation may be less costly to continue as a joint venture with a minority position than to withdraw from the country. A local partner may be an asset if market penetration is difficult or political contacts are critical. But it is unlikely that the parent company will increase its investment or transfer the latest technology to the joint venture enterprise. The foreign entity will thus become quite unlike other wholly owned foreign investments of the multinational. It may remain relatively static while other foreign wholly owned company investments receive any needed additional capital and the latest technology.

If the host nation offers attractive investment incentives, accepting limitations on equity and management participation may be a fair trade, especially if the incentives are available immediately and the joint venture rules are likely to fade in time. If the market in the host nation has good long term prospects, it may be appropriate to accept a joint venture and invest. In Mexico in the 1970s, the willingness of Japanese investors to enter joint ventures with minority participation placed pressure on U.S. firms to accept the same limits on ownership, and even to offer better deals because of the growing Mexican desire to lessen reliance on U.S. investment. But new investment was never as extensive as it would have been without the restrictive laws of the 1970s, illustrated by the rapid increase in new foreign investment since those laws were repealed in the 1990s and Mexico entered both GATT/WTO and NAFTA.

Retroactive Effect of Equity Limitations

To force foreign investment already in existence to convert to joint ventures may give rise to claims of expropriation. Consequently, countries usually applied the laws to new investment, but often added provisions that made it very difficult for current investment to continue without conversion. For example, the Mexican 1973 Investment Law was not retroactive on its face, but regulations denied permission to enter new lines of products or establish new locations without conversion to a joint venture. India's Foreign Exchange Regulation Act of 1975 separately classified existing and new investment, granting the latter favorable treatment because it complied with joint venture mandates. But the Indian government began to place pressure on all foreign investment to convert to joint ventures, leading to conflicts with many companies.

TECHNOLOGY TRANSFERS AND FOREIGN INVESTMENT

Many foreign direct investments include the transfer of technology to a subsidiary or joint venture. Such technology may be patented, copyrighted, a trade secret or simply "know-how". Legal protection for knowhow varies from country to country and is, at best, limited. Unlike patents, copyrights and trademarks, you cannot by registration obtain exclusive legal rights to knowhow. Knowledge, like the air we breathe, is a public good. Once released in the community, knowhow can generally be used by anyone and is almost impossible to retrieve. In the absence of exclusive legal rights, preserving the confidentiality of knowhow becomes an important business strategy. If everyone knows it, who will pay for it? If your competitors have access to the knowledge, your market position is at risk.

Typically, if only for tax reasons, there will be a separate transfer of technology agreement, often subject to regulatory review and approval either in conjunction with the investment or independently. It is not unknown for host developing nations, such as China, to require technology transfers. India demanded in the 1970s that Coca-Cola alter its structure from a wholly foreign owned investment to a joint venture. While the Indian government did not expressly state that the foreign parent would have to share the secret and very valuable Coke formula, the government did say that such sharing would be the natural consequence of the partnership sense of the joint venture. Coca-Cola would not disclose its formula, and withdrew from India, not to return until the 1990s, when India had relaxed its previously strict foreign investment rules.

In countries with extensive counterfeiting and intellectual property piracy, again China, foreign investors may not be willing to transfer frontier technology. The transfer of strategic technology may not be permitted by the home nation, as commonly happens in the United States under its export control regulations. From the licensee's standpoint, and the perspective of its government, there is the risk that the licensed technology may be old or obsolete, not "state of the art." Goods produced under old technology will be hard to export and convey a certain "second class" status. On the other hand, older more labor intensive technologies may actually be sought in the early stages of development. Excessive royalties may threaten the economic viability of the investment and drain hard currencies from the country. The recipient typically is not in a sufficiently powerful position to bargain away restrictive features of standard international licenses.

For all these reasons, and more, developing countries frequently regulate patent and knowhow licensing agreements. Royalty levels will be limited, certain clauses prohibited (e.g., export restraints, resale price maintenance, mandatory grant-backs to the licensor of improvements), and the desirability of the technology evaluated. Regulation of licensing is not limited to the developing world. The European Union extensively regulates patent, knowhow and software licensing. See Chapter 5. In the United States, there is a less direct form of licensing regulation via antitrust law.

The home country investor also faces legal risks. The flow of royalty payments may be stopped, suspended or reduced by currency exchange regulations. The taxation of the royalties, if not governed by double taxation treaties, may be confiscatory. The licensee may abscond with the technology or facilitate unauthorized distribution of "gray market" goods which eventually compete for sales in markets exclusively intended for the source company. In the end, patents expire and become part of the world domain.

Licensing is a kind of partnership. If it succeeds, the parent company's royalties (often based on sales volumes) will increase and a continuing partnership through succeeding generations of technology may evolve. If not, the dispute settlement provisions of the agreement may be called upon as either party withdraws from the partnership. Licensing of patents and knowhow often is combined with, indeed essential to, foreign investments. A foreign subsidiary or joint venture will need technical assistance and knowhow to commence operations. When this occurs, the licensing terms are usually a part of the basic joint venture or investment agreement.

Technology transfers may also be combined with a trade agreement, as where the parent company ships necessary supplies to the joint venture or subsidiary. Such supply agreements have sometimes been used to overcome royalty limitations through a form of "transfer pricing," the practice of marking up or down the price of goods so as to allocate revenues to preferred parties and jurisdictions (e.g., tax havens).

PERFORMANCE REQUIREMENTS AND THE WTO TRIMs AGREEMENT

Trade-oriented foreign investment barriers that individual nations impose have come to be described as "trade-related investment measures" or TRIMs, a title incorporated into the 1995 WTO package of agreements. Led by the United States, the developed nations have tried to limit foreign investor TRIMs through the General Agreement on Tariffs and Trade (GATT)/ World Trade Organization (WTO) process.

Developing nations take a less negative view of TRIMs. They believe TRIMs provide a means of host nation control over various aspects of foreign multinational enterprise activity. Specifically, they believe that TRIMs serve as useful policy tools to promote government objectives in furthering economic development and ensuring balanced trade. Additionally, developing nations have quite vigorously defended the use of TRIMs as an aspect of national sovereignty, historically to maintain control over natural resources and more recently to preserve domestic culture.

TRIMs represents one of the very few areas of foreign investment law where a modicum of unity exists. Although many countries impose TRIMs, the developed and developing countries have different views regarding their economic effects. Developed nations argue that TRIMs cause investors to base their decisions on considerations other than market forces. The TRIMs Agreement embraces the core principle of national treatment, mandating that foreign-controlled enterprises receive no less favorable treatment from governments than their domestic counterparts.

But it is less than clear exactly what form of practice the term TRIMs encompasses. The Uruguay Round of GATT, leading to the creation of the WTO, defined fourteen practices as TRIMs. United Nations and other commentators have broken these into four categories of host country law imposed on foreign investors: local content requirements, trade-balancing rules, export requirements, and mandatory technology transfer/local R & D duties.

The term "performance requirements" generally refers to barriers that governments use to condition entry of foreign investors, often through a "permission to invest" regulatory commission. Trade-related investment practices which are deemed inconsistent with TRIMs are listed illustratively in an Annex. These include minimum domestic content rules (say 50% of the value of the foreign investor's products must be sourced locally), limitations on imports used in production, the linkage of allowable imports to export requirements (known as "trade balancing" requirements), export quotas or percentage of production requirements, employment and training duties, and restrictions on foreign exchange designed to limit imports.

Member states may "deviate temporarily" from national treatment principles, thus undermining the impact of TRIMs. There have been about a dozen TRIMs disputes, all centered on automobiles. For example, the United States and others have succeeded in challenging Indian and Indonesian local content and export requirements for autos through strictly intergovernmental WTO proceedings. See my *International Trade and Economic Relations Nutshell.*

On balance, performance requirements, most notably local content rules, continue to be widely present around the globe, especially under pre-investment clearance controls. Sometimes these requirements are literally impossible to fulfill, such as Indonesia's mandate that all tablets and smartphones sold in that country contain at least 30% local components. Of course, such rules incentivize foreign investment to produce such components in Indonesia.

SERVICES INVESTMENT AND THE WTO GATS AGREEMENT

In the United States, services account for over two-thirds of national GDP and provide jobs for nearly two-thirds of the work force. Services account for almost one-third of U.S. exports in sectors such as tourism, education, finance, construction, telecommunications, transport and health. In contrast, most developing nations are minimal exporters of services, save by means of exporting their people. . . but migration was not included as a subject under the WTO General Agreement on Trade in Services (GATS, 1994). The GATS facilitates foreign investment abroad by selectively enabling the establishment of service-connected foreign branches, offices and subsidiaries.

Market access for services is a major focus of the GATS. The GATS defines the supply of services broadly to include providing services across borders or inside member states with or without a commercial presence therein. The core GATS Article XVII commitment is to afford most-favored-nation treatment to service providers, subject to country-specific, preferential trade agreement or labor market integration agreement exemptions. One such exemption covers provision of audio-visual services in the EU.

In addition, each WTO member state made under GATS a specific schedule of commitments (concessions) on opening up their markets in services' sectors negotiated using the WTO Services Sectoral Classification List. They further agreed under Article XVI to provide national treatment to their services' commitment schedule. Certain mutual recognition of education and training for service-sector licensing occurs. For example, to what degree may foreign banks or foreign economic consultants provide services, and are they entitled to national treatment? The answers to those questions will be found in the specific commitments of each GATS member.

National laws that restrict the number of firms in a market, that are dependent upon local "needs tests", or that mandate local incorporation are regulated by the GATS. Various "transparency" rules require disclosure of all relevant laws and regulations, and these must be administered reasonably, objectively and impartially.

State monopolies or exclusive service providers may continue, but must not abuse their positions. Detailed rules are created in annexes to the GATS on financial, telecommunications and air transport services. Under the Telecommunications Reference Paper (TRP), for example, the United States successfully argued that Telmex had abused its monopoly position in Mexico by charging discriminatory, non-cost-oriented connection fees for foreign calls. *See* Mexico-Telecoms, WT/DS204/AB/R (2004).

Much to its consternation, the United States was found to have failed to exclude Internet gambling services under its GATS commitments' schedule. This caused Antigua-Barbuda to prevail in a dispute that alleged U.S. gambling laws discriminatorily prohibited its right to export such services (owned by U.S. foreign investors) to the U.S. market. *See* U.S.-Gambling, WT/DS285/AB/R (2007). The United States also lost the argument that its Internet gambling services' restraints were justifiable on public morals' grounds. This argument failed as discriminatory under the "chapeau" of the GATS Article XIV general exceptions (similar to GATT Article XX general exceptions).

The U.S. Congress approved and implemented the GATS agreement in December of 1994 under the

Uruguay Round Agreements Act. Subsequently, early in 1995, the United States refused to extend most-favored-nation treatment to financial services. The European Union, Japan and other GATS nations then entered into an interim 2-year agreement which operated on MFN principles. Financial services were revisited in 1996–97 with further negotiations aimed at bringing the United States into the fold. These negotiations bore fruit late in 1997 with 70 nations (including the United States) joining in an agreement that covers 95 percent of foreign trade and investment in banking, insurance, securities and financial information. This agreement took effect March 1, 1999.

GOVERNANCE BY THE UNITED NATIONS AND INTERNATIONAL LAW

The principal multi-nation organization that has attempted to regulate multinationals is the United Nations. The United Nations and its subsidiary organizations, however, have had little success in developing an effective, widely accepted regulatory scheme. This should not be surprising because the United Nations is a large organization with diverse cultural, economic, and political norms. The role of the United Nations, especially the Centre on Transnational Corporations, has become somewhat obscure as developing nations and nonmarket economies increasingly adopted less restrictive investment laws. The aspirations of developing nations of the 1970s to achieve development through transfers (reparations for alleged abuses of colonialism, transfers of technology based on ideas being the patrimony of mankind rather than subject to private ownership, etc.), have been largely subordinated to a desire to achieve development through self-help and encouragement of foreign investment.

Part of the efforts of the developing nations in the 1970s involved the creation of international norms that would control multinationals, such as a UN initiated Code of Conduct. Not only did these efforts fail, but the development of international law in general has been disappointing in its failure to establish legal norms for both multinationals and host nations. For example, the most contentious issue, compensation rights subsequent to expropriation, was before the International Court of Justice in the *Barcelona Traction* decision (1970 I.C.J. Rep. 3), but the ICJ focused on a narrow issue of ownership and did not address compensation.

The earlier focus on investment rules by the United Nations was renewed around the turn of the century, but this time as a joint effort with the International Chamber of Commerce (ICC) in Paris. Rather than the restrictive approach taken by the United Nations in the 1960s and 1970s, the UN-ICC effort sought to produce investment guidelines for the private sector, promoting that sector's involvement in the UN's decision-making processes, and its greater participation in the economic development of the poorest countries. This joint effort has also not been successful. The principal focus of the ICC regarding investment rules by the UN has involved the latter's attempts to control climate, and the former's concern that any such UN controls may harm investment.

The World Bank, home of the successful International Centre for the Settlement of Investment Disputes (ICSID, see Chapter 7), is another organization that has drafted guidelines on foreign investment. They are important to investors seeking World Bank investment assistance. World Bank lending and investment programs have been heavily influenced by U.S. perspectives since its inception post-WWII. As an alternative, China has created and funded the Asian Infrastructure Development Bank (AIDB). The United States elected not to participate in AIDB, but the EU, Japan, Canada and others do.

THE OECD MULTILATERAL AGREEMENT ON INVESTMENT (MAI)

The OECD, an organization comprised of about 35 developed nations, also participated in developing rules governing foreign investment. It conducted extensive work on a proposed Multilateral Agreement on Investment (MAI). The United States urged that this Agreement liberalize foreign investment law, and address such issues as national treatment, standstill and roll-back rules, non-discriminatory most favored nation treatment, and transparency. The OECD considered such issues as free movement of executives, foreign investor rights to participate in privatization, state monopolies, intellectual property rights, portfolio investment, restrictions on investment in sensitive areas, relations with regional organizations, authority over investment by sub-federal government (i.e., states and provinces), protection of culture by limitations on investment, and dispute settlement.

Developing nations expressed concern that the MAI might be an attempt by the OECD to monopolize market share by industrialized nation corporations in the developing world. There were expectations that the MAI would be completed by 1998. But the United States would not agree to EU insistence that an exception be created so that it could deny investment benefits granted exclusively within the EU to non-EU investors The United States further rejected "cultural exception" and "public order" clauses in the proposed MAI. The cultural exception would have allowed nations to limit investment when it had an adverse impact on the host nation's culture (promoted by France and Canada). The public order clause would permit withholding national treatment in industries considered essential to national security, law enforcement, and public order.

The United States tabled many exceptions to the applicability of the proposed Agreement's provisions, and pushed hard for NAFTA-like foreign investor rights. In Europe, major concerns were raised by a NAFTA "investor-state" arbitration dispute (see *Ethyl* in Chapter 8) that implied rather extraordinary rights of foreign investors to challenge national safety, health and environmental regulations. France, decrying the proposed "hyper-rights" of foreign investors under the MAI, withdrew in frustration.

In the course of the debate over the MAI, a Canadian study suggested that it would not have eliminated important foreign investment barriers. The report illustrated that when some barriers, such as mandatory joint ventures or local content requirements, are removed, others arise. Some such barriers represent deeply rooted and long-established practices, never intended as barriers, but which have come to function as such.

The year (1998) ended without completion of the Multilateral Agreement on Investment, and without any expectation that it would ever be concluded. The MAI has since remained dormant, though it remains as close to a Code of foreign investment law rules as has ever been attempted. Its failure returns the focus on foreign investment law to host nations, both developed and developing.

LIMITATIONS ON MERGERS AND ACQUISITIONS

A frequently used method to invest abroad is to acquire a locally owned company in the foreign nation. Foreign acquisitions may provide an infusion of needed capital not available at home, and bring new management ideas where old management has lacked creativity and been stagnant. Foreign acquisitions have many of the characteristics of an acquisition inside the United States. That includes both the loss of an opportunity to increase the number of competitors in the business were the investing company to commence a new company ("greenfields investment"), and the consequences of vertical integration if the company acquired is the distribution channel while the company acquiring is the producer, or vice versa.

The much more common reason has been the replacement of a locally owned business by a foreign owned business. The nation may be particularly concerned where the proposed acquisition is of a large domestic industry that is thought to *be* a domestic industry. For example, a proposed foreign acquisition of General Motors would create far more objection than proposed foreign acquisitions of 1,000 companies, each one-1,000th the size of GM, but not thought of *as American.* That of course did not stop Fiat from acquiring control of Chrysler after the U.S. 2008 meltdown.

One Canadian report noted particular foreign acquisition barriers:

1. Antitrust policies, such as merger controls, that prohibit takeovers for economic or social reasons.

2. Administrative procedures, such as using required takeover reviews to demand performance requirements.

3. Structuring corporations with voting schemes that permit effective control by a small group representing a small proportion of the shares but with ability to block a takeover.

4. Anti-takeover laws that restrict voting rights of individuals or groups, such as in some American states.

5. Restrictions on privatized government companies such as the U.K. and Italian use of "golden shares" to prevent changes of control.

6. Structures such as the Japanese *keiretsu* that essentially precludes a hostile takeover, or large bank holdings that block takeovers.

7. The limited role of stock markets with few listings, and high local concentrations of ownership which are hard to dislodge.

Even more sensitive may be proposed acquisitions of enterprises bearing the name of the nation, such as Mexicana Airlines or Canadian Pacific Railway. U.S. incorporated airlines, wishing to merge or have some close linkage with large foreign airlines, have often been rejected in their attempts. Likewise, many nations will bar the acquisition of "national champions". Japan, for example, took this approach when it sought to block the purchase of Sharp Electronics and its valuable technology by a Taiwanese company in 2016. European governments are also known to protect their national champions. The objection may be cultural and emotional as well as economic. See Chapter 5.

Restrictions on acquisitions are thus often based more on the feared *loss* of a domestic company, than the feared *addition* of a new foreign company. This means foreign investors and their lawyers have a different obstacle to overcome to obtain approval of an acquisition as opposed to a new investment. Examples include mergers and acquisitions laws in China (Chapter 4), Europe (Chapter 5) and North America (Chapter 6). Mergers of global MNE giants can attract scrutiny in dozens of jurisdictions. For example, the GE/Alstom of France merger in 2015 required about 20 approvals, including Brazil, Canada, Israel and South Africa.

Prohibiting *any* foreign investment in a particular sector is protective of domestic industry. Prohibiting foreign investment by means of *acquisitions* does not assure protection for domestic industry, since it allows competition to exist by the establishment of a new industry that is foreign owned. Thus protectionist arguments urge restrictions on all investment, not only acquisitions.

STOCKS, BONDS, AND SOVEREIGN DEBT

The purchase of foreign stocks, bonds and similar investments has become widespread, indeed almost mandatory as pension and mutual funds, insurance companies, hedge funds and money managers seek globally balanced or specific foreign portfolios. The risks inherent in such indirect foreign investments vary with the nature of the stocks and bonds, and the exchanges upon which they are traded. For example, the vast liquidity and for the most part orderly running of the U.S. securities markets is commonly seen as a "safe haven", while the governmentally managed character of Chinese exchanges are perceived to be "risky". Of course, as noted in Chapter 6, foreign businesses may make offerings on U.S. exchanges provided they adhere to U.S. securities law, notably its disclosure rules. Such offerings may reduce the perception that Chinese and other stocks and bonds of foreign origin are risky.

Special problems arise when sovereign debt is purchased. Massive movements of stock and bond investments can de-stabilize developing/emerging nations and their markets. Chile and other countries have imposed transaction taxes in an effort to manage the flow of "hot money" from abroad. Whereas the securities of private and state-owned or controlled enterprises are normally governed by bankruptcy law, sovereign bonds are not. Sovereign state defaults on debt payments have occurred down through history, most recently by Argentina and Greece. Argentina remains in default on some of its un-renegotiated 2001 debt, bought up by speculators, who succeeded in obtaining a federal court order for payments due, and are now in pursuit of Argentinian assets around the world. See *NML Capital Ltd v. Argentina*, 699 F.3d 246 (2012) and *Argentina v. NML Capital Ltd*, 134 S.Ct. 2250 (2014).

In recent years, with United States support, International Monetary Fund (IMF) loans have rescued sovereign debt issuers and owners, "conditioned" upon adoption of specific reforms by debtor states. This occurred widely in Asia and Latin America during the late 1900s, and led to the perception that the IMF is the world's "sheriff", setting the terms for refinancing national debts and protecting the interests of creditors.

The IMF functioned as the first line of negotiation in an international "debt crisis," and commercial and national banks often conformed their loans to IMF conditions. These conditions had dramatic, negative political and social repercussions in debtor nations. From 2006 onwards, nations paid off their IMF debt in record numbers. Argentina did so with an assist from Venezuela. Brazil, Russia, Bolivia, Uruguay, Indonesia, the Philippines and others joined in the flight from IMF loan conditions. The IMF's loan portfolio stood at $100 billion in 2003. By 2008, that portfolio was approaching zero, and the IMF was running a budget deficit, cutting staff and proposing sales of gold reserves. Many commentators wondered aloud what was the role of the IMF without loans?

The global financial and economic crisis that commenced late in 2008 muted this commentary. The IMF "pre-approved" unconditional, short-term loans to nations it deemed sound but facing liquidity problems, such as Mexico, Brazil and South Korea. Conditional IMF loans were made to Iceland, Pakistan, Ukraine and Hungary late in 2008, with others, notably Greece, Portugal, Ireland and Ukraine following. Injections of new capital made it clear that the IMF was back in the loan and loan conditioning business.

For the first time, the IMF joined with the EU and the European Central Bank ("The Troika") to finance a 110 billion rescue of Greece with lots of conditions attached. Indeed, the EU seemed almost grateful that the IMF would enforce dramatic reductions in government spending and employment, improved accounting and anti-corruption measures, privatization, tax increases, monopoly break-ups and structural changes in the Greek economy. The IMF does this through constant monitoring and gradual, contingent release of bailout funds. Despite large social and political protests, Greece has been bailed out *three* times by the Troika under steadily more difficult conditions that make it extremely doubtful Greece will ever be able to pay off its debts without a "haircut" in the total amount due.

The IMF has also drafted a Code of Best Practices for "Sovereign Wealth Funds" (SWFs). Such Funds are said to hold over $3 trillion, and are expanding rapidly. Abu Dhabi, Saudi Arabia, Kuwait, Singapore, Russia, China and Norway all have large SWFs, many of which played an important role in bailing out U.S. banks and securities firms with heavy sub-prime loan exposure. In 2008, developing nations (particularly their central banks) bought over 50 percent of the net foreign purchases of U.S. government securities.

In a role reversal, the United States has become heavily dependent on SWF and developing world (especially Chinese) capital inflows to finance its large national debt and enormous international trade deficit. The primary concern is that SWFs and developing nations might use their power for political purposes. Their emergence further diminishes the need for IMF loans. As yet the SWFs and China have not "conditioned" their lending or investment decisions.

FRANCHISING AS A FORM OF FOREIGN INVESTMENT

One of the easiest ways to invest abroad is franchising. Back in the home country the franchisor has created a "formula for success". Many rightly consider franchising to be a U.S. invention, but foreigners have also rapidly been developing international franchising systems. Exporting that formula, often with adaptations to local laws and culture, requires relatively little capital on either side of the transaction. "Start-up" payments by franchisees can provide a quick infusion of cash to the franchisor, but royalty payments over the life of a profitable franchise are the major goal.

Although patents, copyrights and trademarks may all be involved in international franchising, trademark licensing is at the core of most international franchise agreements. "Famous" trademarks are may be used deceptively, or directly copied, in developing nations. For example, Kentucky "Finger Lickin Good" Fried Chicken became Kenny's "Lip Smackin Good" Fried Chicken, using the same color scheme, in Kenya. Famous marks are granted special status under the 1883 Paris Convention for the Protection of Industrial Property, but of course the operational reality of such protections may be weak in the legal systems of developing nations.

Distribution (wedding gowns) and service (fast food) franchises may differ in purpose and content. In general, franchising is especially useful to facilitate market entry and brand awareness. For example, a principal joint venture investment in Cuba has been hotel franchises. Most franchisors have established fairly standard contracts and business formulae which are utilized in their home markets, and receive counsel on the myriad of laws relevant to their domestic business operations. Approaches to developing, defining and managing franchise relationships that have worked domestically may not work abroad. For example, agreements authorizing development of multiple locations within a given territory and, sub-franchising by a master franchisee, are often used overseas while infrequent in the United States.

International franchising confronts the attorney with the need to research and evaluate a broad range of foreign laws which may apply in any particular jurisdiction. Such laws tend to focus on placing equity and control in the hands of local individuals and on regulating the franchise agreement to benefit the franchisees. The European Union, for example, has a regulation (No. 330/10) that details permissible, prohibited and "gray area" franchise agreement clauses. See Chapter 5. Many jurisdictions, including in the United States, mandate extensive disclosure by franchisors. See Chapter 6. Antitrust and tax law are important in international franchising. Double taxation treaties, for example, will affect the level of taxation of royalties. Antitrust law will temper purchasing requirements of the franchisor, lest unlawful "tying arrangements" be undertaken. Tying arrangements involve coercion of franchisees to take supplies from the franchisor or designated sources as part of the franchise.

In addition, counsel should be sensitive to the cultural impact of foreign franchising. For example, the appearance of a franchise building or trademark symbol may conflict in a foreign setting with traditional architectural forms (such as in European cities) or nationalist feelings hostile to the appearance of foreign trademarks on franchised products (such as in India or Mexico). Cultural conflicts can diminish the value of international franchises. To anticipate and solve legal and cultural problems, foreign counsel is often chosen to assist in the task of franchising abroad.

Because franchising links trademarks with business attributes, there is a broad duty in the law for the franchisor to maintain quality controls over the franchisee, particularly in the business format franchise system. Any failure of the franchisor to maintain such quality controls could cause the trademark in question to be abandoned and lost to the franchisor. In order to maintain adequate quality controls, the franchisor must typically police the operations of the franchisee. Broadly speaking, the duty to maintain quality controls arises because a trademark is a source symbol. The public is entitled to rely upon that source symbol in making its purchasing decisions so as to obtain consistent product quality and attributes.

International franchisors operating at a distance from their franchisees must be especially concerned with quality controls. On the other hand, excessive control or the public appearance of such control may give rise to an agency relationship between the franchisor and the franchisee. Such a relationship could be used to establish franchisor liability for franchisee conduct, including international product and other tort liabilities. It may be possible to minimize these risks through disclaimer or indemnification clauses in the franchise agreement.

Franchise formulae often involve utilization of trade secrets and confidential information. This may range from recipes and cooking techniques to customer lists, pricing formulas, market data or bookkeeping procedures. It is extremely difficult to protect such secrets and information. The first problem arises from the concept of what is a trade secret. Generally speaking, abstract ideas or business practices which do not involve an element of novelty are not considered trade secrets. Some international clarity for defining trade secrets is provided in the WTO TRIPs agreement, and treaties like NAFTA (the first international agreement to include coverage of trade secrets). The European Union, on the other hand, is still struggling to harmonize trade secret law among its members.

When international franchise trade secrets are involved, maintaining such secrets can be difficult given the wide number of persons who may have access to the confidential information. Terminated employees and terminated franchisees are another fertile source of the loss of trade secrets and confidential information. Even though the franchisees may warrant to protect confidentiality, once released there may not be an effective way to recapture the secret or remedy the harm. This is particularly the case in the Internet age.

TRENDS IN FOREIGN INVESTMENT LAW

The enactment of restrictive investment laws was most prominent in the 1970s. Two important events in the 1980s tended to stop the enactment of restrictive investment laws. The first was the debt crisis in the early 1980s, which caused nations to realize that restrictive investment laws did not contribute to economic growth and exports. The second was the dismantling of the USSR and the commencement of the transition of many nonmarket economies to market economies. Even nonmarket economies outside the Eastern Europe and USSR group were making such changes. Vietnam, for example, first adopted a foreign investment law in 1987, and has since amended it several times. Tanzania and Mongolia both enacted investment laws in 1990, neither of which has any reference to mandatory joint ventures.

The former USSR first adopted joint venture legislation in 1987, with modifications in 1988 and 1989, and a new law in 1990. The law was quite liberal, which was the direction taken by the nations that were formerly part of the USSR. Poland enacted a series of investment laws, each more liberal than the previous. The 1991 law eliminated the previously required approval process for many investments.

By the turn of the millennium nearly all developing and nonmarket economies had opened their economies to more foreign direct investment, even though their earlier announced reservations about extensive participation in the means of production and distribution by foreign enterprises remained in many existing written laws. There was a reluctance at first to repeal these laws, which were often popular with the citizens, media and academics. The nations instead began to relax their enforcement of the restrictive laws.

While foreign nations, both developing and nonmarket, previously had brought many, and sometimes all, industries within the ambit of foreign equity limitations or prohibitions, these governments began to administer those laws with increasing flexibility. At times, the way the laws read and the way they were applied seemed quite opposite. Starting in the 1990s, the laws began to be modified to reflect the reality of practice, and to reflect obligations under bilateral and multilateral investment agreements (see Chapter 7).

In the last two decades foreign investment has increasingly been recruited and offered incentives. This amounts to a vastly different picture of foreign investment than existed in earlier times when it was subject to discouraging restrictions in most developing nations, and even in a few developed nations, such as Canada.

The world of foreign investment has changed markedly. Incentives are now the norm, and not only in developing nations. Incentives vary country-by-country, and within a country over time. Tax rates are sometimes reduced for specified periods of time. States or provinces, and counties and cities, offer attractive incentives. BMW autos are being made in South Carolina, and Mercedes-Benz in Alabama, with notable government incentives. Many developing nations offer substantial benefits, such as property tax holidays, special exchange preferences, and labor incentives such as the absence of labor unions.

Incentives are typically given for new greenfields investment, but usually not for acquiring a local company. But governments might offer incentives to buy a state-owned company, perhaps in the form of a more favorable price. If the foreign investor plans to export most of production, the likelihood of receiving incentives rises, especially from federal/central governments.

CHAPTER 2

OPERATIONAL CONTROLS OVER FOREIGN INVESTMENT

Currency Issues	**Taxation**	**Transfer Pricing**
Corruption		**Mass Tort Litigation**

Some nations allow entry with comparative ease. Once established, however, the *operation* of the enterprise may be subject to various restrictions that divert time and resources from the main purpose of the investment. Government oversight may be extensive, with frequent visits from different officials to the degree that it becomes more harassment than regulation. Another form of restriction on operations is performance requirements that mandate minimum local content, specify use of local labor, and mandate levels of technology used in production. The elimination of performance requirements has been a focus of multinational negotiations, especially in the GATT, where the adoption of the WTO TRIMs Agreement (see Chapter 1) targets diminished use of such restrictions.

The worldwide economic declines in 2008 brought more demands for corporate regulation, especially in the financial sector. Most of the discussion was focused on such financial issues as lending practices, hedges, and especially executive compensation that is not linked to performance. The European Union, for example, has legislated pay restraints for business executives, be they foreign or not.

Restrictions are often imposed on repatriating capital or sending profits or royalties abroad, or receiving hard currency to pay for needed imports. Currency restrictions have long been associated with foreign investment in developing nations such as Brazil, less so with Mexico, and have been prominent in China.

CURRENCY ISSUES

Currencies of developing nations are almost uniformly considered to be "soft" currencies, meaning their values tend to be less stable and in less demand than market-driven floating "hard" currencies such as the U.S and Canadian dollars, the Japanese Yen, the Euro and Swiss Franc. Even market-driven, floating currency issues complicate foreign investment by changing costs, revenues and profits. But they do not to halt it unless they become so extreme that they overwhelm principal investment objectives.

Few developing nations have the kind of controls formerly used in nonmarket economies, where entering persons were required to convert so much hard currency for the soft local currency, and where no currency could be taken out of the nation. Every transaction by foreigners had to be accounted for upon exiting the country, and what local currency had not been spent had to be left within the country, often used to purchase tourist items in a shop at the point of departure. Common as such practices were three to four decades ago, they were largely dismantled as part of the transitional process to market economies.

Soft currencies generate significant currency risks as do the super-soft currencies of nonmarket economies. It may be that merely being a developing nation means that the currency is soft. But within the developing world there are soft currencies and there are softer currencies. The softest of these currencies may be as nearly controlled and unwanted as the currencies of a nonmarket economy. One way to deal with the impact on costs, revenues and profits of currency risk is to hedge in the vast currency markets of the world. Another is to contract for and actually receive payments in hard currencies. A third is to engage in "transfer pricing", outlined below.

Currency controls in developing nations often amount to attempts to fix or manage the rate of exchange rather than allow it to freely float, or to link the currency to a hard currency. Hong Kong, for example, has linked its dollar to the U.S. dollar for decades. Mexico for many years linked the Mexican peso to the dollar, and sometimes adjusted the peso daily, often with a slight daily slippage or decline in the peso against the dollar. Denmark and Bulgaria peg their currencies to the Euro.

When the local currency is formally linked to a hard currency, or a hard currency is adopted as the national currency (Ecuador and El Salvador have adopted the U.S. dollar), the local currency has two problems. First, the country's monetary policy effectively is transferred to the linked nation. For example, if the dollar falls against other hard currencies, such as the yen or Euro or Pound Sterling, the linked nation's currency also falls.

Second, the linking may prove to be artificial and cause a parallel free market rate to arise. The parallel market may be allowed to exist, or be suppressed to the extent possible, and become a black market currency. The country may use the parallel free market rate as a guide against which to devalue the fixed official rate.

Many developing nations compound currency problems with high inflation. High inflation tends not to be a characteristic of nonmarket economies, at least until they become nations in transition. A nation with high inflation cannot long keep its currency pegged to that of a low inflation developed nation. There must be periodic devaluations or the developing nation currency will be highly overvalued. This will cause a parallel market at market rates to develop, will encourage nationals to move currency abroad, and may cause the economy to unofficially "dollarize." The latter occurs when there is little faith in the local currency and nationals begin to deal with a hard foreign currency. This is what Venezuela is currently experiencing.

Most transitional nations have attempted to stabilize their currencies. The transitional process has brought some "hardness" to these currencies. One intermediate measure for Eastern European nations in transition from nonmarket to market economies was to peg the domestic currency at a floating rate to a Western hard currency, initially the German Deutschmark, and subsequently the Euro. With later entry into the European Union, the Euro became in most instances the nation's official currency.

Limitations on Management

A limitation on the permitted foreign equity may not mean an inability to control the investment. Host nation majority owners may elect foreign management. Some host nation laws, however, stipulate that the percentage of foreign management may be no greater than the permitted equity participation, a feature of the now repealed 1973 Mexican law. But even this limitation may be unimportant if the local board is dominated by host nation nationals who are all profit motivated entrepreneurs with goals far more aligned with the foreign affiliate than with local government officials who focus on pursuing national social goals.

LIMITATIONS ON TRANSFER OF CAPITAL AND EARNINGS

One aspect of an import/export performance requirement is to alleviate trade imbalances, reflected in part by the flow of capital in or out of a country. Some countries have no systematic restrictions on movements of capital such as foreign exchange controls, limits on borrowing, transfer pricing, as well as repatriation of earnings.

Ironically, restricting remittance of earnings does not always solve balance-of-payments problems. It may rather cause companies to maintain a static position with respect to their capital, and freeze the flow of currency, both inbound and outbound, to the host nation.

Repatriation of assets, profits, or royalties may have to be reviewed by a national bank. This is often the case even where the general policy is to allow relatively free transfer of currencies. Similar approval may be needed to pay for necessary imports. Some countries have been notorious for demanding that all receipts in foreign currencies be converted to the host nation (usually soft) currency. Any foreign currency thereafter needed to pay for imports or to remit home as profits must be approved. This restrictive policy often leads to double billing for exports, with part of the price going directly to the home nation. Such "transfer pricing" (see below) is as commonly practiced as it is commonly deemed unlawful.

Brazil and Argentina are examples of nations that have relied heavily on currency restrictions. The restrictions have been government responses to a frustrating inability to control inflation and indexation. Argentina even partly linked the Argentine currency with the U.S. dollar, which constituted a form of official dual currency in Argentina. Such currency linkages rarely last. Brazil has relatively little in the way of pre-investment clearance procedures, but its Profits Remittance Law requires registration of foreign capital, reinvestment and regulates outgoing payments for dividends, royalties and profits. This Law operates in tandem with Brazilian taxation. Brazil has reduced restrictions on capital and profit repatriations, but it has a history of currency restrictions and investors are always concerned that restrictions will be restored.

Mexico, contrastingly, imposed currency restrictions only during a brief four-month period in 1982. As a result of considerable inflation, capital flight from Mexico increased dramatically in the early 1980s. To conserve remaining hard currency, the government nationalized banks and imposed exchange controls in 1982. The elected but not yet inducted president terminated the controls a few months later. The banking industry was partially opened to foreign investment several years later. Mexico's entry into NAFTA a decade later accelerated Mexico's return to private ownership of and foreign participation in banking.

India seems to have stood somewhere between Mexico and Brazil. While repatriations were generally freely allowable, they were controlled by the Reserve Bank of India and subject to numerous restrictions. Yet the Indian practice was generally thought to be accommodating to foreign investment. If a repatriation or divestment was particularly large, the Indian government might stagger it over several years to cushion its impact on India's persistent foreign exchange difficulties.

China, as part of obtaining export oriented or technologically advanced status, encourages investors to reinvest profits in China rather than remitting them abroad. Such encouragement is generally present in most nations, both because it reduces demand on foreign currency reserves and adds to the industrial base of the nation. Reinvestment is often the only real choice for a foreign investment, since idle funds may be taxed or diminished in value if there is indexation in the nation which does not apply to such funds.

TAXATION OF FOREIGN INVESTMENT, TRANSFER PRICING

A major consideration of any company considering foreign investment is taxation. If a desirable location has exceptionally high corporate income and other taxes (social security, real property, etc.), that desirability may diminish to the point where the nation is rejected as a possible site. Many international business lawyers are uncomfortable with rendering tax advice, and are likely to add the services of a tax specialist. That may include both a specialist on the taxation rules in the foreign nation, as well as a U.S. lawyer familiar with the U.S. tax rules covering such areas as the taxation of income of the foreign investment repatriated (or deemed repatriated) from abroad, income taxation of U.S. employees working abroad in the foreign investment, and the like. As in so many domestic instances, such as mergers, business reasons suggest certain actions but tax rules determine how each action may be carried out.

Many developed nations have concluded tax treaties with nations in which their multinationals invest, essentially to avoid double taxation. Even though a nation may have a liberal foreign investment law, unless there is a reasonably clear expression of the form of taxation facing the investment, investors will be slow to enter. Some nations offer tax incentives to foreign investment, such as tax holidays that defer tax for a certain number of years, or rebates when profits are reinvested rather than repatriated. These tax benefits are often linked to investment in high priority areas, such as those that generate foreign exchange for the host country. Tax benefits may extend beyond a tax on profits to taxation of royalties, taxes on imports and exports, sales and consumption taxes, and taxes on personal income of expatriates. One problem for foreign investors is the dynamics of taxation in foreign nations. Tax burdens change frequently and incentives received one year may be far less valuable in another.

Tax units, whether nations, states or provinces, are always concerned when reporting methods tend to diminish income expectations. Two issues relate to transfer pricing and the unitary tax. If a foreign company reduces its taxable income in a host nation by intracompany transfers at prices which do not reflect arms-length transactions, the host nation may respond with methods to restructure the transfers, and possibly impose sanctions. Secondly, when the subsidiary reports an income that as a percentage of the world-wide corporate entity's income is considerably lower than the percent of assets, employees, and sales within the host nation, the host nation may adopt a unitary tax that replaces a tax based on reported income by adjusting that income to parallel the percent of assets, employees, and sales in the jurisdiction.

"Transfer pricing" is a chronic tax issue associated with foreign investment. Basically, parent companies adjust the price of goods, services, technology or intellectual property rights charged to their foreign subsidiaries or joint ventures in a manner that is "tax efficient". Such adjustments primarily transfer profits as between affiliated business entities. In other words, they are not the product of arms-length negotiations. Transfer pricing can be used to avoid or minimize host nation business taxation, host nation limits on technology and IP royalties, and host nation currency controls. To some degree, transfer pricing issues may be resolved in "double taxation" treaties between developed nations when the flow of foreign investment is two-way.

Section 482 of the U.S. Internal Revenue Code authorizes the IRS to re-allocate gross income, deductions, credits or allowances among entities owned or controlled directly or indirectly by the same interests in order to prevent evasion of taxes or to clearly reflect income. This is easier said than done, and the IRS almost always has numerous "transfer pricing" tax disputes in progress. For example, in 2015 the IRS served a $3.3 *billion* dollar tax liability notice on Coca-Cola for transfer pricing related to sales of its syrup. Not surprisingly, transfer pricing has been widely used to avoid U.S. corporate taxation by transferring royalties and revenues to tax haven entities. California employs "unitary tax rules" to deal with transfer pricing. It taxes foreign subsidiaries, not on earnings, but on the basis of the average amount of the subsidiary's employees, assets and sales in California. Minority shareholders who lose earnings as a result of transfer pricing may want to consider whether transfer pricing involves a breach of fiduciary duties by Boards of Directors.

Other jurisdictions have also followed the IRS re-allocation approach, but the complexity of the issues and accountings mandates a reasonably sophisticated tax service, not always found in the developing world. Developing nations are particularly interested in ensuring that local joint venture partners get their proper share of profits. India has sent transfer pricing tax notices to Microsoft, Shell, GE and others alleging payment of low prices for shares in their respective Indian subsidiaries, a financing technique used by MNE. The EU has challenged very favorable transfer price deals obtained from national tax authorities by Starbucks in the Netherlands, Fiat/Chrysler, Amazon, and McDonald's in Luxembourg, Apple in Ireland, and Anheuser-Busch InBev in Belgium. The EU Commission considers them unlawful state subsidization. Appeals by the companies and national governments involved are pending before EU courts.

In Mexico, "maquiladoras" (assembly plants) were run by foreign investors for decades as break-even cost centers using transfer pricing techniques. This practice avoided relatively high rates of Mexican corporate taxation, and in the early years of maquiladoras, Mexican currency controls and royalty limits. Mexico eventually established "safe harbors" in their tax regulations indicating that minimum, low levels of maquiladora profits were unlikely to attract "arms-length" tax audits. Bingo! Maquiladoras suddenly showed profits slightly higher than those needed to take advantage of the safe harbors.

RESTRICTIONS UPON WITHDRAWAL, BANKRUPTCY SHOPPING

The withdrawal of foreign investment may be subject to restrictions. These restrictions may affect the ability to repatriate capital, the liability of the foreign parent or other subsidiaries in the country for debts of the withdrawing entity, and the removal of physical assets from the country. Potential investors should evaluate the restrictiveness at each level in determining whether or not to invest.

Termination of an investment by bankruptcy may introduce the foreign investor to different theories of bankruptcy, including liability of the parent for debts of the foreign subsidiary. Chapter 11 of U.S. bankruptcy law provides a much used form of reorganizing a corporation. Few other nations have such proceedings. Where a corporation has assets in the United States but is principally a foreign corporation, Chapter 11 may be attractive. For example, in December, 2004, the Russian oil giant Yukos filed for Chapter 11 protection in Houston, where the company claimed it had assets and where its chief financial officer had a residence. The petition asked the U.S. court to stop an auction planned in Russia a few days later of Yukos most valuable asset, Yuganskneftegas. The Russian government scheduled the auction to collect on a tax claim that some officers of Yukos viewed as expropriation. An injunction was issued prohibiting Gazprom, the huge Russian natural gas company, from participating in the auction.

But it was ignored in Russia and the auction was held as scheduled. However, Gazprom apparently was concerned that its gas exports could be threatened by legal actions in Europe. It did not bid. At the auction an unidentified buyer purchased Yuganskneftegas in a six minute auction. The buyer was believed to be a group of individuals who would quickly sell the company to another Russian oil giant, with Kremlin approval. The secrecy of the proceeding illustrates the lack of transparency in Russia in insolvency proceedings, and the need for global bankruptcy rules.

Firms sometimes file for bankruptcy under laws more favorable to restructure the company, and this practice is increasing. For example, an auto parts maker in Germany, Schefenacker, was facing default on a bond debt and moved its headquarters to London, where it filed for bankruptcy and restructured the company in a manner not permitted under German law. A small group of bondholders in Germany might have been able to force a liquidation in German courts, but could not do so in London. Schefenacker already had a plant in the United Kingdom, thus providing a link with Britain. That can be important because EU law limits the filing of insolvency petitions to the "center of a debtor's main interests." Sometimes bonds held in the country from which the company moves are converted into shares, reducing the vote of bondholders in that departed nation. Management is retained as before. In a case involving Parmalat of Italy the Bank of America was able to file to wind up the proceedings of a Parmalat Irish entity located in Dublin. The end result of this global bankruptcy shopping has been revisions to the laws in France, Germany and Italy.

Protocols between governments sometimes can sort out bankruptcy across borders. In 1991–1992 the first significant protocol was used in the Maxwell communications empire insolvency. The protocol was between courts in the United States and the United Kingdom. The function of a protocol is to agree upon how the insolvency will proceed, and avoid the problems discussed above. The Maxwell protocol is an exemplary case and other protocols have followed. Several have involved U.S.-Canadian cases. Some have used satellite television for hearings. Protocols increased after the International Bar Association adopted in 1995–96 its Cross-Border Insolvency Concordat. The Concordat is a set of principles intended to encourage and assist insolvency administration involving more than one country. Protocols have filled an important gap.

In 2000, Mexico was the first major nation to adopt the UNCITRAL Model Bankruptcy Law. Canada has also now adopted the essence of the UNCITRAL Model Law, as has the United States, thus making it effective throughout NAFTA. Japan has adopted legislation based on the Model Law, as has South Africa. UNCITRAL has also developed a Legislative Guide on Insolvency as an assist to the many countries in the process of adapting their insolvency laws to the Model Law.

CORRUPTION AND FOREIGN INVESTMENT

Bribery in some nations has reached epidemic proportions. Visit the Transparency International website for their global maps graphically displaying a Corruption Index for the world's nations. A UK organization, Control Risks, suggests three classes of corruption. First is the payment of bribes to officials and businesses for favorable treatment. Second is nepotism carried to a level of domination of business by clans and families. And third is the evolution of corruption into organized crime, with the participation of officials at the highest levels of government. This last class seems the case with Russia, creating a potentially serious risk of extortion and kidnaping to all persons transacting business in the country.

Disclosures of corruption in China frequently appear to involve government officials. For example, the Chinese People's Procuratorate reported in one year 34,070 cases of economic crimes (bribes, embezzlement, graft, etc.) involving more than 7,000 officials, including 3,017 managers of state owned industries and 2,141 involved with banking and negotiable securities. The current, vigorous anti-corruption campaign of President Xi Jinping has netted an unprecedented number of high-ranking government and military officials.

The regulated nature of foreign investments and the large sums involved invite corruption, be it extortion by government officials or payments made to obtain, maintain or influence business interests. Laws against bribery, starting prominently with the U. S. Foreign Corrupt Practices Act in 1977 (FCPA), have proliferated. Individual and corporate sanctions are almost always severe, and sanctioning under several legal regimes for the same practices is not infrequent.

THE U.S. FOREIGN CORRUPT PRACTICES ACT

Back in the 1970s, as a spin-off of Watergate, secret slush funds used by U.S. companies to pay foreign officials to advance business interests were revealed. There was an outcry by the press within the United States and abroad about the disclosed payments, especially by U.S. aircraft corporations to Japanese and Dutch officials. The response of Congress was the FCPA. But there was almost no legislative response from other nations individually, and only a very modest response internationally. The United States thus stood nearly alone for decades in responding to the general condemnation of payments to foreign officials by enacting the FCPA. Many U.S. businesses objected to the United States adopting a law prohibiting foreign payments. These businesses had to compete abroad for contracts with enterprises from nations which had no such laws, and which in some cases, even allowed foreign bribes to be considered tax deductible ordinary and necessary business expenses.

The current, twice-amended FCPA remains relatively concise. It establishes stringent accounting and disclosure standards supervised by the SEC. The FCPA prohibits payments to foreign officials or political parties directly, or "while knowing" by way of third persons or subsidiaries, when such payments are for the purpose of influencing any act or decision of the foreign official, inducing the foreign official to act or refrain from acting in violation of the official's duty, inducing the foreign official to use influence with a foreign government *or an instrumentality* of that government (interpreted as including state-owned or state-controlled enterprises) to influence that government's or instrumentality's act or decision, or to secure "any improper advantage". For example, procurement contracts, tax benefits, customs preferences, and foreign investment privileges fall within its scope.

The Justice Department enforces the illegal payments prohibitions. Sanctions can include felony criminal penalties for willful violations, civil penalties and jail terms, and even the threat of being denied contracting rights with the U.S. government. Any criminal fine imposed on a person under the FCPA may not be paid or indemnified by the company directly or indirectly. There is an important exception for routine government action ("grease payments"), which is further defined in a separate section. The Act then establishes as an affirmative defense, cases where the payment was lawful under the *written* laws of the foreign country (this defense has never successfully been invoked), or was a "reasonable and bona fide expenditure" for business purposes. Anyone dealing with the FCPA should read the 2012 Department of Justice Resource Guide to the U.S. Foreign Corrupt Practices Act.

Other "sanctions" are less formal, but potentially no less severe. Reputational damage, procurement exclusion, shareholder lawsuits and higher capital costs may follow. FCPA settlements typically also impose ongoing compliance costs. For example, in 2015 a small Florida company (IAP) paid over $7 million to settle criminal charges regarding procurement payments to Kuwaiti officials made via a consultant. In addition, IAP promised high-level commitment against corruption, a clear corporate policy against corruption and regular corruption risk reviews, assignment of compliance responsibilities to a senior executive reporting to independent monitoring bodies, extensive training, reporting and investigation systems, disciplinary procedures, and corruption due diligence in mergers and acquisitions.

When the FCPA was first enacted the U.S. government denied that U.S. businesses would suffer. But that view changed as other nations were urged but failed to adopt similar laws. One argument in favor of the law was that foreign officials would become aware that they should not talk about payments to U.S. business persons, since such payments were prohibited. But that presumed a more perfect world than existed. Some observers believe that payments by U.S. companies to foreign officials have continued, but are made with much greater care and with less of a paper or electronic trail than before.

FCPA prosecutions have risen dramatically in the past 10 years. Most are settled under deferred or non-prosecution agreements. This explains the absence of FCPA case law and reinforces the wide discretion to the SEC and DOJ to interpret the Act as they see fit. At present, for example, whether hiring relatives of Chinese officials is covered by the FCPA is under scrutiny. Here are some settlement examples:

The FCPA can apply to extraterritorial activities of foreign as well as U.S. firms. For example, Siemens AG paid bribes in numerous countries and an agreed to an FCPA fine of $800 million. The 2008 Siemens' FCPA settlement remains the largest to date. German and 20 other anti-bribery law enforcement authorities also pursued Siemens, which is reported to have spent over $1 billion in legal and accounting fees. The Siemens cases involved the Oil-for-Food program, which resulted

in four other settlements against Akzo Nobel of the
Netherlands for $3 million in penalties, against
Flowserve Corporation for $10.55 million of criminal
and civil penalties, against AB Volvo resulting in
$12.6 million in penalties, and against Fiat for $17.8
million civil and criminal penalties.

The French engineering giant, Alstom, pleaded
guilty in 2014 and agreed to pay $772 million in
record FCPA criminal fines. Alstom failed to
disclose its misconduct or cooperate with U.S.
authorities concerning its corrupt payments via
consultants in Indonesia, Egypt, Saudi Arabia and
the Bahamas. The total fines amounted to over 2.5
times Alstom's profits from its corrupt activities and
delayed GE's acquisition of Alstom for several years
pending settlement. Alstom also faces criminal
charges before Britain's Serious Fraud Office. In
2015, Hitachi of Japan agreed to pay $19 million to
settle FCPA charges concerning payments made to
South Africa's ruling party regarding power station
construction contracts.

Significant settlements also include Lucent
Technologies, Inc., involving payments to Chinese
officials and resulting in penalties of $137 million.
KBR/Halliburton settled for $579 million in 2009,
BAE for $400 million in 2010, Johnson & Johnson
for $70 million in 2011. Daimler settled in 2010 with
the SEC, agreeing to pay $185 million in FCPA fines
($96.3 million criminal and $91.4 million civil).
Avon voluntarily reported itself concerning illegal
payments in China leading to a "moderate" FCPA
settlement of $135 million in 2014 along with the

placement of an independent FCPA "monitor" inside the company. In 2010, the FBI conducted its first FCPA sting operation ("Shot Show"), resulting in the arrest of 22 executives from military and law enforcement products companies. The government has also seized personal assets (pensions, cars and homes) of violators as forfeited proceeds of bribery.

There have also been individual prosecutions, including some high profile persons. Albert Stanley, CEO of KBR, a subsidiary of Halliburton, agreed to serve seven years in prison and pay $10.8 million in restitution. In 2010, the FBI conducted its first FCPA sting operation ("Shot Show"), resulting in the arrest of 22 executives from military and law enforcement products companies. The government has also seized personal assets (pensions, cars and homes) of violators as forfeited proceeds of bribery. Corporate compliance personnel may need prior DOJ/SEC approval, and government monitors given unfettered access to records and compliance processes.

A New York Times article in December 2012 covered more than three full pages describing bribes allegedly made by Wal-Mart in Mexico. The payments led to a Department of Justice investigation that is still ongoing, an expensive *global* in-house review of payments' practices by Wal-Mart (reportedly costing over a million dollars a day!), and a dramatic drop in the value of Wal-Mart stock.

FCPA COMPLIANCE PROGRAMS

The dramatic increase in FCPA proceedings during recent years, combined with minimal jurisdictional requirements and major reputational and corrective action costs (not to mention share price declines), have caused widespread adoption of company compliance policies and programs. Training of all employees, especially foreign employees, in contact with foreign officials has become routine. Such training is repeated regularly, and recorded in personnel files. A policy will not assure that illegal payments are not made in an investment context. But even if illegal payments are later found to have been made, a written policy, acknowledged by employees' signatures, will to establish the company's good intentions and should help in minimizing penalties. Morgan Stanley is thought to have avoided penalties completely when one of their Chinese employees "went rogue" despite major repeated training and compliance efforts.

Vendors, customs brokers, transport carriers, construction and other service providers of U.S. corporations engaged are being required to undergo FCPA training. Such third parties must also complete FCPA audits, and sign contract clauses and affidavits as to compliance and awareness of FCPA risks. Some firms decline absolutely to make any grease payments. Dealing with agents and consultants creates special problems. They should be asked for details about the existence of any relatives or business associates who are in the government. The company should contact various persons in the U.S. government, Chambers of Commerce, local counsel, and the like to check on their reputation, and conduct a Google search. All this "due diligence" might help to later establish that the company did not act "while knowing" (the FCPA standard) that payments to third parties would end up going corruptly to officials. Finally, the agreement with the agent or consultant should contain a clause that none of the funds paid to the agent will be used in any manner which might violate the FCPA.

FCPA due diligence in connection with international mergers and acquisitions has become the norm. The resulting business assumes FCPA liabilities, though it may seek indemnification. Record keeping and internal control compliance programs are mandatory and critical to adhering to the strict FCPA accounting and disclosure rules, which require a bribe to be declared a bribe.

OECD, UN AND BRITISH BRIBERY LAW

The 35 or so industrial nations of the OECD, and the United Nations, have attempted to address corruption. The OECD adopted a Convention on Combatting Bribery of Foreign officials in International Business Transactions in 1997, some 20 years after the FCPA. The OECD Convention obligates signatories to criminalize bribery of foreign officials and sanction inaccurate accounts. The OECD also recommended prohibiting tax deductions for bribes, a recommendation that Canada and others have followed. Japan has taken the bribery issue seriously. Japan's Ministry of International Trade and Industry (MITI) began in 1997 to adopt measures consistent with the OECD guidelines. Nigeria's president sent its principal bribery enforcement official on a year-long overseas assignment. Perhaps he had been too effective a leader in combating bribery. Enactment of laws in other OECD countries followed slowly, indeed Britain's Bribery Act did not arrive until 2010 (see below). Adoption and enforcement of anti-bribery policies often differ, but some foreign enforcement actions have gained attention in Brazil, Finland, France, Germany, India, Ireland and the Philippines.

The United Nations finally came into the game in 2004, after years of inability to agree and failure to acknowledge that perhaps some governments were responsible for their officials' actions in receiving bribes from foreign entities. Because the UN Convention went beyond the scope of the FCPA and OECD enactments, including procedures for recouping bribes "hidden" abroad by the officials who received them, it was thought to be the answer to the need for a more multinational approach to bribery. Some 170 nations have subscribed to the U.N. Convention, but many of the worst offending nations have acted to make the UN Convention just so many words. Some $20 to $40 billion a year are lost by developing nations to corruption.

The UN and World Bank are collaborating on a Stolen Assets Recovery Initiative, joined by the U.S. Department of Justice has a Kleptocracy Initiative.

Recoveries of corruptly derived assets are few and far between, and in some countries graft has become openly brazen. While the UN Convention against Corruption is welcome, the OECD appears to have largely preempted the field with respect to serious attention.

The British Bribery Act of 2010 (BBA) may have been late in arriving, but is now widely perceived to be one of the most rigorous in the world. It extends not just to payments to foreign officials, but also to private parties. Its coverage is broad in scope (for example, "grease payments" are not exempted) and its criminal and civil liability is strict, extending to essentially all firms doing business in the U.K. Hypothetically, therefore, the BBA reaches U.S. firms with U.K. stock listings or sales offices, and those processing illegal payments via British banks. The BBA governs the activities of such firms around the world, say bribes in India.

Administered by Britain Serious Fraud Office (SFO), the BBA governs the activities of such firms around the world, say bribes in India. Alstom of France, already having paid the DOJ $772 million for FCPA violations, stands charged under the BBA for making $75 million in payments to secure $4 billion in Egyptian, Saudi Arabian, Bahamian and Indonesian projects. The SFO need not take into account the FCPA fines Alstom has already paid.

The Act applies to solicitation as well as receipt of bribes, and has no statute of limitations! Violators can be disbarred from EU public procurement contracts. It is tempered by an undefined "adequate procedures" compliance defense not found in the FCPA.

In sum, neither the OECD or U.N. Convention, nor the British Bribery Act, is a clone of the FCPA, but the lonely U.S. position on foreign corrupt practices law now has allies.

MASS TORT LITIGATION RISKS: ALLEGED HUMAN RIGHTS AND ENVIRONMENTAL VIOLATIONS

Foreign investors have always faced possible litigation in the host nation. Jurisdiction in the host nation, say for products liability, is rarely a problem because the company is clearly there and doing business. But a subsidiary in the host nation often has few assets. While they may be sufficient to satisfy judgments dealing with such common issues as a job related injury to an employee, or a contract breach, they are insufficient when multiple plaintiff actions are brought for alleged large scale injury such as environmental damage or labor abuses. In such actions the defendants typically include both the parent and the host nation subsidiary, leading to jurisdiction issues over the parent if the suit is brought in the host nation.

Such suits are also brought in the United States, often in state courts where juries are perceived as hostile to multinational corporations, such as South Texas or Mississippi. Initiated by attorneys' with contingent fee contracts and who demand punitive damages, human rights abuses, environmental damages and even cultural genocide have been the charges in an increasing number of suits against some of the largest corporations in the United States, including Del Monte, DuPont, Exxon Mobil Corp., Ford Motor Company, Texaco, Union Carbide, and United Technologies. The principal basis for these suits has been alleged violations of international law and specifically of the Alien Tort Claims Act (ACTA) of 1789 (28 U.S.C.A. 1350). The Act gives U.S. district courts jurisdiction over "any civil action by an alien for a tort only, committed in violation of the law of nations or a treaty of the United States."

Early U.S. Supreme Court ACTA Case Law

Much of the ACTA litigation has evolved since the *Filártiga v. Peña-Irala* decision (630 F.2d 876) by the Second Circuit Court of Appeals in 1980. *Filártiga* did not involve a corporate defendant. It was brought by a Paraguayan citizen, Filártiga, residing in the United States, against one Peña, another Paraguayan citizen in the United States on a tourist visa. Peña had been the Inspector General of the Police in Asunción, Paraguay, and allegedly tortured and killed the son of Filártiga. The case was based principally on violations of the Alien Tort Claims Act, a 1789 enactment of Congress addressing quite different concerns, such as acts of piracy. It was rarely used until *Filártiga*. But its brevity and breadth provided the court a foundation to find Peña in violation. The court had little trouble in holding that death by torture constituted a violation of international law.

The Court indicated that private claims under federal common law should not be recognized for violations of international law norms with "less definite content and acceptance among civilized nations than the historical paradigms familiar when the ACTA was enacted." Nevertheless, when the court rendered its opinion in 1980 the floodgates opened for many suits that tried to enlarge upon the scope of violations of international law.

How expansive an interpretation should be given the ATCA's "violation of the law of nations" language is yet undetermined. Certainly torture and extra-judicial killing are such violations. So perhaps are hostage taking and aircraft sabotage, and acts of terrorism. But the cases have tested the ATCA's language in two ways. One is the scope of acts within a category that appear at first glance to constitute international law violations, but may encompass less clear violations, such as torture (e.g., cutting off hands versus sleep deprivation) and human rights (extra-judicial killing of political dissidents versus "cultural genocide" relocating indigenous people to build a dam).

The second debate is whether to bring within violations of international law areas where there is uncertainty about whether acts violate treaties or customary international law. The most frequently litigated may be violations of environmental laws. While there are many domestic environmental laws, there is considerable debate as to whether there is any international environmental law, especially customary law. Several federal Circuit courts have rejected environmental ACTA claims.

Sosa v. Alvarez-Machain, a 2004 U.S. Supreme Court decision (542 U.S. 692, 124 S.Ct. 2739), limited ATCA. *Sosa* involved an individual claiming that his abduction in Mexico by U.S. federal authorities constituted a violation of international law under the ATCA. The case brought the U.S. Supreme Court into the debate over the limits of the ATCA. The Court rejected the defendant's argument that the ATCA does not provide a cause of action, but found that the abduction of Alvarez-Machain in Mexico and his transportation to the United States for trial did not violate the law of nations. The Court urged judicial caution in applying too broad an interpretation of the ATCA.

While these issues could be debated and litigated in cases against officials of the foreign nations, subject to jurisdiction in U.S. courts, the far deeper pockets are those of multinational corporations. It was inevitable that suits would be brought against corporate defendants. The first to establish corporate liability was *Doe v. Unocal,* 395 F.3d 932 (9th Circ. 2002), brought by Burmese nationals charging human rights violations by the defendant for complicity with the government in using forced labor in the construction of an oil pipeline. Subsequent Federal Circuit opinions stress the need to prove that corporations share the intent of government acts causing harm to ATCA plaintiffs.

Recent U.S. Supreme Court ACTA Case Law

In 2012, the Supreme Court held that only natural persons could be liable under the federal Torture Victim Protection Act of 1992. The issue of corporate liability under the ATCA was raised but not decided by the U.S. Supreme Court in *Kiobel v. Royal Dutch Petroleum Co.*, 133 S.Ct. 1659 (2013). This opinion involved human rights claims by Nigerian refugees against British and Dutch oil companies and their Nigerian subsidiaries for allegedly aiding and abetting human rights violations by the government in Nigeria. Declining to rule on a Second Circuit decision that corporations are not subject to ACTA as a matter of customary international law, the Supreme Court instead ruled unanimously that the ATCA could not be used because there is a presumption against extraterritorial application of U.S. law. That presumption is not easily displaced, and the mere presence of a corporation in a foreign country is not a sufficient reason.

The Court held: "And even where the claims touch and concern the territory of the United States, they must do so with sufficient force to displace the presumption against extraterritorial application." While the decision was unanimous, four justices believed that corporations may be "today's pirates." Immediate reaction was that the decision will substantially eliminate the currently popular ACTA litigation by foreign plaintiffs based on nothing more than a U.S. corporation's presence in a foreign nation.

Forum Non Conveniens (fnc)

Motions for *forum non conveniens (fnc)* rulings are often presented by U.S. defendants as part of mass tort litigation strategy. If they are successful, the case is sometimes moved to a remote foreign forum where the case often dies. The death is because the U.S. attorneys no longer have visions of large punitive damage awards. Indeed, they may have little involvement as attorneys in the foreign forum. For example, an airplane crash affirmative *fnc* ruling never went to trial in Scotland. The notorious *Bhopal* gas explosion *fnc* case resulted in a settlement in India far less than what might have been a jury's award in the United States, and little of the settlement funds ever reached the injured plaintiffs. Moreover, *forum non conveniens* dismissals can be granted prior to consideration of personal and subject matter jurisdiction. . . convenient for the court and the litigants

The law of *forum non conveniens* seems sufficiently elastic that it is hard to predict the outcome, and additionally hard to predict possible conditions that the court may impose upon the defendant in return for granting the *fnc* motion. The law is a product of equity, and is somewhat amorphous. U.S. Courts have thus increasingly asked about the nature of the proceeding in the foreign forum, especially about the nature of the process. If there is a viable legal system that provides for the resolution of disputes of the form presented, the *forum non conveniens* motion may be granted.

One problem for defendants and their attorneys in obtaining a successful *forum non conveniens* ruling is that control over the case may be diminished or lost. If the case is actively pursued abroad, the attorneys likely will not be able to appear before the foreign court, and foreign counsel must be hired. The U.S. defendant will have to learn about the foreign law and legal system. Chevron's successful invocation of *fnc* in an environmental pollution dispute resulted in a multi-billion dollar 2013 judgment against it in Ecuador. A federal district court opinion found the Ecuadorean judge had been bribed and his opinion fraudulently "ghost-written" by plaintiffs' U.S. attorneys. Chevron successfully utilized arbitration proceedings to obtain an interim award ordering Ecuador not to seek enforcement of the judgment until a final decision is reached, but failed to persuade U.S. courts to enjoin enforcement globally in the absence of enforcement proceedings in the United States. Chevron has spent a small fortune defending itself against collection of the Ecuadorean judgment around the world.

As *Chevron* suggests, the better choice for a mass tort defendant may be to keep the matter in the U.S. court, but to seek application of foreign law. Many such cases merit the application of foreign law, and when a court so rules the difficulty of proving foreign law may be an impossible burden for the plaintiff. For an analogous instance also suggesting be careful what you wish for, a U.S. helicopter firm succeeded in obtaining a *forum non conveniens* dismissal against Chinese parties alleging damages from a helicopter crash inside China. This dismissal led to a default judgment of about $650,000 against the firm in Chinese court proceedings. The Chinese judgment was ultimately held enforceable in California under the Uniform Foreign Money Judgments Recognition Act.

For considerably more extensive coverage of international business litigation issues, see R. Folsom, *Principles of International Litigation and Arbitration* (West Academic Publishing).

CHAPTER 3

THE LAW OF AND INSURANCE AGAINST EXPROPRIATIONS

Expropriation Law Standards   **Calvo Clauses**

Compensation   **Claims Settlements**

OPIC and MIGA Insurance

Absent any applicable investor-state treaty rules and remedies, for example arbitration proceedings like those found in BITs or NAFTA (see Chapters 7 and 8), if a taking occurs, there are several issues that will face the expropriated foreign investor. What law will apply: The law of the place of the taking, international law, or the law of the forum? Was the taking for a public purpose, or was it retaliatory or discriminatory? Was proper compensation forthcoming? Must remedies be exhausted in the taking nation? If the investor whose property has been taken attempts to sue the taking government in courts in the United States, or in third nations, what are the likely defenses?

Assuming international law applies or is to be considered, what is the content of that law? For example, the Mexican expropriation of foreign petroleum interests in 1938 commenced a dialogue between Mexico and the United States regarding applicable law. Mexico insisted that Mexican domestic law applied, which required compensation. The United States insisted that international law applied, which also required compensation. The United States argued that compensation had to be made in accordance with an alleged "prompt, adequate, and effective" international law standard. Mexico disagreed that such a standard existed under international law. A vigorous debate over what is the international law of expropriation continues.

Avoiding or insuring against the risk of expropriation may depend upon its form. Most attention focuses on direct expropriation, when part or all of the investment is taken by decree of the host nation government. Indirect or "creeping" expropriations involve various governmental actions that may make continuation of the investment impossible. These actions can include: excessively high tax rates, forced joint ventures, extensive government control, mandatory use of domestic inputs, and mandatory export levels.

The risk of expropriation cannot be fully avoided, and insurance should be considered, especially that provided either by the U.S. Overseas Private Investment Corporation (OPIC) or the World Bank's Multilateral Investment Guarantee Agency (MIGA), discussed below. Taking measures to avoid the risk of expropriation cannot assure a foreign investor that expropriation will not occur. Many of the expropriations of the last century resulted from revolutions (USSR, Cuba, Mexico, Nicaragua) or very significant alterations in the government through elections (Chile), or in post-independence nationalism (Indonesia). More recently, expropriations have tended to be ideologically driven, e.g. in Venezuela, Bolivia and Ecuador. Venezuelan expropriations have hit virtually every major oil company, Cargill, Cemex, Banco Santander and many others.

APPLYING DOMESTIC LAW OF THE TAKING NATION

While there does seem to be agreement that international law is applicable to takings of foreign property, this principle has been challenged in two ways. First, the U.N. Charter of Economic Rights and Duties of States affirms the right of nations to expropriate property, and states that compensation issues are to be settled by "domestic law of the nationalization State", unless otherwise agreed. This Charter, which does not constitute international law, was passed over the objection to this provision by 16 nations, mostly the largest industrialized nations, including the United States. The Charter illustrates the diversity of opinion regarding expropriation arising with the achievement of independence by many former colonies of the industrialized nations.

Second, when a nation expropriates foreign property, it tends to find greater comfort in arguing the applicability of its own law, which invariably is less demanding in requiring compensation than whatever standard the international community has approved.

APPLYING INTERNATIONAL LAW

Even if the parties agree that international law is applicable, it may be difficult to determine what international law requires. It may be "prompt, adequate and effective" compensation, as the United States argues, or "just" compensation, as the Restatement of Foreign Relations suggests, or "appropriate" compensation, as U.N. Resolution 1803 proposed in 1962, and which seems to have been adopted by tribunals and courts more than any other standard.

A sovereign nation has full and permanent sovereignty over its natural resources and economic activities. That principle is clearly stated in the U.N. Resolution on Permanent Sovereignty over Natural Resources (1962). Sovereignty gives the nation the right to take privately-owned property, whether that property is owned by the country's nationals or foreigners. These are long held concepts that exist on both an international and domestic level. Most national (and state or provincial) constitutions express this right. But the theory of taking does not allow the taking for any reason or upon any whim of the prevailing government. There must be a public purpose. There are two problems with the public purpose, however. First is its definition, and second is determining who is to measure public purpose in an international expropriation.

DEFINING PUBLIC PURPOSE

There has never been a very clear definition of public purpose. It is often expressed in such broad words as "improvement of the social welfare or economic betterment of the nation." Does this mean such specific goals as improved infrastructure, better medical care, lower rates for basic services such as electricity, more adequate housing, or a lower infant-mortality rate? Or does it mean something more general, such as a shift to a different fundamental economic theory, by increasing or making exclusive the state ownership of the means of production and distribution. The proper definition may be what the taking nation says it is, but at least there seems to be agreement that some legitimate public purpose is a necessary component of a lawful expropriation, and the taking nation must offer some rational purpose for the taking.

Defining public purpose does not end the problem. When one state has taken the property of nationals of another, what court should sit in judgment of the public purpose issue, both to define it and to determine whether it is likely to be or already has been met? A court in the taking nation is not likely to overrule the taking for lack of public purpose justifications. The ideal setting for establishing these rules is the International Court of Justice. But that court has not yet proven to be an effective body to develop an international law of expropriation.

Such development is thus left to national courts and various tribunals, which have tended to shy away from addressing the public purpose issue. That has been because of both the conceptual difficulty with the issue and the fact that foreign investors whose properties have been expropriated usually are not interested in restitution of their property as long as the taking government is in office. The foreign investors are interested in receiving compensation. Consequently, while the public purpose element of expropriation is present and should be considered, there are other elements of expropriation more likely to be the subject of investor concern.

RETALIATION AND DISCRIMINATION

In addition to lacking a public purpose, an expropriation may be unlawful if it was in retaliation for acts of the government of the person who owned the property, or if it discriminated against a particular person or government. Proof of a retaliatory purpose may actually constitute proof of the absence of a public purpose. If an expropriation is undertaken solely to discriminate against a foreign nation, it may constitute proof of both a lack of a public purpose and retaliation. The three elements, public purpose, retaliation, and discrimination, are thus often quite interrelated.

The Cuban expropriations were examples of both. The first expropriations were exclusively of U.S. property (i.e., discrimination), and were in response to the United States eliminating the Cuban sugar quota (i.e., retaliation). Both were reasons for U.S. courts holding the expropriations to have been unlawful. The taking of some property of only one nation's nationals is not necessarily discriminatory. A country may decide to nationalize one sector, such as mining. That sector might be owned exclusively by nationals of one foreign nation. It could be difficult in such case to conclude whether the taking was based on the desire to have the state own all mining interests, because it was believed more sound economically or preferable for national security reasons, or was based on an intention to discriminate against one nation and take its property, whether it consisted of mining properties or hotels or anything else.

However important it may be to understand the issues of public purpose, retaliation and discrimination, the real issue is likely to be the payment of compensation. If a foreign investor is compensated satisfactorily, there is likely to be little concern with the technicalities of lawfulness or unlawfulness of the taking under international law because of the public purpose, retaliation, or discrimination characteristics of the taking. The investor may be concerned with the loss of future business, however, and may wish to consider the prospects of a return of the property after the new, hostile government is either replaced or adopts a different attitude toward foreign investment or the foreign investor.

THE UNCERTAINTY OF
INTERNATIONAL LAW

As noted above, if the expropriated foreign property owner is satisfactorily compensated, that is likely to end the matter. A ruling by any dispute settling entity, court or tribunal, domestic or international, that the expropriation was unlawful, is a purely pyrrhic victory if there is no satisfactory compensation. What, therefore, is the proper measure of compensation?

The U.S. government's repeatedly stated position regarding compensation is that it is (1) required under international law, and it (2) must be prompt, adequate, and effective. The first view, that international law requires compensation, is generally shared by jurists within the United States and abroad. But the second view, the prompt, adequate, and effective standard, is the subject of vigorous debate and is rejected by many U.S. and foreign jurists. The two parts are often discussed as one issue.

The first international court case usually referred to that discussed expropriation is the 1928 *Chorzów Factory* decision of the Permanent Court of International Justice (PCIJ Ser. A No. 17). That case referred only to a duty of the "payment of fair compensation." That seems less stringent than the "prompt, adequate, and effective" standard alleged to be the prevailing international law by U.S. Secretary of State Hull in 1938 in his notes to the Mexican government. There has been little further guidance from the PCIJ or its successor the

International Court of Justice. The narrow focus in the latter's *Barcelona Traction* decision (1970 ICJ Rep. 3) added very little, if anything, to the international law of expropriation compensation.

A subsequent dispute involving an intervention which allegedly caused the company to file for bankruptcy was decided by a chamber of the International Court of Justice (the ELSI Judgment, 1989 ICJ Rep. 15). It involved the interpretation of the Treaty of Friendship, Commerce, and Navigation between the United States and Italy, most specifically issues regarding interference with the U.S. company's right to "control and manage" its operation in Italy. The measure of damages became an issue, and was not dealt with very clearly, partly because of the uncertainty of the company's ability to function during the period of intervention and the appropriateness of damages after filing bankruptcy. But the ruling was that Italy had not violated international law in its requisition or intervention. Furthermore, since the damages were conditioned upon liability, there was no final decision as to their measure.

Debate over the proper level of compensation continues without anything resembling a consensus. But some standards have developed that might be applied by a court or tribunal. The alternatives seem to use elastic words or terms, but when further defined, there may be less difference than is at first thought to exist.

COMPENSATION

The "prompt, adequate and effective" standard is likely to be applied by U.S. courts or tribunals applying a U.S norm of compensation theory, or searching for an international standard, or U.S. courts or tribunals applying an agreement between the parties or nations that calls for the application of the prompt, adequate, and effective standard, such as a bilateral investment treaty. There is no assurance, however, that a U.S. court or tribunal searching for "the" international law will arrive at a prompt, adequate, and effective standard. The 1981 *Banco Nacional v. Chase Manhattan Bank* decision (658 F.2d 875, 2d Cir.) suggested that the consensus of nations was to apply an "appropriate" standard, quoting one highly regarded American author who rejected the prompt, adequate, and effective standard as a norm of international law

Because of the very limited number of judicial decisions discussing the compensation issue, decisions of arbitration panels are often useful to compare with cases. In the 1981 *LIAMCO* arbitration (20 Int'l Legal Mat. 1), the arbitrator suggested that the prompt, adequate, and effective standard was not the only standard, and interpreted the contract to conclude that under general principles of law only "equitable" compensation was required. But the arbitrator included in the award a substantial amount for lost profits, a conclusion suggesting the adoption of a *full* compensation standard.

"Appropriate" compensation norm is the standard in U.N. Resolution 1803 of 1962, which in the view of many jurists, remains the most likely norm to be applied. It has been suggested as the standard in the *Banco Nacional* decision noted above, and in at least two other important international arbitrations, the *TOPCO/CALASIATIC* and *AMINOIL* cases (17 Int'l Legal Mat. 1 (1978) and 21 Int'l Legal Mat. 976 (1982)).

A "fair" compensation standard was used in the much-discussed but little followed *Chorzów Factory* PCIJ decision, noted above. However, fair compensation has not generally been accepted as the proper standard, and has not become an accepted norm of international law. That is at least partly due to the broad sense of what fair might include. A legal norm deserves greater definition.

The Restatement (Third) of the Foreign Relations Law of the United States adopted "just" in place of "appropriate", largely to avoid a possible inclusion of host nation demanded deductions under an "appropriate" standard. Several expropriating nations had calculated compensation by taking the company's value of the property and deducting what were called "excess profits" or "improper pricing" of resources to arrive at a conclusion that either no compensation was due, or that the company actually owed the expropriating nation. But it is hard to envision a taking nation agreeing that while such deductions could be allowed under an "appropriate" standard, they could not under a "just" standard.

The expropriated foreign investor may prefer to have the property returned rather than receive compensation. This is not likely to be the case where there has been a revolution with an investment-hostile government, such as Cuba, but may be appropriate where a counter-revolution has soon restored an investment welcoming government. There is some precedent for restitution. In the *TOPCO/CALASIATIC* arbitration, following expropriations of Texas Overseas Petroleum Corporation and California Asiatic Oil Company by Libya, the sole ICJ arbitrator, Professor Dupuy (Secretary General of The Hague Academy of International Law), noted that the *Chorzów Factory* decision suggested that *restitutio in integrum* remains international law, and ordered Libya to resume performance of the agreement. Libya actually settled the claims of U.S. oil companies by giving them oil. But in the *BP Arbitration* (53 ILR 297, 1953) the arbitrator, Swedish Judge Lagergren, stated that the *Chorzów Factory* rule of *restitutio in integrum* was meant only to be used to calculate compensation, suggesting adherence to a full compensation theory.

MANDATORY QUESTIONS UNDER ANY COMPENSATION STANDARD

Whatever standard is chosen, three questions must be asked. First, *how much* is to be paid? Second, in *what form* is it to be paid? And third, *when* must it be paid? If the answers to these questions are the full value of the property, in convertible currency, and immediately or very soon, then the standard that is being applied seems to be the "prompt, adequate, and effective" standard argued by the United States to constitute international law. The Iran-United States Claims Tribunal, meeting in The Hague for over three decades, never formally applied a "prompt, adequate, and effective" standard.

The Tribunal used a "just" standard, which is stated in the U.S.-Iran Treaty of Amity, Economic Relations and Consular Rights. The standard is stated as "prompt payment of just compensation." But it goes on to state that it must be paid in "an effectively realizable form" and must be for the "full equivalent of the property taken", thus becoming nearly a prompt, adequate, and effective standard. Claims approved by the tribunal have been paid *promptly* from the funds established for the purpose, they have been paid in dollars (that surely constitutes *effective* payment), and the methods of valuation used seem to satisfy any reasonable *adequacy* standard. All that said, the Iran-United States Tribunal is quite unique, however, because of the initial agreement to deposit considerable funds to meet approved claims.

If the consensus is an "appropriate" standard, tribunals that have gained the respect of the majority of the international community, including the main industrialized nations, seem to be applying a standard that is "fair, just, and appropriate" as well as "prompt, adequate, and effective". For now, and perhaps until or unless the investment restrictiveness of the 1970s returns, the demand for

a norm allowing only partial compensation has little
backing.

EXHAUSTION OF LOCAL REMEDIES

Seeking compensation from the expropriating
government is not only appropriate, but may be a
precondition for initiating an insurance claim. It is
reasonable to first seek compensation from the one
who has committed the wrong. That idea makes
sense when the expropriation is not part of a total
change in economic theory following a revolution
that includes the expropriation of all private
property. The taking nation may be prepared to
compensate properties taken in a selective
nationalization, such as a taking of all
telecommunications or air transportation
enterprises. But when a nationalization occurs of
the dimensions of those in the former Soviet Union,
China, Eastern Europe, and Cuba, there is little
reason either for the expropriated property owner to
attempt to exhaust local remedies, or for that party
to be forced to do so before the presentation of
insurance claims.

Nevertheless, it is probably appropriate for the
expropriated party to make some attempt against
the taking government, if nothing more than a
formal written protest of the taking and a demand
for compensation. The problem arises when the
nation expresses a willingness to hear such claims,
but the circumstances and unfolding facts seem
clearly to suggest that the willingness to discuss
compensation is illusory. Cuba, for example, offered

compensation in the form of bonds that deserved the term "junk bonds" long before Wall Street popularized these words decades later.

The expropriated property owner may have to be prepared to establish that local remedies are inadequate before seeking remedies at home or in third party nations. Adequate proof justifying the futility of pursuing local remedies may take time to accumulate. The proof should illustrate deficiencies with the court or tribunal system of the taking nation, the method of valuation, the ability of the country to pay settled claims, and the appropriateness of the form of any payment the taking nation can afford. The experience with taking nations where the taking is part of a major economic, political, and social revolution clearly suggests that local remedies are likely to very unsatisfactory to the expropriated property owners, and that they will have to seek assistance outside the taking nation.

ASSISTANCE OF THE GOVERNMENT— THE "CALVO CLAUSE"

Expropriated U.S. investors usually report the expropriation to the U.S. Department of State. Diplomatic pressure may be essential to success in dealing with the taking nation. The U.S. executive has frequently intervened subsequent to foreign nationalizations of U.S. property. While diplomatic intervention may be helpful and may lead to government sanctions against the taking nation, there is one concern that frequently faces the U.S.

investor abroad—the application by the taking nation of the "Calvo Clause", or something comparable.

The Calvo Clause espouses a theory, sometimes expressed in an agreement signed by the foreign investor, that a foreign investor is entitled to treatment no different than that given domestic investors. This part of the concept means that the foreign investor is entitled to no better treatment than a national, and thus is left exclusively to local remedies. It is consequently interrelated with the exhaustion of local remedies concept and recourse to one's diplomatic channels may result in a *forfeiture* of the property. The Calvo Clause was included in Article 3 of the restrictive 1973 Mexican Investment Law, but there is no instance of any property forfeiture in Mexico, or in other nations which have either adopted the Calvo Clause concept formally in investment legislation, or made it a part of investment rhetoric. The concept was not included in the 1993 Mexican Investment Law, which is more investor friendly than the 1973 law. The NAFTA foreign investment provisions eliminate the Calvo Clause as a threat to a Canadian or U.S. investor, a major concession by Mexico.

The concept of the Calvo Clause improperly frustrates the right of a nation to diplomatic intervention to protect property of its citizens. If a government does intervene, it may not be clear whether it does so at the request of the expropriated foreign investor, or on its own initiative. If the latter, it is unfair to conclude that the property is therefore forfeited because of any act of the investor. While the idea that foreign investors ought to be entitled to no better treatment than nations may seem sensible, the real world does give foreign investors alternatives not available to nationals. One is diplomatic negotiations. When the Calvo Clause goes beyond being a statement of exhaustion of local remedies to being an exclusionary rule precluding any other subsequent remedies, it loses much of its respect and viability.

LUMP-SUM AGREEMENTS AND U.S. CLAIMS COMMISSIONS

U.S. Claims Commissions. A mixed U.S. and British commission to settle claims was created following the U.S. revolutionary war primarily to settle claims of British sympathizers whose lands were seized by the States. But it was not effective and was followed by a *national* commission to determine claims after a lump-sum settlement agreement was concluded in 1803. Over the next century and a half the United States established national commissions to distribute funds received in settlements with Great Britain, Brazil, China, Denmark, France, Mexico, Peru, the Two Sicilies, Spain and the Soviet Union (The Litvinov Assignment).

The U.S. Foreign Claims Settlement Commission was established in 1954 as a separate entity when the earlier International Claims Commission was abolished. Its function is essentially judicial, and the benefit of its existence (as opposed to using the district courts, for example) is its ability to acquire expertise in the narrow area of adjudication of foreign claims. Evidence of valuation of property lost abroad is difficult to obtain, and that form of evidence demanded in the courts is rarely available. In 1980, after a number of years of relative inactivity, the FCSC was transformed into a separate and independent agency within the Department of Justice. Any sums obtained by the United States are distributed according to the statute.

Special funds have been created in the Treasury for specific claims, relating to claims and agreements with Yugoslavia and the People's Republic of China. Each real or expected settlement with an expropriating nation must necessarily be kept separate from another, thus the statutes have titles covering special procedures for various specific takings. These include claims against: (1) Bulgaria, Hungary, Romania, Italy, and the Soviet Union; (2) Czechoslovakia, Cuba and China; (3) The German Democratic Republic; and (4) Vietnam. Each is related to takings following significant disturbances, principally war and revolution. The statute illustrates a pattern of procedural provisions which will likely be adopted for any future losses by U.S. citizens abroad where the takings are of all the property of U.S. citizens.

Post WWII, when there has been an extensive nationalization of foreign property, such as by China and Cuba, the most frequent settlement has been by a lump-sum under the terms of a binational agreement. Lump-sum settlements are common, but they remain questionable as a part of the jurisprudence of the international law of compensation. Any agreed upon lump sum is subsequently divided among claimants who have quite likely filed claims years earlier, soon after the expropriations occurred. For example, the Cuban nationalizations occurred between 1959 and the early 1960s. The Cuban Claims Act was passed in 1964, providing for claims to be filed between 1965 and 1967, extended later to 1972. The valuation method ranged from strict reliance on book value to a usually much higher going concern value.

The Cuban Claims Act process is part of the larger U.S. Foreign Claims Settlement Commission. If Cuba is willing to negotiate the claims, it will not likely agree that the amount as determined by the United States is correct, partly because there was never any Cuban representation at the claims hearings. Cuba will not be able to afford to pay the some $2 billion (and counting) in claims, and the experience of U.S. claims commissions is the ultimate payment of a substantially lower negotiated amount than the full value of previously documented claims.

The Iran-United States Claims Tribunal. Foreign countries often prefer the use of a national claims commission to distribute an agreed upon total sum as the country prefers. The Iran-United States Claims Tribunal is quite unique in this respect, it varies from the norm at least partly because the U.S. hostages were involved, and there was no time to conduct a lengthy process to determine how much money to demand from Iran. The Iran-United States Claims Tribunal was created in 1981 as part of the settlement of the crisis between Iran and the United States arising from the 1979 hostage taking at the U.S. Embassy in Tehran. The only reason Iran agreed to the tribunal was because the United States had frozen Iranian assets. Claims had to be filed by January 19, 1982, and approximately 1,000 were so filed for amounts of $250,000 or more, and 2,800 were filed for smaller claims. Most claims have been satisfied but a few large and complex claims remain.

The Iran-U.S. Tribunal has tended to interpret its obligation to provide full compensation to mean something closer to going concern value than book value. Arguing for acceptance of a claim under a going concern value does not assure that one will receive that higher amount, but it may mean a claim accepted for an amount higher relative to other U.S. claimants, and thus ultimate receipt of a higher amount in the pro rata apportioning of any agreed settlement.

Lawsuits. Some claimants might prefer bringing their own suits against the foreign government if they are able to locate property owned by that foreign government situated in the United States. That has not proven very successful in most cases. When a nation undertakes a massive expropriation of the property of a foreign nation it usually removes as much property as possible from that nation. The inability of Iran to do so motivated Iran to agree to the Iran-United States Claims Tribunal. Cuba successfully transferred large sums out of the United States before remaining assets were frozen by the Congress.

Thus, there may be little sense in seeking a judgment in a U.S. court if there is no property to attach and it is evident that the hostile taking nation will reject any attempt to enforce the judgment in the taking nation. Furthermore, the United States may make filing claims before a national commission the only available procedure. Many investors who were in the process of suing Iran at the time of the resolution of the hostage dispute and the establishment of the claims tribunal were angered that the agreement included removal of their claims from courts to the tribunal. Requiring all U.S. claimants to use this same process may benefit relations between the nations, but may not satisfy some claimants who were able to attach specific property of the foreign government, and who believe they might receive a greater share of their claim by separate litigation.

Separate litigation will often be attempted by expropriated investors, perhaps more successfully when the expropriations have not been massive takings as discussed above, but more selective takings of only certain property. For example, owners of Chilean copper mines expropriated under the Allende regime were compensated after they attached the proceeds of sales by the successor state-owned copper company. Some thought should also be given to individual suits against foreign governments for expropriation. For immunity and act of state reasons, collecting on judgments against foreign sovereigns is extremely difficult. See R. Folsom, *Principles of International Litigation and Arbitration* (West Academic Publishing).

OPIC INSURANCE PROTECTION
FOR U.S. INVESTORS

The Overseas Private Investment Corporation's (OPIC's) mandate is to "mobilize and facilitate the participation of U.S. private capital and skills in the economic and social development of less developed friendly countries and areas, thereby complementing the development assistance objectives of the United States." Guided by the expected economic and social development impact of a project, and its compatibility with other U.S. projects, preferential consideration is given to investment projects in countries having low per-capita income. But, the President may designate other countries as beneficiaries under separate authority. Countries may be denied OPIC insurance if they do not extend internationally recognized workers' rights to workers in that country, but the President may waive this prohibition on national economic interest grounds.

OPIC began as a government entity to insure U.S. investment abroad against (1) inconvertibility of local currency, (2) expropriation or confiscation of U.S. owned property, or (3) war, revolution, insurrection, or civil strife. All are subject to definition, generally left to principles of U.S. or international law. Claims would be paid by OPIC, which would then be subrogated to the investor's claims against the government. The U.S. government had far more leverage in exacting compensation than single investors.

OPIC operates with a fifteen member Board of Directors that includes eight appointed by the President from outside the government. At least two of the eight must be experienced in small business, one each in organized labor and cooperatives. Other Board members include the Administrator of the U.S. Agency for International Development, the U.S. Trade Representative or the Deputy, the President of OPIC, and four members who are senior officials of such entities as the Department of Labor. The OPIC President and CEO is appointed by the President, taking into account private business experience. It is this composition that causes it to be referred to as a "quasi-private/quasi-public" organization.

OPIC is a U.S. program for U.S. business. Eligibility is limited to U.S. citizens, U.S. corporations, partnerships, or other associations "substantially beneficially owned" by U.S. citizens. "Substantial beneficial ownership" ordinarily means that more than 50 percent of each class of issued and outstanding stock must be directly or beneficially owned by U.S. citizens. Foreign corporations, partnerships and other associations are also eligible if they are 95 percent owned by U.S. citizens. If it appears from all the circumstances that foreign creditors can exercise effective control over an otherwise eligible corporation, no insurance will be written.

As is the case of so many organizations formed for a specific purpose, OPIC began to assume roles related and sometimes unrelated to its original mandate. OPIC has become a broader "development" agency. Building upon its guarantees and political risk insurance OPIC has assumed a lending role (with loan guarantees) for such projects as the Kenya Women's Finance Trust, a water desalination plant in Algeria, and constructing four solar power plants in Peru. The role of risk insurance which was OPIC's initial function has continued, and has become at least partially shared with the successful Multilateral Investment Guarantee Agency (MIGA), discussed below.

OPIC has broad power to engage in such insurance activities as to insure, reinsure, cooperate in insuring, enter into pooling or risk-sharing agreements, and hold ownership in investment insurance entities. But its role is not limited to insurance. In addition to insuring investment risks, OPIC has some financing authority. It provides loans which are sponsored by or significantly involve U.S. small businesses. OPIC may also guarantee loans, regardless of the size of the company. Although OPIC currently provides financing worldwide, much of its initial focus was for investments in Latin America.

Foreign policy often seems to influence OPIC decisions. When the Wall came down, there was a dramatic increase in financing in Eastern Europe.

Relatively recently, OPIC created new private equity investment funds—the Modern Africa Growth and Investment Company Fund, and the New Africa Opportunity Fund. These two funds address nations long thought overlooked. In 2008, OPIC announced over $200 million in investment support in Africa, plus almost $150 million in the Middle-East. The Arab Spring has led OPIC to continue focusing on the Middle-East and North Africa.

OPIC—PROGRAMS AND TERMS

The three principal investment risks noted above (1) inconvertibility of currency, (2) expropriation or confiscation of property, and (3) property loss caused by war, revolution, insurrection, or civil strife) were the initial reason for the existence of OPIC. A fourth class has been added called "business interruption" due to any of the principal three risks. OPIC insurance is limited to 90% of the book value of the investment. Its premiums are not cheap, commonly 1.5% to cover all of these risk categories.

Inconvertibility. Before insurance against inconvertibility of currency is approved, the investor must obtain assurance from the host country that investor earnings will be convertible into dollars and that repatriation of capital is permitted. If the currency thereafter becomes inconvertible by act of the government, OPIC will accept the foreign currency, or a draft for the amount, and will provide the investor with U.S. dollars.

Expropriation. Expropriation is broadly defined and "includes, but is not limited to, any abrogation, repudiation, or impairment by a foreign government of its own contract with an investor with respect to a project, where such abrogation, repudiation, or impairment is not caused by the investor's own fault or misconduct, and materially adversely affects the continued operation of the project." OPIC contracts have followed a more specific and enumerative approach, because the law does not define specifically what actions constitute expropriation. OPIC's standard insurance contract contains a lengthy description of what is considered to be expropriatory action sufficient to require OPIC payment. That definition may help an investor in drafting a contract with the foreign host government, because that government will have to deal with OPIC once OPIC has paid the investor's claim.

The OPIC insured U.S. investor must exhaust local remedies before OPIC is obligated to pay any claim. All reasonable action must be taken by the investor, including pursuing administrative and judicial claims, to prevent or contest the challenged action by the host government.

War, Revolution, Insurrection or Civil Strife. The third form of coverage, "war, revolution, insurrection, or civil strife," (political violence) is not defined by the statute. The usual OPIC contract provides protection against:

   injury to the physical condition, destruction, disappearance or seizure and retention of

Covered Property directly caused by war (whether or not under formal declaration) or by revolution or insurrection and includes injury to the physical condition, destruction, disappearance or seizure and retention of Covered Property as a direct result of actions taken in hindering, combating or defending against a pending or expected hostile act whether in war, revolution, or insurrection.

Civil strife is politically motivated violence (e.g., civil disturbances, riots, acts of sabotage, terrorism). Added to the OPIC statute in 1985 was a provision providing:

Before issuing insurance for the first time for loss due to business interruption, and in each subsequent instance in which a significant expansion is proposed in the type of risk to be insured under the definition of "civil strife" or "business interruption", the Corporation shall . . . submit to [Senate and House Committees] . . . a report with respect to such insurance, including a thorough analysis of the risks to be covered, anticipated losses, and proposed rates and reserves and, in the case of insurance for loss due to business interruption, an explanation of the underwriting basis upon which the insurance is to be offered.

Since its inception, OPIC has funded, guaranteed, or insured billions worth of investments, not all of them in accordance with standard insurance risk management principles. For example, OPIC insured a GE Hungarian investment for $141 million, but the World Bank's MIGA reinsured $50 million of this project, thus lessening the full exposure of OPIC.

OPIC—ELIGIBLE INVESTMENTS

Upon payment of a claim, OPIC is subrogated to all rights to the investor's claim against the host government. Because the United States (OPIC) must deal with the foreign government, OPIC will not write any insurance in a foreign country until that country agrees to accept OPIC insurance and thus to negotiate with OPIC after claims have been paid.

Legislation authorizes OPIC to carry out its functions "utilizing broad criteria". OPIC must consider investment eligibility in accordance with extensive guidelines that provide that OPIC conduct operations on a self-sustaining basis. It must consider the economic and financial soundness of the project; use private credit and investment institutions along with OPIC's guarantee authority; broaden private participation and revolve its funds through selling its direct investments to private investors; apply principles of risk management; give preferential consideration to projects involving small business (at least 30 percent of all projects); and consider less developed nation receptiveness to private enterprise.

OPIC must also consider whether projects foster private initiative and competition and discourage monopolistic practices; further balance of payment objectives of the United States; support projects with positive trade benefits to the United States; advise and assist agencies of the United States and other public and private organizations interested in projects in less developed nations; avoid projects which diminish employment in the United States; refuse projects which do not have positive trade benefits to the United States; and refuse projects which pose an unreasonable or major environmental, health, or safety hazard, or result in significant degradation of national parks and similar protected areas.

OPIC must also operate consistently with the goals of U.S. law relating to protection of environment and endangered species in less developed nations. Additionally, it must limit operations to nations which provide or are in the process of providing internationally recognized rights for workers. That includes right of association, right to organize and bargain collectively, prohibition of forced or compulsory labor, minimum age for employment, and acceptable conditions of work. Such requirement is often observed more on paper than in practice in many of the countries listed as acceptable for OPIC assistance. Finally, OPIC must consider the host nation's observance of and respect for human rights.

OPIC participates only in *new* investments (loans or insurance) because its role is to encourage new investment, not facilitate existing investment. Each proposed investment is evaluated by OPIC to consider, in addition to the above eligibility requirements, the extent to which the U.S.

participant has long-term management arrangements with the new enterprise, the extent of private participation and whether the project is likely to assist further development of the host nation's private sector. Loans or the contribution of goods or services to foreign governments will not be insured unless they are part of a construction contract. Nor will OPIC insure the credit or solvency of the foreign government.

OPIC—CLAIMS AND DISPUTE SETTLEMENT

Claims presented by insured investors are "settled, and disputes arising as a result thereof may be arbitrated with the consent of the parties, on such terms and conditions as OPIC may determine." OPIC insurance contracts have stated that "any controversy arising out of or relating to this Contract or the breach thereof shall be settled by arbitration in accordance with the then prevailing Commercial Arbitration Rules of the American Arbitration Association." The arbitration process is important: OPIC has challenged a number of claims presented to it by U.S. companies claiming to have lost property through expropriations.

From 1966 to 1970, $3.5 million was paid to settle eight claims. From 1971 through most of 2012, OPIC agreed to 292 insurance claim settlements which totaled $970.8 million, constituting either cash settlements to investors or OPIC guaranties of host nation obligations. OPIC had denied twenty-eight claims, fourteen of which had been submitted to arbitration by the investors.

Since 1978, OPIC has had the authority to deny loss claims if the investor, a controlling shareholder, or any agent of the investor has engaged in any act which resulted in a conviction under the 1977 Foreign Corrupt Practices Act, and such act has been the "preponderant" cause of the loss. There have been few convictions under the FCPA, however, since most charges lead at most to a consent decree involving a fine. See Chapter 2.

INVESTMENT INSURANCE ON AN INTERNATIONAL LEVEL

The concept of offering insurance for various investment risks which led to the creation of OPIC in the United States, and to similar programs in several other nations, has been built upon on an international level by the World Bank's 1988 creation of the Multilateral Investment Guarantee Agency (MIGA). This organization, part of the World Bank, was intended to encourage increased investment to the developing nations by offering investment insurance and advisory services. Voting power is equally divided between the industrial and developing nation groups. Shares are proportional to member nations' shares of World Bank capital. Unlike OPIC, MIGA is not a lending agency, but its parent organization the World Bank serves principally as a lender.

Creating MIGA within the World Bank structure offers benefits a separate international organization lacks. MIGA has access to World Bank data on nations' economic and social status. This gives considerable credibility to MIGA, and encourages broad participation. It is not certain how MIGA has affected national programs, such as OPIC. A U.S. based company, for example, may prefer dealing with OPIC because of greater confidence of claims being paid, of maintaining information confidentiality, and benefiting from legal processes established in bilateral investment treaties. But U.S. companies may find MIGA insurance available where OPIC is not. Rather than being an alternative to OPIC, MIGA should be viewed as compatible with OPIC. For example, International Paper Investments of the United States obtained MIGA insurance for risks of currency transfer, expropriation, and war and civil disturbance, plus additional political risk insurance from OPIC.

Banks have found MIGA attractive because bank regulators in some countries have exempted commercial banks from special requirements for provisioning against loss where loans or investments are insured by MIGA. Furthermore, investors in nations without adequate national insurance programs have very much welcomed MIGA's creation. But even some of the newly industrializing nations, such as India and South Korea, have adopted national programs. MIGA is not intended to replace national programs, but to extend the availability of investment insurance to many areas where it was not previously available, which in turn is expected to assist economic development in those areas. MIGA's success will likely be where it fills gaps rather than where it competes with established and successful national insurance programs. Those gaps are substantial and MIGA has a very major role to play in the world.

Unlike national programs, such as OPIC, MIGA has the leverage of a large group of nations behind it when it presses a claim. The clear intention of MIGA is to avoid political interference and consider the process solely as creating legal issues. The last three decades have been quiet times for foreign investment with regard to the risks insured against by OPIC and MIGA. But the risks are perceived as sufficiently likely that OPIC and MIGA have been quite busy writing new insurance.

MIGA—INSURANCE PROGRAMS

Risks covered by MIGA are noncommercial and include risks of currency transfer; expropriation; war, terrorism, and civil disturbance; breach of contract; and failure to honor sovereign financial obligations, all actions by the host government. Only developing nations are eligible locations for insured investments.

Currency Transfer. This insurance is similar to that offered by OPIC. It covers losses incurred when an investor is unable to convert host nation currency into foreign exchange and transfer that exchange abroad. Host nation currency may be that obtained from profits, principal, interest, royalties, capital, etc. The insurance covers refusals and excessive delays where the host government has failed to act, where there have been adverse changes in exchange control laws or regulations, or where conditions in the host nation that govern currency transfer have deteriorated. Currency devaluations are *not* covered. Such devaluations are often the cause of substantial losses, but these are commercial losses attributed to changes that are to some extent predictable, and are not carried out by host nations to harm investment. Indeed, currency devaluations are usually extreme measures to address changing demand for the nation's currency.

Expropriation. This is insurance for partial or total loss from acts that reduce ownership of, control over, or rights to the insured investment. Included is "creeping" expropriation, where a series of acts has the same effect as an outright taking. Not covered are nondiscriminatory actions of the host government in exercising its regulatory authority.

Valuation for compensation is net book value; that may mean inadequate compensation where book value reflects historic costs. Loans and loan guarantees are compensated to the extent of the outstanding principal and interest. Compensation is paid at the same time as the insured assigns its rights in the investment to MIGA, which then may take action against the expropriating government.

War, Terrorism, and Civil Disturbance. This insurance covers losses for damage, disappearance, or destruction to tangible assets by politically motivated acts of war or civil disturbance, such as revolution, insurrection, *coups d'état*, sabotage, and terrorism. Compensation is for the book value or replacement cost of assets lost, and for the repair of damaged assets. This insurance also covers losses attributable to an interruption in a project for a period of one year. This is business interruption coverage, and becomes effective when the investment is considered a total loss. Book value is the measure of compensation.

Breach of Contract. This special insurance covers losses caused by the host government's breach or repudiation of a contract. When there is an alleged breach or repudiation, the foreign investor must be able to invoke an arbitration clause in the contract and obtain an award for damages. If that award is not paid by the host government, MIGA provides compensation.

Failure to Honor Sovereign Financial Obligations. More recently added, this insurance is for losses from the failure of a government to make payments when due where there is an unconditional (not subject to defenses) obligation or guarantee related to an eligible investment. The investor does not need to obtain an arbitral award.

MIGA—ELIGIBLE INVESTMENTS AND INVESTORS

MIGA insurance may cover, to a maximum of U.S. $220 million per project and usually for a maximum of fifteen years, new equity investments, shareholder loans or guaranties, and non-shareholder loans. Also covered are technical assistance and management contracts, asset securitization, capital market bond issues, leasing, services, and franchise and licensing agreements.

MIGA will insure acquisitions under a state privatization program, an important program.

Two member countries are involved. First, investors must be from a member country, and only foreign investors qualify. With Agency approval, however, domestic investors may receive coverage for projects where they bring assets back to their nation. This special allowance is intended to promote the return of capital transferred to safe havens during times of political or economic uncertainty. Second, the location of approved investments must be in developing member nations which approve the insurance. There was considerable discussion regarding insuring only in developing nations which adopted standards for protecting foreign investment, but the final Convention did not include any such standards. Member nation standards for protecting foreign investment may nevertheless be a factor in writing insurance, if any measure of risk management principles is to be followed. Since the viability of MIGA is dependent both on its care in selecting risks, and on its ability to negotiate settlements after paying claims, the right of subrogation is extremely important.

An investor seeking MIGA insurance must be a national or member country *other than* the country in which the investment is to be made. The test of nationality for corporations is incorporation and having its principal place of business in the member nation, *or* being majority owned by nationals of the member nation. Commercially operated state owned corporations are eligible if it operates on a commercial basis. Even non-profit organizations are eligible if they operate on a commercial basis.

MIGA—SCOPE OF COVERAGE

MIGA covers investments under a standard term of fifteen years, which may be increased to twenty years if MIGA determines that the longer term is justified by the nature of the project. If the insurance is for a loan, the term follows the duration of the loan agreement. Once written, MIGA is not able to terminate the coverage except for default by the investor. The insured investor, however, is entitled to cancel the insurance on any anniversary date after the third.

Premiums are based on a risk assessment which includes consideration of the political and economic conditions in the host nation. They average about one percent of the insured amount per year. Rates vary, however, depending on the industry and type of coverage. MIGA can insure equity investments to ninety percent of the initial contribution, plus 180 percent to cover earnings. Contracts such as for technical assistance are covered to ninety percent of the value of the payments due under the agreement. Loans and loan guarantees are also insured to ninety percent of the principal and interest that will accrue over the term of the loan. These figures are maximum available guarantees. The *current* amount is that in force for the given year. The difference between the maximum and current amount is referred to as the *standby* amount of guarantee, and constitutes a reserve coverage that the investor may place in effect each year to cover changes in the value or amount of investment at risk.

MIGA—CLAIMS

In all but two cases, MIGA has resolved disputes that would have led to claims. It has paid additional claims related to damage from war and civil disturbance. The first was for an equity investment in a power corporation in Indonesia, which was suspended by a presidential decree due to an economic crisis. The second was for war and civil disturbance, a guerilla attack in Nepal had damaged a hydroelectric plant, and also dealt with a power project. The third claim involved a toll road project in Argentina when the nation faced yet another financial crisis.

MIGA's success lies in finding a resolution without the investor resorting to the claims process. Thus MIGA appears to be a successful entity and a welcome addition to OPIC for U.S. investors. Choosing MIGA or OPIC for a U.S. investor planning an investment abroad is not a coin toss. In one case MIGA may be the better or only choice. In another OPIC may be better. In still other cases, either OPIC or MIGA may be appropriate. Finally, there may be instances when a project has several aspects which call for use of both MIGA and OPIC.

CHAPTER 4
INVESTING IN CHINA

WTO Membership   Foreign Economic Contracts

Special Economic Zones (SEZs)   Guanxi

Equity Joint Ventures   Contractual Joint Ventures

Wholly Foreign-Owned Enterprises (WFOEs)

Technology Transfers   Hong Kong and Macau

According to the 1982 Constitution, the state sector is the leading force in the economy of the People's Republic of China. Starting in the early 1980s, there was a quiet retreat from this position. The amount of China's industrial output produced by state enterprises steadily dropped. Correspondingly, during the 1980s, there was rapid growth in the number and economic significance of foreign, private and collective enterprises. These enterprises accounted for over half of the gross domestic product (GDP) of the People's Republic by the late 1980s. They were an engine of economic growth and jobs. In 1988 and again in 1993, the Constitution of the PRC was amended to affirm the development of these sectors as a supplement to the state economy. That said, large well entrenched state-owned or state-controlled enterprises continue to dominate certain sectors, such as banking. State banks in turn have lent copiously to state manufacturing "dinosaurs," such as shipbuilding. The market viability of these loans and the state enterprises they support, absent further underwriting, is doubtful.

Ever since Mao died in the 1970s, and a receptive environment was created, China has been taking in foreign investment at a phenomenal pace. Initially, many investors chose the equity joint venture (EJVs) format, though wholly owned subsidiaries (WFOEs) were also an option. The arrival of foreign investors brought a wave of capital, technology and talent in the midst of a policy retreat from state-owned enterprise. . . close to $120 billion in 2014 foreign direct investment. Wal-Mart, KFC (Yum Brands), Volkswagen, General Motors and GE exemplify China investment success stories. But Revlon and Best Buy came and then left China as strong local brands emerged.

A significant number of EJVs have been undertaken in partnership with Chinese governmental entities, particularly local governments. Such entities often provided "guanxi", that is to say connections necessary to China's foreign investment approval and implementation process. In more recent years, foreign investors have tended to favor WFOEs, more confident of their ability to navigate China's bureaucratic and cultural maze. In addition, a number of EJVs have converted to WFOEs.

This chapter has been adapted from R. Folsom, *International Business Agreements in the People's Republic of China* (Kluwer Law).

PRICES AND MARKETS

A broad trend towards free market economics (taking goods off "the plan") was apparent in the People's Republic during most of the 1980s. The number of products allocated through central planners dropped from 250 to 20 by 1988. The share of industrial output and retail sales subject to state planning dropped to 30%. Nevertheless, China's economy remains regulated. The government's central administration fixes prices for important consumer and producer goods, and local economic bureaucrats also set prices and control supplies. The fixed price has little to do with actual costs. Reregulation of previously deregulated areas was the trend between 1988 and 1992. Late in 1992, the PRC lifted price controls on most production materials, including petroleum, copper, lead, aluminum, certain types of steel, and many machinery and electronics goods. This left about 110 production items subject to central or provincial price controls. By the end of 1992, only seven agricultural commodities (including grain, cotton and tobacco) continued to be regulated in price.

Price controls go to the heart of government regulation of the Chinese economy. No other area has provoked more controversy in the drive for economic reform. Price controls are a litmus test on the progression or regression of the economic reform movement. The status of these reforms sends important signals to foreign investors in the PRC.

Broad price reforms were tested in the city of Guangzhou (Canton). The *Beijing Review* reported

in 1987 on some of the problems encountered with
Guangzhou's price controls:

> Under China's old price structure, prices
> reflected neither the true value of the goods nor
> the relationship between their supply and
> demand. . . .
>
> —The purchasing prices for farm and
>   sideline products were unduly low, and
>   selling prices were still lower than the
>   purchasing prices. The state had to
>   subsidize them.
>
> —The prices of manufactured goods were
>   high, but the prices of minerals, energy
>   and raw materials were too low. For
>   example, the 1978 profit rate for state-
>   owned industrial enterprises was 21
>   percent, 43.19 percent for light industry,
>   47.68 percent for the textile industry and
>   only 0.46 percent for coal. Due to their low
>   prices and meager profits, household goods
>   like soap, matches and toilet paper were
>   often out of stock.
>
> —The price of commodities bore no relation
>   to quality. For a long time the state set a
>   unified price for every kind of commodity.
>
> —Charges for transport, urban public
>   utilities and services were unduly low. For
>   example, it cost just five to 20 fen to ride a
>   bus. Every year the municipal
>   transportation and communications
>   company lost 1 million yuan.

The Guangzhou reforms involved far fewer fixed prices on agricultural and industrial goods than previously. There were instead, more prices floating within limits and more free market prices. Indeed, the overall proportion of goods subject to fixed prices decreased dramatically. Only key commodities such as grain, oil, fuel and medicines, along with transport fares, rent, water rates, electricity, tuition and postage were subject to fixed prices. Floating prices were allowed for services and recreational activities such as hotel rooms, concerts and the theatre. Free market prices governed more than half of all prices, including most food items. However, the state still buys some foodstuffs and subsidizes their retail price in off-seasons. The total amount of subsidization has declined.

The Guangzhou experiment in broad price deregulation provided a model which has spread throughout China. China's accession to the World Trade Organization in 2001 cemented these reforms.

CARTELS, MONOPOLIES AND COMPETITION

The tensions inherent in moving China's planned economy into the marketplace are evident in its regulatory law. China has, for example, an unusual collection of laws supporting competition and encouraging collaboration. Regulations Concerning the Promotion of Economic Combinations were first adopted in 1980. These regulations encourage state enterprises to voluntarily participate in economic

combines by signing a contract. Producers and
processors of raw materials might, for example,
execute such a cartel agreement. The regulations
provide that combines can enjoy incentives in the
marketing and supply of products.

Regulations Concerning Development of Socialist
Competition were also provisionally issued in 1980.
Under these regulations, state enterprises are given
more power to decide on production, marketing,
finance, and the like without interference from local
authorities. No monopoly of any commodity is
allowed other than those (such as the state tobacco
monopoly) designated by the government. Although
these regulations give priority to the government's
economic plans, state enterprises may produce in
excess of plan quotas. In addition, authorities
cannot create local monopolies, or forbid the sale
locally of products that are made elsewhere. These
regulations were incorporated into the Anti-
Improper Competition Law of December 1993. This
Law does not address abuses of market power by
state enterprises.

A new Anti-Monopoly Law emerged in 2008.
Coca-Cola's attempted acquisition of a leading
Chinese soft drinks company was blocked under this
law in 2009. A number of major companies have
been fined or are being investigated by China's
"antitrust" regulators, including Microsoft,
Volkswagen and Chrysler. Qualcomm recently paid
approximately $900 million in fines for asserted
monopoly violations.

The government is thus in a legal position which allows it to choose between economic combines or socialist competition. Prior to 1989, the trend was clearly in the direction of more competition and fewer state-authorized cartels. Indeed, as market forces increasingly came into play the capitalist phenomenon of "multifarious monopolies" reared its head. New regulations were adopted by the State Council to combat these practices. No enterprises or trade associations may establish a "monopoly price," regardless of whether the state has set a ceiling price for the relevant product or decreed that it is subject to a floating or free market price. The state will punish offenders and replace monopoly prices with "reasonable" ones.

China's answer to monopoly pricing is thus in part re-regulation of markets, not a greater promotion of competitive alternatives. This is a step backwards from the development of a market economy, one which the Chinese explain by reference to the infant state of their economic system. There may be some legitimacy to this explanation, but monopoly pricing controls could undercut the progress toward deregulation of markets and attraction of foreign investors.

CHINA: FROM ISOLATION TO OPEN DOORS

Under Mao Zedong, China followed trade and investment policies of economic isolation and self-sufficiency. These policies were partly a response to past economic exploitation of the country by foreigners. They also reflected communist ideology and a rejection of the economic tenets of modern capitalism. Since the Cultural Revolution, the People's Republic has opened its doors and law to world trade and investment as part of its modernization and development strategy. This reversal is most evident in its relations with Hong Kong, Japan and the United States, China's three leading trade partners. Roughly one-third of China's GNP is now involved in foreign trade.

Even after the 1989 resurgence in the power of economic traditionalists, the PRC continued to be receptive to world trade and investment. In the period following Tiananmen Square, however, once enthusiastic foreign investors became cautious and were constrained by their banks and governments. Recentralization, austerity and contractions in China's economy hurt their existing investments. Though the doors remained open, many though not all foreigners hesitated to enter. The Taiwanese, Singaporeans, South Koreans and (more deliberately) the Japanese led the return to trading and investing in China.

Until the relatively recent "normalization" of PRC-Taiwan (Chinese Taipei) relations, Taiwanese investors often set up shell companies in Hong Kong to funnel investments into China, principally in Fujian province across the straits from Taiwan. By 2014, Taiwanese firms based in China were employing over 15 million workers, Japanese companies about 11 million, and South Korean enterprises had approximately 2 million Chinese employees. Broadly speaking, this reflects a growing trend, the Asianization of China's international economic relations. It portends diminished influence for the United States in Chinese trade and investment policies.

THE UNITED STATES AND CHINA: TRADING AND INVESTING

Prior to 1972, according to United States' policy, trading with the PRC was treated as trading with the enemy. Trade relations between the U.S. and the PRC began to improve following the signing of the Joint Communiqué (Shanghai Communiqué) by President Richard Nixon and Premier Zhou Enlai on February 28, 1972, in Beijing. The Communiqué focused primarily on a summary of the U.S. and Chinese points of view on global politics (e.g., the war in Vietnam, the situation in Korea, and the status of Taiwan) without attempting to reconcile them. In addition, it suggested the desirability of increasing people-to-people contacts, trade between the PRC and the U.S., and exchanges in "science, technology, culture, sports and journalism."

However, the United States continued to enforce numerous restrictions on trade with the People's Republic after 1972. Export controls limited the shipment to the PRC of most United States goods. High tariffs (known as "Column Two" or "Smoot-Hawley" tariffs) prevented substantial import of Chinese products into the United States. Trade relations changed dramatically, however, in 1979 with the resumption of formal diplomatic relations between the U.S. and the PRC and the adoption of the United States-People's Republic of China Agreement on Trade Relations.

Under the 1979 Agreement, the United States granted most-favored-nation tariff status ("Column One" tariffs) to goods of PRC origin. Tariffs on Chinese goods dropped dramatically and U.S. imports quickly rose. The United States also removed most of its export controls over nonstrategic trade to China. U.S. export control regulations were amended to create a unique category ("Group P") for the PRC which permitted more exports to China than to many other communist nations. A further loosening of controls occurred in 1983, just before President Reagan visited the PRC, when export trade with China was shifted to "Group V." This shift allowed exports to the PRC on a basis comparable to most other noncommunist nations with which the United States trades.

Indeed, the Departments of Commerce and Defense, which principally administer U.S. export controls, even authorized the export of substantial quantities of military products to China. Transfers of strategic technology also expanded. Much of the liberalization in trade, especially that relating to military equipment, can be attributed to the desire of the U.S. government to sway the PRC towards its side in what it saw as a triangular power relationship involving the U.S., China and the former Soviet Union. In June of 1989, however, the Bush administration suspended military cooperation with the PRC in response to events surrounding the 1989 Democracy Movement. Goods on the munitions control list were banned from China trade. These limitations also affected nonmilitary sales, such as Boeing 757s, because any product with a component on the munitions control list could not be sold to the PRC. While munitions exports to China remain controlled, they are no longer as severe as the post-Tiananmen Square restraints.

Since 1980, Chinese imports and exports have benefited from U.S. Export-Import Bank financial support, although this was slow in forthcoming after Tiananmen Square. Because the United States and China exchanged diplomatic notes in 1980 on investment guarantees, U.S. Overseas Private Investment Corporation (OPIC) loans, insurance and guarantees have also been extended to China. See Chapter 3. Should OPIC make payment to any U.S. investor or trader in China, the PRC will recognize OPIC's rights to the claims of that person. Participation in OPIC programs was denied after Tiananmen Square, though subsequently renewed.

There are additional gaps in China's foreign investment relations with the United States. One notable omission is the absence of a bilateral investment treaty (BIT) with the United States. Negotiations on such a treaty have been ongoing for several years. In sum, but for Democracy Movement sanctions, U.S. trade and investment relations with the PRC more closely resemble those of an ally than an enemy. China's admission to the World Trade Organization in 2001 solidified this alliance.

UNITED STATES—PRC TRADE AND INVESTMENT DISPUTES

Trade and investment disputes between the United States and the People's Republic regularly emerge. For example, private U.S. investors owning property in prerevolutionary China or holding imperial government bonds commenced litigation in the early 1980s against the PRC in the federal courts. This litigation threatened to undermine the lump-sum claims settlement agreed upon in 1979 by the U.S. and the PRC. That settlement released assets frozen by both governments since 1949 for the purpose of paying claimants. U.S. litigants were disgruntled with their return of only 40 cents on each dollar of their investments. One default judgment was actually entered against the PRC, which has always disclaimed liability for the "odious debts" of prerevolutionary China. The lump-sum claims settlement was eventually upheld by the U.S. federal courts, but not before economic relations were frayed.

In recent years, disagreements have arisen about the volume of Chinese imports of United States grain, the export of Chinese textiles and goods produced by prison labor to the U.S., Chinese shipment and of military goods and technology to the Middle East, and the alleged subsidization and dumping of Chinese goods in the United States. China ameliorated some of these concerns by signing the Nuclear Nonproliferation Treaty in 1991 and by agreeing to multilateral controls over the shipment of missiles in 1992. Apparent breaches of these commitments caused President Clinton to further restrain in 1993 the flow of military goods and technology to the PRC.

In addition, the United States, after goods shipped through Hong Kong are considered, finds itself with a massive trade deficit with the PRC. However, when the corresponding *declines* in trade deficits with Taiwan and Hong Kong are factored in, the U.S. trade position since 1987 with "Greater China" is less overwhelming. This pattern reflects the movement of export industries to the mainland as Hong Kong and Taiwan have become high-cost centers.

Since 2001, China and the United States have taken nearly all their trade disputes to the WTO. For details, see my *International Trade and Economic Relations Nutshell.*

UNITED STATES TARIFFS ON PRC GOODS: THE ISSUE OF HUMAN RIGHTS

Another divisive trade-related issue involved U.S. application of the "Jackson-Vanik amendment," part of the 1974 Trade Act, to China's tariff status. This provision requires the President in most cases to annually review the emigration policies of communist nations granted most-favored-nation (MFN) now called "Normal" tariff status. Such status can be denied if the communist nation's emigration policies do not pass muster. This happened in 1988 with Romania under President Nicolae Ceausescu, for example, causing U.S. tariffs on its goods to skyrocket.

Questions surrounding China's emigration policies, and its general human rights record, were downplayed by U.S. authorities for many years prior to Tiananmen Square. Events in Tibet and those in connection with the 1989 Democracy Movement moved the Jackson-Vanik amendment to the forefront of Sino-American trade relations. President H. W. Bush's renewal of the waiver of Chinese compliance with Jackson-Vanik and the resulting continuation of China's most favored nation status in June of 1990, 1991 and 1992 was heavily criticized on human rights, arms control and trade deficit grounds. The breadth of this criticism suggested that Jackson-Vanik had moved beyond a mere examination of emigration questions and become a political fulcrum of Sino-American trade relations.

Early in 1992, Congress agreed upon a conference committee version of the United States-China Act of 1991. This legislation was initiated in August of 1991 as a rebuke of the President's extension of the PRC's MFN tariff benefits in June of 1991. The conference committee version prohibits the President from further extending China's MFN status unless he or she reports that the PRC has accounted for citizens criminally detained or accused in connection with the 1989 Democracy Movement and that the PRC has made significant progress in achieving Congressionally specified objectives on human rights, trade and weapons proliferation. President Bush vetoed this legislation in March of 1992. As predicted, the House of Representatives mustered the two-thirds votes needed to override, whereas the Senate did not.

The political battle over China's MFN trade status continued even though President Clinton attached general human rights conditions to its renewal in 1993. This seemed to pacify Congress for the moment. But it engendered hostility and resistance in China. Less publicly, the United States business community opposed the linkage of human rights to MFN tariffs as its PRC trade and investment commitments and opportunities were endangered. China, meanwhile, had developed the world's fastest growing economy and it decided to force the issue. If anything, abuse of human rights in the PRC actually increased early in 1994, notably prior to a well-publicized visit of the U.S. Secretary of State. With Congress increasingly split on the issue, President Clinton made what proved to be an historic reversal in policy. In June of 1994, he renewed China's MFN tariff status without human rights conditions, limiting imports only as regards Chinese-made ammunition and guns.

China's admission to the WTO in 2001 mooted Jackson-Vanik. Since then, Chinese goods are generally entitled to MFN treatment.

THE PRC PRIOR TO WTO MEMBERSHIP

In the fall of 1991, the United States Trade Representative (USTR) initiated a prominent

investigation into the restrictive trade practices of
the People's Republic of China under Section 301 of
the Trade Act of 1974. This investigation was
undertaken in part to mitigate Congressional
frustration over President Bush's continued
willingness to grant most-favored-nation tariff
status to Chinese goods. The Section 301
investigation focused upon PRC import quotas,
prohibitions and licensing procedures, and PRC
technical barriers to trade (e.g., standards, testing
and certification requirements). It also challenged
the failure to publish PRC laws, regulations, judicial
decisions and administrative rulings relating to
import restraints. Additional issues concerned PRC
tariffs ranging up to 200% and PRC import taxes.
The main thrust of the proceeding was to open up
China's markets to U.S. exports. It caused the
United States and the PRC to undertake intensive
trade negotiations.

Since China was not then a member of the
GATT/WTO, and in spite of U.S. bilateral trade
agreements with the PRC, the USTR proceeded
with this investigation on an unfair practices' basis.
This meant that no trade agreement dispute
settlement procedures were triggered. The Section
301 investigation was in addition to the Special 301
priority country investigation of PRC practices in
the intellectual property field commenced in the
spring of 1991. For more on Section 301, see my
*International Trade and Economic Relations
Nutshell.*

In October of 1992 the United States and China signed a memorandum of understanding that narrowly avoided massive, unilateral Section 301 trade sanctions. The People's Republic agreed to phase out by the end of 1977 numerous nontariff trade barriers, including import licenses, quotas and bans as well as regulatory restraints. The removal of these barriers improved U.S. export possibilities for telecommunications equipment, airplanes, machinery, agricultural goods, electrical appliances, computers, auto parts and pharmaceuticals. Furthermore, China promised to undertake a series of significant tariff cuts no later than the end of 1993. All of China's import-substitution regulations and policies were eliminated. In particular, the PRC did not condition entry into its market upon technology transfers.

China promised that all laws, regulations, policies and decrees dealing with China's import and export system would be published on a regular basis, and no such rules would be enforced unless they had been made readily available to foreign traders, investors and governments. The goal was complete "transparency" of PRC trade and investment law, and an end to the use of secret internal directives ("neibu"). For its part, the United States committed itself to full GATT/WTO membership for the PRC.

GATT/WTO MEMBERSHIP FOR THE PRC

While the Chinese were concerned about their future bilateral trading relations with the U.S., they also took steps to integrate their trade law into that of the world community. The PRC applied to join the General Agreement on Tariffs and Trade (the "GATT"), known since 1995 as the World Trade Organization (WTO). The WTO has over 160 member states and customs territories (including Hong Kong and Taiwan) and is the core of the world trading system. The WTO, for example, is the source of many trade rules on tariffs, quotas and nontariff trade barriers. It is responsible for the levels of tariffs applied to trade in goods among its members. The benchmark WTO level is most-favored-nation (MFN) ("Normal") tariffs. This is applied automatically among the WTO signatories. Thus, when the United States first debated MFN tariffs for China under Jackson-Vanik (above), it was considering a special application of that tariff level because the PRC was not a member in good standing of the GATT/WTO.

Prior to Mao's assumption of power in 1949, China was a signatory to the GATT. There was a sense, therefore, that its present application was merely a question of reactivation of its membership. China had to pay "a price" to join the GATT/WTO. Joining in 2001 was an important step in the development of PRC trade and investment law and relations. Full participation in world tariff and nontariff trade barrier negotiations came with membership. One dramatic benefit for the PRC arrived in 2005 when the WTO Textiles Agreement eliminated longstanding quotas on trade in apparel goods. Chinese exports mushroomed. WTO membership also affected a vast range of PRC laws on dumping practices, subsidies and countervailing duties, import injury ("escape clause") proceedings and the like. Similarly, WTO membership influenced the applicability of the laws of many nations trading with the PRC.

In order to make trading with China more attractive to foreigners and to help facilitate China's entrance into the GATT/WTO, the PRC undertook a series of trade reforms. For example, subsidies from the central government compensating foreign trade enterprises for losses suffered from exports were stopped. While the removal of subsidies helped the cash-strapped central government and helped convince China's trading partners that it will abide by the free-trade rules associated with the GATT/WTO, it caused economic problems for many of China's trading enterprises. In some instances, provincial governments subsidized selected businesses in order to meet state export targets.

In addition to pressures from the U.S. and other partners regarding its trade practices, there has also been continuing debate within the Chinese leadership on the extent to which the country should remain open to foreign trade and investment. The position of the Chinese government is to continue to open up to the outside world in order to absorb capital and technology that will continue to help the PRC grow, thus reinforcing Chinese Communist party rule. However, a more conservative minority element within the Chinese leadership advocates greater caution in dealing with foreigners in order to protect the PRC from "spiritual pollution" and possible exploitation.

FOREIGN ECONOMIC CONTRACTS
OF THE PRC

Contracts between foreign companies and PRC foreign trade enterprises are the source of most Chinese trading. Until recently, there were significant moves away from centralization of Chinese trading through selected national and regional state enterprises. Local officials and local trading companies were given foreign trading authority. Exports and imports grew rapidly. However, this trend has been partly reversed as the central government has reasserted control over China's trade.

The Chinese are shrewd trade negotiators, as many a foreign executive has learned the hard way. They deal from a fundamentally different perspective on time and its value. To them, quite literally, time is not money and they exploit the advantages of delay in negotiations. In addition, the Chinese often deliberately cultivate a sense of friendship and obligation in their negotiating opposites, relationships which can promote guilt or dependence to their advantage. Many a foreign trader has been "shamed" into a contract term it later regrets.

Fundamental cultural clashes about the meaning of a contract can also serve to undermine the significance of concluding a China trade agreement. For many foreigners, the signing of a contract culminates the negotiations—they have a deal. The terms of the deal are to be found strictly within the four corners of the agreement. To many Chinese, the same event merely signals that the two parties have established "a relationship," one which allows either to call upon the other for tolerance, flexibility and favors. Much to the surprise of foreign parties, these calls often run counter to the very heart of their hard-won agreement. They find themselves involved in endless rounds of frustrating negotiations. They get worn down, tired of losing money and skeptical of the wisdom of doing business in China. Some pull out, but many hang on—waiting for that pot of gold that surely must be at the end of their Chinese rainbow.

Many Chinese trading companies have developed standardized international contracts with which they usually commence negotiations and from which they are often unwilling to deviate significantly. Use of standard form contracts provides uniformity of terms, and perhaps more importantly, security for the Chinese negotiators. Deviations from the standard form run the risk of sanctions later should the deal turn sour. As might be suspected, there are major differences between standard contracts depending whether China is the seller or purchaser. In purchase contracts, for example, a strict penalty clause applies to foreigners for failing to deliver on time. The Chinese find it commercially advantageous to omit such clauses from their international sales contracts.

The law applicable to international trade contracts is of major concern to both parties. For political reasons, the Chinese always insist that contracts with Hong Kong companies be governed by PRC law. This is consistent with the PRC view that Hong Kong is part of China. Hong Kong firms have, largely for economic reasons, acquiesced in this choice of law. Many other Chinese trade agreements, however, omit any designation of applicable law because neither party wants the other's law to govern. When a United States entity is involved, this omission is now generally covered by U.S. and PRC accession to the United Nations Convention on the International Sale of Goods (1980) ("CISG"). Since 1988, most trade contracts between United States and Chinese parties omitting a choice-of-law clause are governed by the CISG. It becomes the law of the contract. For more on CISG, see my co-authored *International Business Transactions Nutshell*.

FOREIGN ECONOMIC CONTRACT LAW

One of the most important developments in PRC international trade law since the Cultural Revolution was the enactment of the Foreign Economic Contract Law of 1985 (FECL). This law and its successors, notably the 1999 Contract Law (CL), govern procedures for drafting international contracts for goods and services (excluding transport contracts). The FECL/CL allows the parties to choose the substantive law governing their trade contracts, and this choice can be made by mutual agreement after concluding the contract. In the absence of such a choice, the law of the country "most closely related to the contract" applies.

Chinese law permits any choice of controlling language. It also covers the enforceability of foreign economic contracts, including *force majeure*. An exemption from liability for damages flowing from the fact of *force majeure* is created, and the contract is not void or terminated. The duty to mitigate damages, the enforceability of liquidated damages, and the right to recover damages in the People's Courts for breach or invalidity of a contract are part of the law. This emphasis on damages as the primary remedy for breach of foreign economic contracts differs from the focus of domestic contract remedies which stress specific performance. The different contexts and PRC interests at stake in domestic versus foreign economic contracts may explain this dichotomy.

Chinese law mandates that foreign economic contracts contradicting the laws or social or public welfare of the PRC are invalid. Although consultation by the parties can remove the effects of any such invalidity before judicial remedies are pursued, this provision is so broad that nearly all Chinese contracts are at risk. Chinese law further provides that in the absence of relevant Chinese law and regulations, "international norms" apply to foreign economic contracts. Indeed, when Chinese law conflicts with PRC treaty obligations, the latter prevails. This is an especially significant provision because of China's ratification in 1987 of the United Nations Convention on the International Sale of Goods (CISG). Although the 1985 FECL, the 1999 CL and the 1980 CISG are quite similar in many respects, they are not identical. The CISG, for example, favors specific performance remedies in ways that are absent from Chinese law. Nevertheless, the preference for damages does not undermine China's commitment to participation in world trade law since the CISG provisions prevail in the event of a conflict.

The relationship between the Foreign Economic Contract Law of 1985 and the General Principles of Civil Law adopted in 1986 was not especially clear. The Civil Law established basic contract law doctrines. However, it gave no indication whether these doctrines prevail in the event of a conflict with the FECL. Perhaps the best interpretation is that the Civil Law was intended to expand upon the FECL, not limit its terms or applicability. Civil Law rules on void and voidable contracts and secured transactions, for example, filled gaps in the FECL. Another important issue, the applicability of the FECL to foreign investment enterprises located in China, was not resolved. For equity or contractual joint ventures and wholly-owned foreign enterprises, the contracts of these entities are now governed by the 1999 Contract Law of the PRC.

The Supreme People's Court interpreted the FECL by issuing a 1987 Notice entitled "Responses to Certain Questions Concerning the Application of The Foreign Economic Contract Law." All lower courts were instructed to follow this Notice in resolving FECL cases. The Notice covers six legal questions:

- Which contracts are governed by the FECL?
- What are the applicable conflict of law rules?
- When may certain foreign economic contracts be voided?
- When may such contracts be rescinded and cancelled?
- What are the consequences of the voiding or rescinding of foreign economic contracts?
- What relief is available for breach of contract?

The 1987 Notice supplemented the FECL in a number of ways, drawing particularly on the contract principles enunciated in the 1986 Civil Law and the CISG. The 1987 Notice was one of the Supreme Court's first attempts at broad judicial control over the "interpretation" of Chinese laws. This interpretation clearly involved judicial lawmaking in areas not covered by the FECL. The Notice clarified the meaning and considerably expands the scope of the law on foreign economic contracts and it still provides an immediate and useful supplement to publication of individual decisions of the Supreme Court. Much of its content was incorporated in the 1999 Contract Law which followed the FECL.

PREFERENTIAL TRADE AND INVESTMENT ZONES

Businesses are treated preferentially in China's Special Economic Zones (SEZs), Economic and Technological Development Zones (ETDZs) and selected "open" coastal cities. In these zones and cities, enterprises are granted preferences and subsidies concerning employment of workers, taxation, utilities, land use, export permits and such. Four rural SEZs were created in 1979. Fourteen coastal cities the government hoped to industrialize with foreign capital were "opened" in 1984. In addition, thirteen ETDZs were authorized in 1985 and an additional SEZ, Hainan Island, was established in 1987. In 2013, the Shanghai Free Trade Zone was established with much publicity intended to become a "shining example of market reform," especially financial reform.

One of the most important of these areas is the Shenzhen SEZ in Guangdong Province located directly across the border from Hong Kong. This is where considerable growth and development within China's enterprise zones has taken place. Substantial investment and trading in Shenzhen comes from Hong Kong sources. The Hong Kong dollar is accepted as currency there.

There has also been a substantial surge in Taiwanese investment in the Xiamen SEZ in Fujian Province on the mainland just across from Quemoy. Smaller sums are being invested in the Zhuhai SEZ adjacent to Macao and the Shantou SEZ in Guangdong Province. Shenzhen and Zhuhai were set up as multipurpose zones incorporating a variety of economic activities such as industry, commerce, housing, agriculture and tourism. Shantou and Xiamen were to focus on the processing of exports.

Some of the commerce in the SEZs is "compensation trade." As applied to the PRC, compensation trade refers principally to a contract whereby a foreigner supplies capital equipment (e.g., textile machinery) which is paid for in installments with goods produced by that equipment. The great advantage of such contracts is their avoidance of foreign exchange and debt problems. A variation on the compensation trade theme involves "assembly operations." Here the foreigner supplies component parts (e.g., electronics) processed or assembled in China for a fee.

In theory, the PRC's preferential economic zones are to be used principally to attract foreign commerce and to serve as "bridges" for introducing foreign capital and advanced technology into the rest of China. In addition, they are seen as classrooms for training Chinese personnel in management techniques and in the use of advanced technology. Deng Xiaoping referred to the Shenzhen SEZ as a "bold experiment" which he hoped would succeed but "if it fails, we can draw lessons from it." These words reflect the negative side of Shenzhen and other SEZs as they have become shopping and employment centers for well-connected Chinese.

For example, about three-fourths of all Shenzhen SEZ production is sold to Chinese buyers, leading to a net outflow of money from the rest of the country to the SEZ. Thus Shenzhen has mostly succeeded in attracting domestic capital to purchase imported or SEZ consumer goods. A fence has actually been constructed to isolate Shenzhen from the rest of

Guangdong Province. Hainan Island was so consumed with illegal trading of foreign goods and illegal currency exchanges that the Party leadership released details of multimillion dollar scandals involving local officials, including the People's Army and Navy. Crackdowns followed, but the general pattern of opportunistic abuse of the SEZs by those with connections (*guanxi*) continues. In spite of these and other problems with China's preferential zones, the Chinese government has re-endorsed its support for their continuation.

Investment, licensing and trading in SEZs and ETDZs are subject to zone regulations. An early example was the Shenzhen SEZ Regulations for Foreign Economic Contracts (1984) issued by Guangdong Province. These regulations govern joint ventures, cooperative ventures, compensation trade, and assembly agreements in Shenzhen. The regulations require certain clauses for each type of SEZ contract, including dispute settlement clauses. The Guangdong government has also adopted Importation of Technology, Bankruptcy, and Shareholding Company Regulations for Shenzhen. Regulations of this type have often preceded national laws covering the same subjects.

Thus, the SEZs and ETDZs are not only economic experiments, they are also legal experiments. Some of the lessons drawn from such experiments found their way into the Foreign Economic Contract Law of 1985 (FECL). For example, the Shenzhen contract regulations emphasize formalities, whereas the FECL did not. The Shenzhen regulations mandate that the Chinese language version of the contract govern. The FECL left that issue to the parties' choice.

The economic and legal futures of Hong Kong and Macao under Chinese rule may be forecasted, perhaps, from China's preferential economic zones. In a reversal of what might be feared in Hong Kong, the Guangdong authorities incorporated a number of Hong Kong ordinances into the Shenzhen legal regime. These primarily concern economic legislation, but also include civil service rules. In the long run, mergers of Hong Kong and Shenzhen SEZ and Macao and Zhuhai SEZ are not inconceivable.

GUANXI TRADING AND INVESTING

There is a difference between PRC trade and investment law on the books and in operation. This difference is most evident in the practice known as "trading or investing through the back door." Such practices constitute a return to the venerable *guanxi* system of private "relationships." The *guanxi* system breeds corruption, inefficiency and illegal behavior. Some instructive examples of trading and investing through the back door are given by Walter Keats, writing in the *China Business Review*:

How does *guanxi* manifest itself today in China trade? It can be seen in high officials who pass the word to favor certain vendors with whom they have a special "relationship." It reveals itself in the way some overseas Chinese agents represent Chinese units that are perfectly capable of dealing with foreign companies on their own—simply because the agent has a "relationship" with one of the Chinese officials. It can be seen in the willingness of officials in Guangdong Province to permit the import of agricultural material in violation of Chinese quarantine restrictions because of their "relationship" with the vendor or vendor's agent.

Sometimes the price asked in exchange for buying your product or service is sponsoring an official's child to attend college overseas. Or a foreign business partner may be asked not only to invite certain officials in his country, but expected to give them special favors including "gifts", such as stereos, TVs, washing machines, refrigerators, cars and even money. All too often, the abuses are even more blatant. A financial official may delay approval of a contract or letter-of-credit until he or she is invited to join a delegation going overseas. Or a visiting delegation may demand that each of its members receive a percentage of the value of a contract in US dollars. And worst of all for China, certain projects receive approval or foreign exchange allocations based on who knows whom, not the true merits of the project.

Guanxi practices, combined with the cumbersome bureaucracy the Chinese have been cultivating for generations, create major problems for foreigners (particularly United States attorneys and executives who face severe penalties under the U.S. Foreign Corrupt Practices Act). *Guanxi* practices challenge the very idea of a rule of Chinese law governing trade and investment relations. Much of the progress represented by the FECL/CL, China's accession to the CISG and the WTO, and the PRC investment laws discussed below could be undermined if *guanxi,* not law, prevails.

FOREIGN INVESTMENT ENTRY AND OPERATIONAL CONTROLS

The foreign investment climate in the People's Republic of China changed dramatically after the Cultural Revolution. The country moved from a position of outright hostility and suspicion of foreign investors to an open though selective embracement of their capital, talent and technology. The degree of enthusiasm depends generally on whether a proposed foreign investment is deemed to fall within one of three regulated categories: "Encouraged, Permitted or Prohibited". At the central government level, MOFCOM (China's Ministry of Commerce) is typically the gatekeeper. Local entry controls may also apply. In recent years, controversial VIEs ("variable interest entities", discussed below) have been used to circumvent China's regulatory restraints on foreign investment.

Political and economic stability has always been a basic premise upon which most China investment is undertaken. With this premise in doubt after Tiananmen Square, the investment climate was initially perceived by foreigners as risky. Some new foreign investments and loans were delayed, cancelled or made prohibitively expensive.

Nevertheless, while North American and European investment in China at first declined or plateaued, capital and technology imports from Hong Kong, South Korea, Taiwan, and Singapore (the "Four Dragons") increased. Since South Korea and Taiwan were not officially recognized by the PRC, much of this trade and investment was channeled through Hong Kong companies. From China's perspective, the Four Dragons of East Asia represent an increasingly desirable alternative for foreign investment resources, an alternative which brings with it far less criticism of domestic policies.

Time has also brought North Americans, Europeans and the Japanese actively back into the Chinese market. Early in 1992, for example, General Motors announced a new joint venture to make pickup trucks in the PRC. GM is now heavily invested in auto production in China though Volkswagen remains China's top seller of cars.

The embracement by the People's Republic of foreign investors is mirrored in the progression of laws, regulations and treaties on foreign direct investment since the Cultural Revolution. For example, State Council regulations adopted in 1986 (known as the "22 Articles"), favor "export" and "technologically advanced" enterprises with reduced land use fees, more independence from the state, the right to hire and fire at will, lower labor and utility costs and less taxation. Many existing investments have been certified by local authorities as qualifying for such benefits. Indeed, cities and provinces have competed for foreign investment in offering these types of incentives.

They also compete among themselves in enacting liberal investment regulations. Guangdong Province and the Shenzhen SEZ adjacent to Hong Kong have attracted the most foreign investment using these techniques. However, in the changing investment climate after Tiananmen Square, Shanghai issued new regulations which subject foreign enterprises to more government controls over price, transport, labor, supplies and sales. The main thrust of these regulations was to remove the preferential treatment once accorded foreign investment and subject it to "equal treatment" with domestic enterprises. The central government also announced an important policy change; all foreign investment enterprises (like their domestic counterparts) must have unions to represent their work forces. They are also required to have an internal "Chinese Communist Party Committee" whose task is to monitor compliance with CCP policies.

There is a broad trend in Chinese law and policy, encompassing tax, land use and labor law for example, towards "leveling the playing field" between domestic and foreign enterprises operating in China.

FOREIGN INVESTMENT OPTIONS: JOINT VENTURES, SUBSIDIARIES AND VIEs

China has created three basic foreign direct investment options. These are equity joint ventures

(EJVs), contractual joint ventures (partnerships, CJVs) and wholly-owned foreign owned subsidiaries (WFOEs). Each investment option is discussed below along with its governing law and implementing regulations. As you will observe, foreign investment in China is heavily regulated. Essentially no foreign investment can be undertaken without appropriate approvals. Many of these approvals must be obtained at provincial, city or preferential development zone levels.

There is a broad trend in Chinese foreign investment law to level the playing field between domestic and foreign investors and as between China's foreign investment options. Since 2008, for example, China has applied a uniform basic tax rate of 25% to both domestic and foreign investors.

In 2015, a draft of a new Foreign Investment Law was released for public comment. This Draft Law would consolidate coverage of Chinese investment options into one law, and abandon the case-by-case approval system for foreign investments not on a negative list of prohibited and restricted sectors. National security reviews would be more demanding. Use of "viable interest entities" (VIEs) to circumvent foreign investment regulatory controls would be circumscribed. VIEs involve setting up a WFOE which contracts with a Chinese-owned VIE operating company that invests in sectors where foreign ownership is restricted. The contracts give the WFOE effective control of the operating company, but not ownership. Amazon,

CBS, Pearson and others are said to operate in China under VIEs.

EQUITY JOINT VENTURES

The first major step taken by the Chinese to open their economy to foreign investors was the passage of joint venture legislation in 1979. The Law on Joint Ventures Using Chinese and Foreign Investment ("JVL") and its successors allows joint ventures, known as "equity joint ventures," to be established between foreign corporations and Chinese enterprises. The JVL is accompanied by its own income tax law and a number of implementing regulations. Equity joint ventures must be approved by the central government. Prior to 1988, this power had been increasingly delegated to local government organizations. Such delegation was part of the general trend toward decentralization of economic controls in China, a trend recently reversed as the government's central planners attempt to get a stronger grip on foreign investment decisions.

The most distinguishing features of Chinese law on equity joint ventures have traditionally been:

- 10- to 30-year terms
- Profit and risk sharing proportionate to share capital
- Limited access to sales in the Chinese market
- Arbitration of labor disputes
- Non-negotiable shareholdings

- Regulated debt-equity ratios

- Flexibility in terms of types of capital contributions (technology included)—25% foreign capital minimum

- Priority to Chinese sources of materials

- Foreign currency account must be balanced, including remission of profits

- Foreigners could not (prior to 1990) serve as chairs of boards of directors

- 33% maximum tax rate

Amendments to the Equity Joint Ventures Law were adopted in 1990 which reduced the differences between it and the Contractual Joint Ventures Law (infra). No "nationalization" may take place. But any "requisition ... when the public interest requires" is subject to a duty to pay "appropriate compensation." One suspects that the difference between "nationalizations" and "requisitions" may be lost on foreign partners to PRC joint ventures. Foreigners may now serve as chairs of the board of directors. Joint ventures may run beyond their original term with special permission, and may bank at any approved foreign exchange institution.

Equity joint ventures, as the oldest form of foreign investment in the PRC, have the longest track record. Partly because of the early adoption of the JVL and the legal security it created, equity joint ventures have become the most popular Chinese investment vehicle of multinational corporations. Thousands of well-known firms have agreed to equity ventures in the PRC. Thus one can find the label "Made in The People's Republic of China" on such diverse products as Camel cigarettes, Nike shoes, Kodak film, Otis elevators, Jeep trucks, Xerox copiers, Singer sewing machines and Heinz baby foods.

Within the limits of the JVL and its implementing regulations, and taking into consideration the model contracts the Chinese have developed, the terms of these joint ventures are negotiable. The regulated nature of joint venture investments in China often requires that local government representatives be brought into the negotiations. Although various central investment authorities will be involved, local officials typically hold important keys to approval of the venture, and most critically, its successful operation in the future. They will, for example, heavily influence such variables as taxation, labor supply, utilities, land use permits and the like.

The equity joint venture bargain thus determines much of its future viability. But, as many foreign investors have discovered, reaching agreement is just the beginning of an equity venture in the PRC. The Chinese often perceive that the agreement merely provides a framework within which negotiations are ongoing. Foreign investors tend to be less flexible and are more likely to want to stick to the terms of the deal and accompanying government representations. These differing perspectives frequently produce disputes.

In addition, the PRC is simply a difficult place to invest. The abruptness of the change in China's investment outlook and laws since the Cultural Revolution has left some uneven edges. Governmental interference with joint ventures is common, quality control problems with inputs and outputs endemic, the necessary infrastructure, managerial talent, skilled labor and hard currency absent, and so on. Repatriating profits (if there are any) is an art form. Government credit squeezes, combined with rising inflation and corruption, remain particularly painful to many joint ventures. Government insistence since 1989 upon adding a Communist Party member responsible for Party organization and loyalty to the management team at joint ventures has increased the discomfort level of foreign investors. When these general "environmental" difficulties are combined with differing contract perspectives, it is not surprising that serious disruptions can occur.

PROBLEMS AT THE CHRYSLER JEEP JOINT VENTURE

One of the most publicized disruptions was that of the highly favored American Motors Corporation (now owned by Chrysler/Fiat) "model" equity joint venture in Beijing. It is representative of the problems encountered by many other investors in the People's Republic of China. This excerpt appeared in a 1986 edition of the *Shanghai World Economic Herald:*

The original contract called for the Chinese and American sides to jointly design a new jeep using only Chinese components. However, according to the Beijing Review, 'after several months of work by Chinese and American engineers ... it was found that the vehicle designed was defective in such areas as its exhaust system, noise, visibility, and speed, none of which could match international standards. ... AMC suggested that the idea of joint design be postponed. ... The Chinese, however, took AMC's suggestions as a symbol of the Americans' unwillingness to cooperate on a jointly designed vehicle and ... of AMC's desire to control China's market.' Ultimately, the Chinese agreed to build AMC's XJ model series, including the Cherokee jeep, using imported components—but clearly in a suspicion-marred environment that foreshadowed the more serious troubles that arose later.

. . .

In mid-1985 the Beijing International Trust and Investment Corporation—an arm of the Beijing city government—reportedly loaned the venture $8.5 million to buy equipment for a new Cherokee jeep assembly line and to import kits. At that time, AMC chipped in an additional $6 million for the assembly line. But recent indications are that the loan was made under the assumption that the vehicles could be sold to end-users in China for foreign exchange. Since December 1985, these end-users have proven unwilling or unable to buy the vehicles with foreign exchange—chiefly because foreign exchange allocations to enterprises have been slashed across the board, but perhaps also because a 60 percent duty on imported parts makes the Beijing price considerably higher than the North American price. During the first part of 1986, local authorities were unwilling to renew foreign exchange allocations or loans to the venture, since the venture's expected foreign exchange earnings were not forthcoming.

This forced a major showdown in which AMC allowed its grievances to leak into American newspapers and, according to numerous reports, threatened to pull out of the venture. The gesture aroused enough high-level concern in China to guarantee the venture renewed foreign exchange for kit purchases, at least for the time being. According to Chinese press reports, the central government has offered $2 million for jeeps already assembled, in addition to an unspecified amount for further kit imports. But the venture's Cherokee jeep production will almost certainly fall well short of the earlier 4,000 unit target.

. . .

The Chinese argue that AMC should also take some responsibility for maintaining the venture's foreign exchange flow. And a number of foreign observers point out that AMC's initial cash contribution—$8 million—was very small in relation to its goal of building an export-quality jeep in China. The corporation has apparently agreed to increase equipment supplies to the joint venture as part of the settlement of the foreign exchange dispute.

Despite such obstacles, foreign firms continue to invest in the PRC in record numbers. Surprisingly, many of these investments are *not* covered by political risk insurance against expropriation, civil unrest and other such contingencies. See Chapter 3. United States' investors, for example, have channeled billions into uninsured Chinese equity joint ventures. This response may have more to do with evaluations of China's market potential than its investment laws. Nevertheless, the sustained, substantial effort on the part of PRC lawmakers to improve the legal environment within which equity joint ventures function is impressive.

WHOLLY FOREIGN-OWNED SUBSIDIARIES

Joint ventures with foreign investors are often found in developing countries like the PRC. Such joint ventures were reasonably common in Eastern Europe before the Iron Curtain came down, and were permitted in the former Soviet Union. There is a sense therefore in which China's 1979 equity joint venture law was merely catching up to world trends. The 1986 law allowing wholly foreign-owned enterprises (WFOEs) was another matter. With this law, China leaped ahead of other socialist countries and many developing nations as well. WFOEs are indicative of just how open and embracing the country can be to foreign investment.

Beginning in 1980, wholly-owned enterprises were allowed in a few preferential economic zones, such as the Shenzhen near Hong Kong. These were often small companies established in Shenzhen by Hong Kong Chinese. Success with this experiment led, in 1983, to the designation of a number of coastal cities where wholly foreign-owned enterprises could be established. The first wholly-owned enterprise outside a SEZ was that of 3M in Shanghai. For 3M in China, the need to balance foreign exchange receipts, uncertainty over applicable tax law, and labor relations proved troublesome. From the Chinese perspective, however, the march forward was not to be denied. In 1986, a general law was passed permitting WFOEs *anywhere* in the PRC. WFOEs can also be used by foreigners with more than one investment in the PRC to unite the management and operations of those enterprises.

The Law on Wholly Foreign-Owned Enterprises and its implementing regulations (particularly those issued in 1990) and their successors create the most restrictive of all of the PRC's foreign investment rules. These rules reflect caution and concern about total foreign ownership of enterprises located in China. The main legal features of the law on WFOEs have been as follows:

- Foreigners may serve as chairs of boards of directors

- Importation of advanced technology and equipment and substantial exportation of products (these rules have recently been relaxed)

- Protection of investment, profits and other rights "under Chinese law"

- Expropriation in "special circumstances," with "commensurate compensation"

- "For the record" submission of production and operational plans to the government—noninterference is to be the rule

- Chinese tax and financial supervision, 50% maximum tax

- Chinese insurance required

- Priority to local sourcing if terms are competitive with international market

- Foreign exchange account must be balanced

- Mandatory trade union facilities

- General supervision by approving authorities

To some extent, the restrictive terms of Chinese law on WFOEs have deterred multinational foreign investors. In general, however, their preference for equity joint ventures is primarily based upon a desire to have a Chinese partner escort them through the bureaucratic and political maze that foreign investors encounter. Lately, however, the "carrying costs" of a Chinese partner and growing familiarity with doing business in China has led many foreign investors to switch to WFOEs.

CONTRACTUAL JOINT VENTURES (PARTNERSHIPS)

Hong Kong, Overseas Chinese and other foreign investors have often preferred "contractual joint ventures." Historically, this has been a less regulated form of doing business in China. A large number of such enterprises (many of them hotel investments) have been established since the Cultural Revolution. Because there are no equity shares, contractual joint ventures resemble partnership agreements. Prior to 1988 a principal attraction of such agreements was the *absence* of a basic law governing them. Even after the adoption in 1988 of a contractual joint venture law, flexibility is still their chief attraction. The 1988 Law on Chinese-Foreign Contractual Joint Ventures (CJV) and its successors were promulgated after years of experience with cooperative enterprise agreements. Viewed together with the 1986 General Principles of Civil Law, the most notable features of the law on CJVs have been as follows:

- Any split of profits may be chosen

- Limited liability is available to CJVs qualifying as legal persons under the Civil Law

- Protection of the rights and interests of the CJV and its parties "according to the law"

- Noninterference with operational and managerial decisions

- Trade unions required

- Balance in foreign exchange receipts required, subject to state assistance

- No minimum percentage of foreign capital

- Foreigners may serve as chairs of boards of directors

- No limit on duration of contractual agreement

Contractual joint ventures are the principal form of small business investment in the PRC. Until 1986, they easily outnumbered equity joint ventures. The return of sovereignty over Hong Kong and Macao by the end of the century caused Chinese investors from those cities to want to be on friendly terms with the mainland. The most common means for such investments is the CJV.

PRC STOCK COMPANIES AND CLASS B SHARES

Opportunities for foreigners to invest in Chinese companies have been increasing. Foreigners have since late 1991 been able to buy "Class B" shares in selected companies publicly traded on the Shanghai and Shenzhen stock exchanges. These shares are denominated in renminbi but can have dividends that are remittable abroad. Class B shares cannot be swapped for purely domestic Class A shares, but they can be traded among overseas investors. Such investors include persons from Hong Kong, Taiwan and Macao. The first Class B offering was that of the Shanghai Vacuum Electronic Device Corporation. Class B shares have generally been in short supply relative to foreign demand to purchase them. An alternative is to purchase Class H shares in Chinese companies listed on the Hong Kong stock exchange.

Regulations issued in 1992 authorize the creation of stock companies with foreign participation. Thousands of PRC state enterprises have been "corporatized" in this manner. Foreigners may invest in the shares of such companies. If the degree of foreign ownership exceeds 25%, the enterprise is then treated as if it were a joint venture receiving tax and other benefits. These are referred to as "foreign-invested" enterprises. Such investments have at least two features that distinguish them from the traditional options available to foreign investors in the PRC. First, both management and workers may take equity interests in the company and, second, much greater flexibility regarding transfers of interests is achieved. Equity and contractual joint ventures may be converted to foreign-invested stock companies.

Starting in 2014, a special Hong-Kong/Shanghai Stock Exchange link was established. This link is intended to foster more "cross-border" investments, but the Shanghai Stock Exchange crash of 2015 has reduced its attractiveness, at least concerning inflows into Shanghai listings, many of which are state-owned or controlled companies.

TECHNOLOGY TRANSFERS TO THE PRC

Major changes have been undertaken in the licensing and intellectual property law of the People's Republic of China since the Cultural Revolution. These changes reflect China's desire to create a modern economy by importing technology and by fostering its development. According to a report issued by central authorities in Beijing, the importation of technology augments China's modernization program in four ways: (1) By decreasing the gap on product quality and standards between China and the developed world; (2) By helping to promote the technological upgrading of Chinese enterprises; (3) By enhancing the ability of Chinese enterprises to independently develop their own new products and technology; and (4) By improving enterprise management.

China's desire to modernize its economy through technological imports is most evident in PRC patent and licensing law. A host of technology import regulations authorizing license agreements with foreign sources has been enacted. These regulations are not a blank check permitting technology importation at any cost. Rather, they are carefully constructed rules intended to promote technology transfers to China under acceptable terms and conditions.

In recent years, China has developed policies favoring "indigenous innovation" over technology importation. China also sometimes requires technology transfers or disclosures in connection with foreign investment approvals.

TECHNOLOGY PIRACY IN THE PRC

Despite the adoption of major PRC patent, trademark, copyright and technology transfer laws and their implementing regulations, a dark shadow hangs over much of Chinese intellectual property practice. Counterfeiting of goods and unlicensed use of technology is approaching epidemic proportions. Computer software is perhaps the most prominent victim. The official remedies discussed below, however diligently applied, seem inadequate to the task of dealing with this problem. Partly, one suspects, there are cultural forces at work. To copy another's work is traditionally a compliment in China. Partly also, the economics of development fuel piracy in the PRC. It is simply much less expensive to "borrow" from foreigners and (increasingly) domestic entities whatever can be reverse-engineered and imitated.

Foreign investors should very carefully consider what level of technology they transfer to their joint ventures and WFOEs. Even "Beijing Jeeps" have been reportedly knocked off by a number of township enterprises. There are no quick solutions to an environment that is fundamentally hostile to intellectual property. In this area, Chinese law will take a long time to mature.

PRC REGULATION OF TECHNOLOGY IMPORT CONTRACTS

As in many developing countries, there is a fear in China of paying excessive royalties for potentially redundant, outdated or inappropriate technology under oppressive contract terms. Likewise, there is a fear of standardized licensing contracts created by attorneys of foreign licensors. The principal objective of China's technology import regulations is to insure that such contracts do not contain restrictive clauses and to increase the bargaining power of Chinese licensees. Although pure licensing agreements are reasonably common, many technology transfers take place in the context of equity or contractual joint venture investments.

The 1985 Regulations for the Administration of Technology Import Contracts, now superseded by the 1999 Contract Law, are an important example of China's approach to licensing agreements. Similar regulations exist in some of China's economic development zones and coastal cities, notably Shenzhen, Xiamen and Guangzhou (Canton), which compete for technology transfers. Chinese law governs patent, trademark, knowhow and technical service contracts with foreigners. They also apply to technology transfers in connection with foreign investment. Once the parties have reached agreement, all such contracts must be examined and approved by government authorities before implementation. Since 1988, in a welcome reform, any technology transfer contract not disapproved after filing is deemed approved. Most Chinese licensing agreements are essentially installment sales. This is achieved by limiting the licensing agreement to a maximum of 10 years followed by the absence of restraints on the licensee's use of the technology after expiration of the agreement. The result is truly a technology transfer.

Chinese law stipulates that the imported technology must be "advanced," "appropriate" and "necessary" to modernization of China's industrial base. To this end, a feasibility study (which can be conducted by foreign experts) precedes the contract. The licensing agreement must contain certain terms, such as a guarantee by the supplier that the technology is "complete, free of error, effective and can achieve the objectives stipulated in the contract." This is an important representation and probably the most common source of lawsuits and arbitrations initiated by the Chinese in the technology transfer area.

Certain terms cannot appear in the agreement. These include restraints on the Chinese recipient's ability to choose the sources of relevant raw materials, spare parts or equipment. Such restraints are generally called "tying arrangements." However, the Chinese licensee can choose to take such supplies from the foreign licensor. In that case, the supplies must be offered at competitive international prices, itemized in the contract and are subject to special approvals. Chinese law also prohibits contract terms that are harmful to the public interest, that violate China's sovereignty, or that are unclear, unequal or unreasonable. In general, these regulations are designed to promote economic modernization in China while protecting it from foreign exploitation.

In other areas, either by law or practice, greater flexibility has been shown. For example, there is no legally stipulated maximum royalty payment.

Royalties of 2% to 5% of net sales value have been routinely approved. Higher royalties get close scrutiny by the examining authorities. Given China's shortage of foreign exchange, barter and countertrade are often substituted for cash royalties. Chinese law prohibits unreasonable restraints upon the Chinese recipient's domestic or export sales. Nevertheless, as a matter of practice, contract terms which effectively eliminate sales competition with the foreign licensor's products have often been permitted.

Once approved and executed, PRC technology transfer contracts are subject to ongoing regulatory approvals. The contract will often stipulate that certification of the delivery of the technology and its integration into the existing Chinese facility is required before payment to the licensor is allowed. This can get complicated because most technology importation is done by central or regional trading companies, not the end user. These trading companies often lack sufficient knowledge of the application of the technology by a factory hundreds or thousands of miles from their offices. Yet they are the ones who typically must make the necessary certifications.

The level of Chinese sophistication about licensing agreements is increasing. They have developed model patent and knowhow licensing contracts with which they frequently initiate negotiations. In their negotiations, and in the administration of their technology transfer law, the Chinese have so far successfully walked a fine line between providing sufficient incentives to bring foreign licensors into a bargain and discouraging them altogether.

HONG KONG AND MACAO

Hong Kong was acquired from the Manchus by Great Britain during the nineteenth century. The island of Hong Kong was ceded in perpetuity after the Opium War of 1839–42. Kowloon on the mainland and Stonecutter's Island were acquired in perpetuity under the 1860 Convention of Peking. In 1898, the Manchus leased to Great Britain the "New Territories" for 99 years. This lease covered approximately 350 square miles, numerous islands and a large body of sea. It encompassed 92% of the area of modern Hong Kong. China always considered these acquisitions the product of "unequal treaties" obtained during periods of weakness. From the Chinese perspective, they were forced to submit to these losses of territory in order to further British trading interests.

Over the years, China (including the PRC) settled into a reasonably comfortable acceptance of the benefits of Hong Kong under British rule (not at all democratic) as a trading center linking it to the West in many profitable ways. For example, the PRC earned large sums of hard currency through Hong Kong for its exports. Hong Kong also served as an important center for training mainland Chinese in marketplace skills and commercial transactions, shipping and the like. And it is through Hong Kong that large quantities of foreign investment capital and technology entered the PRC, particularly coastal and southern China, since 1976. The Hong Kong business community financed or operated industries located in the PRC employing millions of people. At the same time, however, Hong Kong increasingly exported the values and ideology of capitalism to the PRC. This "spiritual pollution" still worries China's more orthodox leadership, and there is ample evidence of its fallout in adjacent Guangdong province.

Macao was a Portuguese overseas territory located on a mainland peninsula of the PRC slightly west of Hong Kong. It also includes two adjacent islands in the South China Sea. In another moment of weakness, China ceded Macao in perpetuity by treaty to Portugal in 1887 after decades of open Portuguese claims of sovereignty. Unsuccessful attempts were made periodically by Holland and Britain to capture Macao.

Modern Macao is a gambling mecca with about a million inhabitants: the vast majority are ethnic Chinese. It has attracted major foreign investments by U.S. and other casino operators and, until the recent anti-corruption campaign of President Xi Jinping, dwarfed Las Vegas gambling revenues.

THE RETURN OF CHINESE SOVEREIGNTY IN 1997 AND 1999

The prospect of the New Territories' lease terminating in 1997 led Britain and the People's Republic of China to begin negotiations on the future of Hong Kong. British Prime Minister

Margaret Thatcher and the Chinese leader Deng
Xiaoping met in September of 1982 for this purpose.
Formal negotiations continued through 22 rounds
with the government of Hong Kong participating as
a member of the British delegation. The goal of both
sides in these negotiations was to create a system
that would maintain the stability and prosperity of
Hong Kong.

On December 19, 1984, British Prime Minister
Thatcher and Chinese Premier Zhao Ziyang
formally signed the Sino-British Joint Declaration
on the Question of Hong Kong. It was ratified by
both sides in 1985. The Declaration covers Hong
Kong Island, Kowloon, Stonecutter's Island as well
as the New Territories. It resulted in the return of
sovereignty over *all* of these areas (including those
ceded in perpetuity) to the People's Republic on July
1, 1997. The more than five million inhabitants of
Hong Kong in 1984, many of them refugees from the
mainland, had no material input into the terms of
the Declaration. They were presented with a *fait
accompli.*

Under the Sino-British Declaration, Hong Kong
became a "special administrative region" of the PRC
"with a high degree of autonomy." While the degree
of the autonomy is much debated, it is more than
that enjoyed by the various autonomous regions of
the People's Republic. Indeed, the Chinese took
great pains to avoid analogies to the terms and
operational realities of Tibet's "autonomy." Hong
Kong was the PRC's first attempt at its "one
country, two systems" policy. This policy is premised

upon the idea that the communist political and economic system of the PRC can coexist with a democratic and capitalistic system in Hong Kong. The policy is ultimately targeted at Taiwan.

In March of 1987, the "one country, two systems" policy was extended to Macao when Portugal agreed to return control over it to the PRC on December 20, 1999. Except for special arrangements concerning the rights of ethnic Chinese who are also Portuguese citizens (dual nationals), Macao became a special administrative region under conditions substantially the same as those for Hong Kong. Mismanagement of the "special status" of Hong Kong and Macao to the PRC will complicate immensely any hope of reunifying Taiwan with the mainland.

The Declaration reached in 1984 between China and Britain on the return of Hong Kong promised significant autonomy for the Hong Kong Special Administrative Region (HKSAR). Most importantly, it provided a list of "policies" that the PRC agreed to incorporate into a "Basic Law" for the HKSAR and to maintain for 50 years after 1997. These policies provide that the HKSAR will have "independent" executive, legislative and judicial power. Whether this independence has been achieved is debatable. The legislature is elected, although the exact method and degree of such elections were not specified in the 1984 Declaration. Extended street protests in 2014/2015 contested China's control over the list of candidates allowed to run for office.

China's pre-approved candidates naturally favor the PRC, and not the Hong Kong democracy movement.

The legislature has the power to create HKSAR law, but foreign affairs and defense matters are reserved to the central people's government (the PRC). The chief executive was appointed by Beijing first on the basis of local consultations, and later by elections. This executive appoints the principal officials in the HKSAR government. The 1984 Declaration specifies that the HKSAR courts are to be independent and possess a power of final adjudication, but their relationship to Chinese legal institutions is ambiguous. The PRC's policy is that "the laws currently in force in Hong Kong will remain basically unchanged" for 50 years. After that, China has made no promises.

CHAPTER 5
INVESTING IN EUROPE

The EU Customs Union and Common Market

Goods and Services   **Nontariff Trade Barriers**

Employment Law   **The EURO**

Mergers and Acquisitions

Hostile Takeovers and National Champions

With 28 member states and over 500 million
residents, the European Union is a powerful
investment magnet containing enormous wealth
and purchasing power. Investing in the EU jumps
over tariff and other trade barriers exporters
typically face when shipping goods into the Common
Market. This chapter focuses upon investing in
Europe and is adapted from R. Folsom, *Principles of
European Union Law* (West Academic Publishing).

This chapter is written primarily for an audience
located outside Europe. The underlying assumption
is that foreign investors will treat Europe as a
regional market, not a series of individual national
markets. Thus, although the relevant laws and
bilateral investment treaties (BITs, see Chapter 7)
of the European country where the investment will
be made always need to be consulted and can vary
greatly, this chapter primarily covers European

Union investment and trade law. It is this body of law that governs the operational realities of the market called Europe. And it is this market potential that so attracts foreign investors to the world's largest common market.

Business executives tend to think in terms of markets. Lawyers tend to think in terms of jurisdictions. From either perspective, Europe since 1950 has been a puzzle whose pieces sometimes change shape or fracture, sometimes disappear or reappear, and are generally hard to fit together. The timeline that follows takes an historical approach to understanding the European puzzle. This approach helps to answer the most basic of investment decisions: *Where in Europe shall we invest?*

1951—European Coal and Steel Community ("Treaty of Paris")

1957—European Economic Community (EEC) ("Treaty of Rome"), European Atomic Energy Community Treaty (EURATOM)

1959—European Free Trade Area Treaty (EFTA)

1968—EEC Customs Union fully operative

1973—Britain and Denmark switch from EFTA to EEC; Ireland joins EEC; Norway rejects membership; remaining EFTA states sign industrial free trade treaties with EEC

1979—Direct elections to European Parliament

1981—Greece joins EEC

1983—Greenland "withdraws" from EEC

1986—Spain and Portugal join EEC, Portugal leaves EFTA

1987—Single European Act amends Treaty of Rome to initiate campaign for a Community without internal frontiers by 1993

1990—East Germany merged into Community via reunification process

1993—Maastricht Treaty on European Union (TEU), EEC officially becomes EC

1995—Austria, Finland, and Sweden join EU, Norway votes no again

1999—Amsterdam Treaty

1999—Common currency (EURO) managed by European Central Bank (ECB) commences with 11 members

2003—Treaty of Nice, draft Constitution for Europe released

2004—Cyprus, Estonia, Slovenia, Poland, Hungary, the Czech Republic, Slovakia, Latvia, Lithuania, Malta join EU

2005—Constitution for Europe overwhelmingly defeated in France and Netherlands

2007—Accession of Bulgaria and Romania

2009—Reform Treaty of Lisbon takes effect Dec. 1, 2009. Treaty of Rome becomes Treaty on the Functioning of the European Union

2010—Greece and Ireland bailed out, 1 trillion EURO safety net created for financial crises

2011—Portugal bailed out, EURO in crisis

2012—Spanish and Italian banks bailed out, Greece bailed out again, EURO in extreme crisis, Treaty on Stability, Coordination and Governance (TSCG) adopted by 25 member states creating permanent European Stability Mechanism crisis loan fund and a Fiscal Compact with balanced budget rules, ECB agrees to buy unlimited short-term national bonds

2013—Croatia joins EU, Cyprus bailed out

2014—Latvia joins EURO zone, Scotland votes against independence from the UK

2015—Lithuania joins EURO zone, ECB commences bond buying ("quantitative easing"), Greece bailed out a third time, massive waves of migrants enter Europe

2016—British referendum in June on withdrawing from the EU ("Brexit")

This timeline suggests where and where not to invest in Europe. Consider the following investment issues:

Would you invest in Norway, a country whose 3–4 million people have twice voted against membership in the EU? Would you invest in Switzerland, which is an equally small market that is not part of the European Union? FYI, some firms manufacturing in Switzerland have "disinvested" and relocated their operations inside the EU. Inside the EU, would you invest in bail-out prone Greece, a country that may not remain in the EURO zone ("Grexit")? What about the UK, with "Brexit" prospects on the horizon? Just the possibility of Britain exiting the EU has already caused foreign investors to postpone additional or new investments in that nation.

What about the EURO crisis? Many U.S. investors have traditionally favored EURO zone countries like Ireland, saving considerable sums trading in a zone that does not require currency exchanges. Of course it does not hurt that Ireland is English-speaking, a short plane ride, and has one of the very lowest corporate taxation rates (12.5%) in the EU as well as reduced taxation of patent income (known as "patent box" taxation). Modest *flat* taxation rates on corporate and personal income as well as VAT transactions exist in some of the states formerly behind the Iron Curtain, Slovakia and Estonia for example. Slovakia has attracted substantial foreign and EU auto industry investments.

High tax EU countries such as Germany and France have seen foreign and domestic investment exit their markets in favor of lower tax and lower wage Eastern European member-states. Costs of operation and prices of goods and services in member states which are not part of the EURO zone, such as Hungary and Poland, are reduced when national currencies float down against the EURO. Consider whether investing outside the EURO zone is a plus?

A series of "right of establishment" decisions by the European Court of Justice indicate that investors can incorporate almost anywhere they wish regardless of where their principal place of operations is located inside the EU. Hence careful evaluation of corporate law questions concerning capital requirements, capacity to sue, liability risks and the like, as well as taxation, needs be undertaken. Thousands of U.K. companies are thought to have been set up to avoid German paid-in capital requirements.

Where to invest may also be influenced by less tangible factors, such as the preference of executives for an EU location and lifestyle. Access to major financial markets, such as the City of London, could be an important element. U.K. corporate law is also thought to be flexible and accommodating, allowing for example the choice of maintaining operational headquarters elsewhere in a lower tax jurisdiction provided the board of directors meets there.

THE EU COMMON MARKET

Investors in the European Union have a great interest in how well its common market works. Their basic goal is to sell in a regional (not a national) market. This section highlights the law governing free movement of goods, money and services. It also very selectively focuses upon the development of common policies of particular concern to foreign investors (with emphasis on U.S. interests).

Space does not permit treatment of European law governing medical and food products, free movement of people, worker and professional rights, banking, insurance, investment advisors, transportation, value-added and excise taxation, broadcasting and media products, computer software, commercial agents, corporate taxation, subsidies, industrial and intellectual property, procurement, products liability, consumer protection, advertising, companies, the environment, energy, telecommunications, agricultural and fisheries policy, customs, trade, franchising, patent and know-how licensing, distribution agreements and antitrust. All of these topics, which may well influence investment in Europe decisions, are covered in R. Folsom, *Principles of European Union Law* (West Academic Publishing).

The campaign for a European Community without internal frontiers was the product of Commission studies in the mid-1980s which concluded that a hardening of the trade arteries of Europe had occurred. The Community was perceived to be stagnating relative to the advancing economies of North America and East Asia. Various projections of the wealth that could be generated from a truly common market for Western Europe suggested the need for revitalization. A "white paper" drafted under the leadership of Lord Cockfield of Britain and issued by the Commission in 1985 became the blueprint for the campaign.

The Commission's white paper identified three types of barriers to a Europe without internal frontiers—physical, technical and fiscal. Physical barriers occur at the borders. For goods, they include national trade quotas, health checks, agricultural monetary compensation amount (MCA) charges, statistical collections and transport controls. For people, physical barriers involve clearing immigrations, security checks and customs. Technical barriers mostly involve national standards and rules for goods, services, capital and labor which operate to inhibit trade among the member states. Boilers, railway, medical and surgical equipment, and pharmaceuticals provide traditional examples of markets restrained by technical trade barriers. Fiscal barriers centered on different value-added and excise taxation levels and the corresponding need for tax collections at the border. There were, for example, wide value-added tax (VAT) differences on auto sales within the Common Market.

The Commission (Cecchini Report) estimated that removal of all of these barriers could save the Community upwards of 100 billion ECUs (European Currency Units) in direct costs. In addition, another roughly 100 billion ECUs may be gained as price reductions and increased efficiency and competition take hold. Overall, the Commission projected an increase in the Common Market's gross domestic product (GDP) of between 4.5 to 7 percent, a reduction in consumer prices of between 6 to 4.5 percent, 1.75 to 5 million new jobs, and enhanced public sector and external trade balances. These figures were thus said to represent "the costs of non-Europe."

Major amendments to the Treaty of Rome (now the Treaty on the Functioning of the European Union, TFEU) were undertaken in the Single European Act (SEA) which became effective in 1987. Amendments to the Treaty can occur by Commission or member state proposal to the Council which calls an intergovernmental conference to unanimously determine their content. The amendments are not effective until ratified by all the member states in accordance with their respective constitutional requirements. Proposals originating in the Commission's 1985 white paper on a Europe without internal frontiers were embodied in the Single European Act.

The SEA amendments not only expanded the competence of the European institutions, but also sought to accelerate the speed of integration by relying more heavily on qualified majority (not unanimous) legislative voting principles in Council decision-making. The Single European Act envisioned the adoption of hundreds of new legislative measures designed to fully integrate the Common Market by the end of 1992. Nearly all of these measures and more were adopted by the

Council, thus increasing the power of the EU to attract foreign investment.

THE EU CUSTOMS UNION

North American traders and investors should understand that the free movement of goods within Europe is based upon the creation of a customs union. Under this union, the member states have eliminated customs duties among themselves. They have established a common customs tariff for their trade with the rest of the world. Quantitative restrictions (quotas) on trade between member states are also prohibited, except in emergency and other limited situations. The right of free movement applies to goods that originate in the Common Market *and* to those that have lawfully entered it and are said to be in "free circulation." In other words, all goods lawfully inside the EU may be freely traded. In contrast, NAFTA has no such universal rule.

The establishment of the customs union has been a major accomplishment, though not without difficulties. The member states not only committed themselves to the elimination of tariffs and quotas on internal trade, but also to the elimination of "measures of equivalent effect." The elastic legal concept of measures of equivalent effect has been interpreted broadly by the European Court of Justice and the Commission to prohibit a wide range of trade restraints, such as administrative fees charged at borders which are the equivalent of import or export tariffs. Charges of equivalent effect to a tariff must be distinguished from internal taxes that are applicable to imported and domestic goods. The latter must be levied in a nondiscriminatory and non-protective manner while the former are prohibited entirely. There has been a considerable amount of litigation over this distinction.

The elasticity of the concept of measures of an equivalent effect is even more pronounced in the Court's judgment relating to quotas. This jurisprudence draws upon an early Commission directive (no longer applicable) of extraordinary scope. In this directive, the Commission undertook a lengthy listing of practices that it considered illegal measures of effect equivalent to quotas. It is still occasionally referenced in Commission and Court of Justice decisions. Its focus is on national rules that discriminate against imports or simply restrain internal trade. This "effects test" soon found support from the ECJ. In a famous case, the Court of Justice ruled that Belgium could not block the importation of Scotch whiskey via France because of the absence of a British certificate of origin as required by Belgian customs law.

The Court of Justice has held that any national rule directly or indirectly, actually or potentially capable of hindering internal trade is generally forbidden as a measure of equivalent effect to a quota. However, *if* European law has not developed appropriate rules in the area concerned (here designations of origin), the member states may enact "reasonable" and "proportional" (no broader than necessary) regulations to ensure that the public is not harmed. This is often referred to as the "*Cassis* formula". See the "Cassis de Dijon" case, *Rewe Zentral AG v. Bundesmonopolverwaltung für Branntwein* (1979) Eur.Comm.Rep. 649 (German *minimum* alcoholic beverage rule not reasonable). Products meeting reasonable national criteria, the *Cassis* opinion continues, may be freely traded. This is the origin of the innovative "mutual reciprocity" principle used in significant parts of the legislative campaign for a Europe without frontiers.

The *Cassis* decision suggests use of a Rule of Reason analysis for national fiscal regulations, public health measures, laws governing the fairness of commercial transactions and consumer protection. Environmental protection and occupational safety laws of the member states have been similarly treated. Under this approach, for example, a Danish "bottle bill" requiring use of approved containers was therefore unreasonable. However, the Danes' argument that a deposit and return system was environmentally necessary prevailed. This was a reasonable restraint on internal trade recognized by the Court under the *Cassis* formula.

Under *Cassis*, national rules requiring country of origin or "foreign origin" labels have fallen as measures of effect equivalent to quotas. So have various restrictive national procurement laws, including a "voluntary" campaign to "Buy Irish." Minimum and maximum retail pricing controls can also run afoul of the Court's expansive interpretations. Compulsory patent licensing can amount to a measure of equivalent effect nullified by operation of regional law. The U.K. could not compulsorily require manufacturing within its jurisdiction. Member states may not impose linguistic labelling requirements so as to block trade and competition in foodstuffs. In this instance, a Belgian law requiring Dutch labels in Flemish areas was nullified as in conflict with the Treaty. These cases vividly illustrate the extent to which litigants are invoking the Treaty and the *Cassis* formula in attempts at overcoming commercially restrictive national laws.

There are cases which suggest that "cultural interests" may justify national restrictions on European trade. For example, British, French and Belgian bans on Sunday retail trading have survived initial scrutiny under the *Cassis* formula. French legislation prohibiting the sale or rental of cassettes within one year of a film's debut also survived such scrutiny. And British prohibitions of sales of sex articles except by licensed sex shops are compatible. National laws prohibiting sales below cost, when applied without discrimination as between imports and domestic products, are not considered to affect trade between the member states. In *Keck*, a remarkable decision signaling a jurisprudential retreat, the ECJ ruled that such laws may not be challenged under the traditional *Cassis* formula. See *Re Keck & Mithouard* (1993) Eur.Comm.Rep. 6097 (Cases C–267/91, C–268/91). Deceptive trade practices laws ordinarily do not amount to "selling arrangements," but national laws regulating outlets and advertising may.

In recent years, member state regulations capable of being characterized as governing "marketing modalities" or "selling arrangements" have sought shelter under *Keck*. For example, the French prohibition of televised advertising (intended to favor printed media) of the distribution of goods escaped the rule of reason analysis of *Cassis* in this manner. Some commentators see in *Keck* and its progeny an unarticulated attempt by the Court to take subsidiarity seriously. Others are just baffled by its newly found tolerance for trade distorting national marketing laws. But the Court of Justice has poignantly refused to extend *Keck* to the marketing of services.

The Court has made it clear that all of the Rule of Reason justifications for national regulatory laws are temporary. Adoption of Common Market legislation in any of these areas would eliminate national authority to regulate trading conditions under *Cassis* and (presumably) *Keck*. These judicial mandates, none of which are specified in the TFEU vividly illustrate the powers of the Court of Justice to expansively interpret the Treaty and rule on the validity under European law of national legislation affecting internal trade in goods.

ARTICLE 36 AND THE PROBLEM OF NONTARIFF TRADE BARRIERS (NTBS)

The provisions of the Treaty on the Functioning of the European Union (TFEU) dealing with the establishment of the customs union do not adequately address the problem of nontariff trade barriers NTBs. As in the world community, the major trade barrier within Europe has become NTBs. To some extent, in the absence of a harmonizing directive completely occupying the field, this is authorized. Article 36 TFEU permits national restraints on imports and exports justified on the grounds of:

(1) Public morality, public policy ("ordre public") or public security;

(2) The protection of health and life of humans, animals or plants;

(3) The protection of national treasures possessing artistic, historical or archeological value; and

(4) The protection of industrial or commercial property.

Article 36 amounts, within certain limits, to an authorization of nontariff trade barriers among the member nations. This "public interest" authorization exists in addition to, but somewhat overlaps with, the Rule of Reason exception formulated in *Cassis* above. However, in a sentence much construed by the European Court of Justice, Article 36 continues with the following language: "Such prohibitions or restrictions shall not, however, constitute a means of arbitrary discrimination or a disguised restriction on trade between member states."

In a wide range of decisions, the Court of Justice has interpreted Article 36 in a manner which generally limits the ability of member states to impose NTB barriers to internal trade. Britain, for example, may use its criminal law under the public morality exception to seize pornographic goods made in Holland that it outlaws, but not inflatable sex dolls from Germany which could be lawfully produced in the United Kingdom. Germany cannot stop the importation of beer (e.g., Heineken's from Holland) which fails to meet its purity standards. This case makes wonderful reading as the Germans, seeking to invoke the public health exception of Article 36, argue all manner of ills that may befall their populace if free trade in beer is allowed. Equally interesting are the unsuccessful Italian health protection arguments against free trade in pasta made from common (not durum) wheat.

But a state may obtain whatever information it requires from importers to evaluate public health risks associated with food products containing additives that are freely traded elsewhere in the Common Market. This does not mean that an importer of muesli bars to which vitamins have been added must prove the product healthful, rather that the member state seeking to bar the imports must have an objective reason for keeping them out of its market. Assuming such a reason exists, the trade restraint may not be disproportionate to the public health goal. A notable 2002 ECJ opinion invalidated a French public health ban on U.K. beef imports maintained after a Commission decision to return to free trade following the "mad cow" outbreak.

Public security measures adopted under Article 36 can include external as well as internal security. An unusual case under the public security exception contained in Article 36 involved Irish petroleum products' restraints. The Irish argued that oil is an exceptional product always triggering national security interests. Less expansively, the Court acknowledged that maintaining minimum oil supplies did fall within the ambit of Article 36. The public policy exception under Article 36 has been construed along French lines (ordre public). Only genuine threats to fundamental societal interests are covered. Consumer protection (though a legitimate rationale for trade restraints under *Cassis*), does not fall within the public policy exception.

INTELLECTUAL PROPERTY RIGHTS AS COMMON MARKET TRADE BARRIERS

A truly remarkable body of case law has developed around the authority granted national governments in Article 36 to protect industrial or commercial property by restraining imports and exports. These cases run the full gamut from protection of trademarks and copyrights to protection of patents and knowhow. There is a close link between this body of case law and that developed under Article 101 concerning business restraints on competition (antitrust).

Trade restraints involving intellectual property arise out of the fact that such rights are nationally granted. As an alternative national IP rights, late in

1993 the Council reached agreement on a Common
Market trademark regime that has been widely
used, especially by U.S. firms. The Council also
adopted Directive 89/104, which seeks to harmonize
member state laws governing trademarks. Decades
were spent by the Commission on developing
Common Market patents to provide an alternative
to national intellectual property rights. These
proposals finally matured in 2014 with the creation
of the EU Unitary Patent regime (not applicable in
Spain and Italy). In the copyright field, several
directives have harmonized European law, perhaps
most importantly on copyrights for computer
software. All of these efforts have helped reduce the
potential for trade restraining impact of national IP
rights.

Perhaps more importantly, the European Court of
Justice has directly addressed Article 36 and
generally resolved against the exercise of national
intellectual property rights in ways which inhibit
free internal trade. In many of these decisions, the
Court acknowledges the existence of the right to
block trade in infringing goods, but holds that the
exercise of that right is subordinate to the TFEU.
The Court has fashioned a doctrine which treats
national intellectual property rights as having been
exhausted once the goods to which they apply are
freely sold on the market. One of the few exceptions
to this doctrine is broadcast performing rights which
the Court treats as incapable of exhaustion. CDs
and the like embodying such rights are, however,
subject to the exhaustion doctrine once released into
the market. Such goods often end up in the hands of

third parties who then ship them into another member state.

The practical effect of many of the rulings of the Court of Justice is to remove the ability of the owners of the relevant intellectual property rights from successfully pursuing infringement actions in national courts. When intellectual property rights share a common origin and have been placed on goods by consent, as when a licensor authorizes their use in other countries, then infringement actions to protect against trade in the goods to which the rights apply are usually denied. It is only when intellectual property rights do not share a common origin or the requisite consent is absent that they stand a chance of being upheld so as to stop trade in infringing products. Compulsory licensing of patents, for example, does not involve consensual marketing of products. Patent rights may therefore be used to block trade in goods produced under such a license. But careful repackaging and resale of goods subject to a common trademark may occur against the objections of the owner of the mark.

An excellent example of the application of the judicial doctrine developed by the Court of Justice in the intellectual property field under Article 36 can be found in *Centrafarm BV and Adriann de Peipjper v. Sterling Drug Inc.* (1974) Eur.Comm.Rep. 1147. The United States pharmaceutical company, Sterling Drug, owned the British and Dutch patents and trademarks relating to "Negram." Subsidiaries of Sterling Drug in Britain and Holland had been respectively assigned the British and Dutch trademark rights to Negram. Owing in part to price controls in the UK, a substantial difference in cost for Negram emerged as between the two countries. Centrafarm was an independent Dutch importer of Negram from the UK and Germany. Sterling Drug and its subsidiaries brought infringement actions in the Dutch courts under their national patent and trademark rights seeking an injunction against Centrafarm's importation of Negram into The Netherlands.

The Court of Justice held that the intellectual property rights of Sterling Drug and its subsidiaries could not be exercised in a way which blocked trade in "parallel goods." In the Court's view, the exception established in Article 36 for the protection of industrial and commercial property covers only those rights that were specifically intended to be conveyed by the grant of national patents and trademarks. Blocking trade in parallel goods after they have been put on the market with the consent of a common owner, thus exhausting the rights in question, was not intended to be part of the package of benefits conveyed. If Sterling Drug succeeded, an arbitrary discrimination or disguised restriction on Union trade would be achieved in breach of the language which qualifies Article 36. Thus the European Court of Justice ruled in favor of the free movement of goods within the Common Market even when that negates clearly existing national legal remedies.

Only in the unusual situation where the intellectual property rights in question have been acquired by independent proprietors under different national laws may such rights inhibit internal trade. While the goal of creation of the Common Market can override national intellectual property rights when internal trade is concerned, these rights apply fully to the importation of goods (including gray market goods) from outside the European Union. North American exporters of goods subject to rights owned by Europeans may therefore find entry challenged by infringement actions in national courts. This is notably true regarding unauthorized trade in gray market goods and can benefit U.S. companies. Using its UK trademark rights, Levi Strauss, for example, successfully kept low-price (Made in the USA) Levi's out of the EU.

LEGISLATIVE SOLUTIONS TO NTBS

Nontariff trade barrier problems were the principal focus of the campaign for a fully integrated Common Market. Many legislative acts have been adopted, or are in progress, which target NTB trade problems. There are basically two different methodologies being employed. When possible, a common European standard is adopted. For example, legislation on auto pollution requirements adopts this methodology. Products meeting these standards may be freely traded in the Common Market. Traditionally, this approach (called "harmonization") has required the formation of a consensus as to the appropriate level of protection.

Once adopted, harmonized standards must be followed. This approach can be deceptive, however. Some harmonization directives contain a list of options from which member states may choose when implementing those directives. In practice, this leads to differentiated national laws on the same so-called harmonized subject. Furthermore, in certain areas (notably the environment and occupational health and safety), the TFEU expressly indicates that member states may adopt laws that are more demanding. The result is, again, less than complete harmonization.

Many efforts at the harmonization of European environmental, health and safety, standards and certification, and related law have been undertaken. Nearly all of these are supposed to be based upon "high levels of protection." Many have criticized what they see as the "least common denominator" results of harmonization of national laws under the campaign for a Europe without internal frontiers. One example involves the safety of toys. Directive 88/378 permits toys to be sold throughout the Common Market if they satisfy "essential requirements." These requirements are broadly worded in terms of flammability, toxicity, etc. There are two ways to meet these requirements: (1) produce a toy in accordance with CEN standards (drawn up by experts); or (2) produce a toy that otherwise meets the essential safety requirements.

The least common denominator criticism may be even more appropriate to the second legislative methodology utilized in the internal market campaign. The second approach is based on the *Cassis* principle of mutual reciprocity. Under this "new" minimalist approach, European legislation requires member states to recognize the standards laws of other member states and deem them acceptable for purposes of the operation of the Common Market. However, major legislation has been adopted in the area of professional services. By mutual recognition of higher education diplomas based upon at least three years of courses, virtually all professionals have now obtained legal rights to move freely in pursuit of their careers. This is a remarkable achievement.

SERVICES ACROSS BORDERS AND FOREIGN INVESTORS

Bankers, investment advisors and insurance companies have long awaited the arrival of a truly common market. Their right of establishment in other member states has existed for some time. The right to provide services across borders without establishing local subsidiaries was forcefully reaffirmed by the Court of Justice in 1986. This decision largely rejected a requirement that all insurers servicing the German market be located and established there.

Legislative initiatives undertaken in connection with the single market campaign promise to create genuinely competitive cross-border European markets for banking, investment and insurance services. Licensing of insurance and investment service companies and banks meeting minimum capital, solvency ratio and other requirements as implemented in member state law is done on a "one-stop" home country basis. Banks, for example, cannot maintain individual equity positions in non-financial entities in excess of 15 percent of their capital funds, and the total value of such holdings cannot exceed 50 percent of those funds. They can participate and service securities transactions and issues, financial leasing and trade for their own accounts. The proposed investment services directive requires home country supervision of the "good repute" and "suitability" of managers and controlling shareholders.

Member states must ordinarily recognize home country licenses and the principle of home country control. For example, Council Directive 89/646 ("the Second Banking Directive") employs the home country single license procedure to liberalize banking services throughout the region. However, host states retain the right to regulate a bank's liquidity and supervise it through monetary policy and in the name of the "general good." Similarly, no additional insurance permits or requirements may be imposed by host countries when large industrial risks (sophisticated purchasers) are involved. However, when the public at large is concerned (general risk), host country rules still apply. Major auto and life insurance directives employing one-stop licensing principles were adopted in 1990. The auto insurance directive reproduces the large versus general risk distinctions found in the Second Non-Life Insurance Directive. Host country controls over general risk auto insurance policies were retained until 1995. Host country permits are also required when life insurers from other member states actively solicit business.

There was a rush by foreign bankers, investment advisors and insurers to get established before January 1, 1993 in order to qualify for home country licenses. North Americans and others have been particularly concerned about certain features of the legislation mandating effective access in foreign markets for European companies before outsiders may benefit from the liberalization of services within the Common Market. This problem is generally referred to as the "reciprocity requirement." It is this kind of requirement that gave the campaign for a Europe without internal frontiers the stigma of increasing the degree of external trade barriers. Many outsiders, in rhetoric which sometimes seems excessive, refer to the development of a "Fortress Europe" mentality and threat to world trading relations.

Since state and federal laws governing banking, investment services and insurance are restrictive, and in no sense can it be said that one license permits a company to operate throughout the United States, one result of European integration has arguably been reform of United States regulatory legislation. Since 1994, the U.S. has noticeably relaxed its rules on interstate banking, and largely repealed the Depression-era Glass-Steagall Act limitations on universal banking.

EQUAL PAY AND EQUAL TREATMENT
("COMPARABLE WORTH")

Once invested inside the European Union, the law of equal pay and equal treatment of men and women in the workforce is perhaps the most startling "operational reality" foreign investors encounter. This area is a prominent element in wide-ranging European social policies. It is derived from International Labor Organization Convention No. 100 which three states, including France, had adopted by 1957. The French were rightfully proud of this tradition of nondiscrimination between the sexes on pay. They also appreciated that gender-based inequality in pay in other member states could harm the ability of their companies to compete. EU law thus enshrines a rough equivalent to what is termed "comparable worth" in the United States and a brave new world for investors in Europe.

EU equal pay rules have been the subject of voluminous legislation and litigation. They applies, quite appropriately, to the European Community as an employer. Early on, the Court of Justice decided that equal pay for equal work is directly effective EU law. This decision allows individuals to challenge pay discrimination in public and private sector jobs. The ruling was applied prospectively by the Court of Justice so as to avoid large numbers of lawsuits for back pay.

In an early case, a flight attendant for Sabena Airlines was able to allege illegal discrimination in pay and pension benefits (as a form of deferred pay) to stewards and stewardesses before a Belgian work tribunal. European law in this area enshrines the principle of "comparable worth," a most controversial issue in United States employment law. Furthermore, women who are paid less than men performing work of less worth may claim relief. The hard questions are how to determine what constitutes "equal work" requiring equal pay or what "women's work" is worth more than that being done by men (again requiring pay adjustments). For example, does secretarial work equal custodial work? Is the work of an airline attendant worth more than that of an airline mechanic?

Council Directive 75/117 (now Directive 2006/54) makes the principle of equal pay apply to work of *equal value* (to the employer). This mandates establishment of nondiscriminatory job classifications to measure the comparable worth of one job with another. The Commission successfully enforced Directive 75/117 in a prosecution before the European Court of Justice against the United Kingdom. The Sex Discrimination Act of 1975, adopted expressly to fulfill Article 157 obligations, did not meet European standards because employers could block the introduction of job classification systems. Danish law's failure to cover nonunionized workers also breached the equal pay directive. But its implementation under German law, notably by constitutional provisions, sufficed to meet regional standards.

In determining equal or greater values, most states favor a job content approach. Content is determined through job evaluation systems which use factor analysis. For example, in Great Britain a job is broken down into various components such as skill, responsibility, physical requirements, mental requirements, and working conditions. Points or grades are awarded in each of these categories and totaled to determine the value of the job. Different factors may be balanced against each other. In Ireland, the demand of physical work can be balanced against the concentration required in particular skills. This is known as the "total package" approach. The equal job content approach relies on comparisons.

This raises the question of which jobs should be deemed to be suitable for comparison. The member states have taken different approaches to this question. In Britain the comparison must be drawn from the same business establishment. In contrast, the Irish Anti-Discrimination Pay Act provides for "comparisons in the same place," and "place" includes a city, town or locality. This approach is designed to ensure that legitimate regional differences in pay are not disturbed.

Employer defenses also vary from member state to member state. In Ireland, employers may justify a variation if they can show "grounds other than sex" for a disputed variation in pay. In Britain, employers will succeed if they can prove a "genuine material factor which is not the difference of sex." In Germany, the employer can prove that "material reasons unrelated to a particular sex" justify the differential. A further consideration in the implementation of equal pay laws has been the existence of pre-existing wage schedules set by collective agreement. In Britain and Italy, courts have held that collective agreements relating to pay cannot be changed or altered except where direct discrimination can be shown.

The burden of proving "objectively justified economic grounds" to warrant pay differentials is on the employer. When a woman succeeds a man in a particular position within a company (here a warehouse manager), she is entitled to equal pay absent a satisfactory explanation not based upon gender. The same is true of part-time (female) workers doing the same job as full-time (male) workers. Free travel to railway employees upon retirement cannot go only to men. And "pay" includes retirement benefits paid upon involuntary dismissal, which cannot be discriminatory. But a protocol adopted at the 1991 Maastricht Summit makes this ruling prospective only. Pay also includes employer-paid pension benefits which cannot be for men only. In this decision the Court refused to remove the retroactive effect of its judgment. Mobility, special training and seniority may be objectively justifiable grounds for pay discriminations.

The principle of equal pay for equal work has been extended by Council Directive to *equal treatment* regarding access to employment, vocational training, promotions, and working conditions (e.g. retirement deadlines). This directive (now 2006/54) prohibits discrimination based upon sex, family or marital status. The Equal Treatment Directive is limited by three exceptions. Member states may distinguish between men and women if: (1) sex is a determining factor in ability to perform the work; (2) the provision protects women; or (3) the provision promotes equal opportunity for men and women. Equal treatment must be extended to small and household businesses.

Dutch Law compulsorily retiring women at age 60 and men at age 65 violated the directive. Women cannot be refused employment because they are pregnant even if the employer will suffer financial losses during maternity leave. Maternity and adoption leave benefits for women, however, need not be extended to men. The dismissal of a woman because of repeated absences owing to sickness is lawful provided the same absences would lead to the dismissal of men. General prohibitions against night work by women but not men violate equal treatment Directive 76/207. The French government failed to justify this criminal law on any special grounds.

Equality also governs social security entitlements such as disability or caring for the disabled pay. Social security benefits cannot be based upon marital status. Women police officers cannot be denied arms when men are not, even in the interest of "public safety" and "national security." Equal treatment requires the elimination of preferences based upon gender in laws governing collectively bargained employment agreements. The Council adopted a declaration in December 1991 endorsing the Commission's recommended Code of Practice on sexual harassment. This Code rejects sexual harassment as contrary to equal treatment law, specifically Council Directive 76/207. But the equal pay and equal treatment directives fail to cover significant categories of women workers; part-time, temporary and home workers. Additional legislation in these areas can be expected.

Although Article 157 on equal pay is directly effective law binding upon public and private employers, it is not yet clear to what degree the equal treatment directives discussed above have that effect. Clearly these directives are binding on the member states and public corporations as employers. The private sector must comply after national implementing legislation is adopted, but if that legislation is deficient the only remedy is a prosecution of the member state by the Commission. There is a trend within the jurisprudence of the Court of Justice towards recognition of a broad human right of equality before the law. This is evidenced in a number of cases, which suggests that the private sector will eventually be bound by all European legislation on equal pay and equal treatment even in the absence of or in spite of national implementing law.

Predictably, questions of "affirmative action" have arisen. A controversial decision of the Court of Justice invalidated a Bremen regulation giving women of equal qualifications priority over men where women made up less than half the relevant civil service staff. While not strictly a quota, the Court found that Bremen had exceeded the limits of the equal treatment directive in promoting equality of opportunity. Article 157(4) attempts to address such issues. It allows member states to maintain or adopt "measures for specific advantages" in order to make it "easier" for the "under represented sex" to pursue vocational activity or to prevent or compensate for "disadvantages" in professional careers. Specific reservation of University professorships for women in Sweden likewise fell upon ECJ review. Sweden now uses increasing targets for women in full professorships.

Transsexuals and homosexuals have begun to benefit from this trend. But the Court notably refused to require equal employer travel benefits for same sex partners. Likewise the Court of First Instance refused to recognize homosexual partnerships as the equivalent of marriage for household allowance purposes. Revisions of the 1976 equal treatment directive emphasizing an approach called "gender mainstreaming" have been adopted. Directive 2000/43 broadly provides for equal treatment irrespective of racial or ethnic origin. Directive 2000/78 more narrowly prohibits employment discrimination on the grounds of religion or belief, disability, age or sexual orientation.

THE EURO—ADMISSION TO THE EURO ZONE

One critical element to foreign investors in the European Union is the status and stability of its currency, the EURO. All member states wishing to join the EURO Zone at its creation in 1999 had to meet strict economic convergence criteria on inflation rates, government deficits, long-term interest rates and currency fluctuations. To join the third stage, a country was supposed to have an inflation rate not greater than 1.5% of the average of the three lowest member state rates, long-term interest rates no higher than 2% above the average of the three lowest, a budget deficit less than 3% of gross domestic product (GDP), a total public indebtedness of less than 60% of GDP, and no devaluation within the ERM during the prior two years. These criteria continue to govern admission of other member states into the EURO zone. One could argue they have been honored more in the breach than conformity.

The economic performance of member states in 1997 became the test for admission to the economic and monetary union. Since both France and Germany had trouble meeting the admissions criteria, this opened a window for much more marginal states such as Belgium, Italy and Spain to join immediately in 1999. Eleven of the then fifteen EU members commenced the EURO Zone. Greece subsequently in 2001 was deemed "qualified" for the EURO Zone based upon (as we now know) dubious financial data. As expected, Denmark, Britain and Sweden opted out of initial participation in the common currency. The Danes did so by voting No in a year 2000 national referendum. The Swedes voted similarly in 2003. By 2015, Slovenia, Malta, Latvia, Estonia, Lithuania, Cyprus and Slovakia had joined the EURO zone, for a total of 19 out of 28 member-states of the Union. The world financial crisis of 2008–09 initially increased the interest of some outside the EURO zone, notably Iceland, to partake of its relative stability. Denmark and Bulgaria have pegged their national currencies to the EURO.

On January 1, 1999, the participating states fixed the exchange rates between the EURO and their national currencies. National notes and coins were removed from the market by July 2002 as the EURO was installed. The EURO has been used for most commercial banking, foreign exchange and public debt purposes since 1999. It has also been adopted (voluntarily) by the world's securities markets, and by Monaco, San Marino, the Vatican, Andorra, Montenegro and Kosovo.

The arrival of the EURO had important implications for United States investors and the dollar. For decades, the dollar had been the world's leading currency, although its dominance has been declining since the early 1980s. Use of the Deutsche Mark and Yen in commercial and financial transactions, and in savings and reserves, had been steadily rising. The EURO was expected to continue the dollar's decline in all of these markets. It was certainly the hope of many Europeans that they had successfully created a rival to the dollar.

THE EURO—EUROPEAN CENTRAL BANK

It was also agreed at Maastricht that in the third stage the European Central Bank (ECB) and the European System of Central Banks (ECSB) would start operations. The ECB and ECSB are governed by an executive board of six persons appointed by the member states and the governors of the national central banks. The ECB and the ECSB are independent of any other European institution and in theory free from member state influence. Their primary responsibility is to maintain price stability, specifically keeping price inflation below two percent per year. In contrast, the U.S. Federal Reserve has two primary responsibilities: maximum employment and stable prices.

The main functions of the ECB and ECSB are: (1) define and implement regional monetary policy; (2) conduct foreign exchange operations; (3) hold and manage the official foreign reserves of the member states; and (4) supervise the payments systems. The ECB has the exclusive right to authorize the issue of bank notes within the Common Market and must set interest rates to principally achieve price stability. The Court of Justice may review the legality of ECB decisions.

Under the EURO's founding rules, the ECB worked closely with the Ecofin Council's broad guidelines for economic policy, such as keeping national budget deficits below 3% of GDP in all but exceptional circumstances (2% decline in annual GDP). If the Ecofin considered a national government's policy to be inconsistent with that of the region, it could recommend changes including budget cuts. If appropriate national action did not follow such a warning, the Ecofin could have required a government to disclose the relevant information with its bond issues, blocked European

Investment Bank credits, mandated punitive interest-free deposits, or levied fines and penalties.

Regrettably, the fiscal enforcement system established when the EURO was created did not work. Sanctions for failure to comply with the 3% budget deficit rule were held unenforceable by the Court of Justice. Since 1999, many EURO states have been under threat of sanctions for failure to comply with the 3% budget deficit rule, most notably Greece, Portugal, Spain, Italy and Ireland after the global financial meltdown of 2008–09. Yet no EURO Zone member state was ever sanctioned, suggesting this system for controlling national deficits is toothless. It has essentially been replaced by the 2012 Treaty on Stability, Coordination and Governance, discussed below.

THE EURO—FINANCIAL BAILOUTS

The global meltdown also caused financial markets to finally realize that national debt issued in EUROs by different Zone members came with different levels of risk. Interest rates rose on Greek, Portuguese, Irish and other bonds, while German, and to a lesser extent French, EURO bonds held firm. Despite a specific TFEU Article 125 prohibition against Union bailouts of member state governments, as the market-driven European financial crisis of 2010/11 demonstrated, bailouts of debt-ridden EURO zone members may occur. Joining with the IMF, a 110 billion EURO rescue package for Greece was organized over German laments. Fearing a cascade of financial crises in

Spain, Portugal, Italy and Ireland, a 1 trillion EURO liquidity safety net (EFSF) was devised using EU-backed bonds, special purpose EU-guaranteed investment loans, and more IMF funds. In addition, the ECB for the first time began buying EURO zone national government bonds in the open market.

All this caused Germany to publicly re-think its traditional role as paymaster and proponent of the European Union and EURO. Clearly the EURO was not as good as the fondly remembered Deutschmark. Sure enough, Ireland tapped into this safety net for over 100 billion EUROs late in 2010, followed by Portugal in 2011. In 2012, massive loans to Spanish and Italian banks and their governments staved off bailouts and moderated interest rates, and Greece was bailed out a second time. In 2013, Cyprus was bailed out under a plan that "bailed in" some bank depositors and creditors. In 2015, Greece was bailed out for a third time. These actions ran down the safety net and ECB resources.

Most private holders of Greek debt have been pushed into a renegotiated deal with roughly a 50% "haircut" in the value of their holdings. Since 2013, EU bailouts require sovereign bond holders to take losses under "collective action clauses" designed to keep individual investors from blocking restructured debt deals. Mandatory losses can be imposed when Euro-zone nations are deemed insolvent by the European Central Bank, the European Commission and the IMF ("The Troika"), acting somewhat like a "bankruptcy court," and the

Euro-zone finance ministers unanimously are in accord.

THE EURO—TREATY ON STABILITY, COORDINATION AND GOVERNANCE (TSCG), ECB BOND BUYING

In March of 2012, with market pressures and threats of a Greek default or exit from the EURO Zone escalating, 25 of the 27 EU members (minus Britain and the Czech Republic) adopted a Treaty on Stability, Coordination and Governance (TCSG) to provide a "permanent" solution to the EURO crisis. Only Ireland allowed its voters a referendum on this Treaty, which was negotiated outside the regular TFEU framework. The Irish, their bailout in progress, voted in favor of ratification by approximately a 60% margin. Importantly, ratification by the German Parliament was upheld by Germany's Constitutional Court under that country's eternal democracy" clause. The TCSG has two principal components: The European Stability mechanism (ESM) and a "Fiscal Compact."

Effective in 2013, the ESM created a permanent 900 billion EURO loan fund, 27% of which is financed by Germany. Any increase in the ESM fund must be approved by the German Parliament. EURO Zone countries may apply for bailout loans conditioned upon fiscal and economic reforms. As a general rule, all EURO Zone national parliaments must approve of any ESM rescue package. Finland has indicated its approval may require loan collateral. The "Fiscal Compact" incorporates a "balanced budget" rule. "Automatic corrective measures" apply if excessive budgets are reached. The EU Commission monitors national budget deficits and breach of the Compact can result in enforcement actions before the European Court of Justice with penalties payable to the ESM.

In addition, since 2012, the European Central Bank has demonstrated its willingness to buy national government and even corporate bonds under "quantitative easing" programs. Germany's revered Bundesbank has openly opposed these developments, which have the support of the Merkel government. Like ESM loans, such purchases will be conditioned upon fiscal and economic austerity commitments with the ECB serving as the regulator of Zone banks. The extent of the ECB's regulatory powers was much debated, though ECB licensing and penalty powers over large banks represented a regulatory base line.

Thus there is a three-part attempt at "permanently" solving the EURO crisis: The ESM, the Fiscal Compact and ECB bond buying. This attempt once again seeks to come to grips with systemic flaws that have haunted the EURO since its creation. . . . Can national spending policies be stabilized, coordinated and governed in support of a common currency? Since all EURO Zone countries are jointly liable for ESM and ECB monies, this amounts to a partial mutualization of national debt risk. It is not, however, as some have suggested is needed, EURO bonds backed by the EURO Zone.

That said, the TGSG is certainly a step in that direction.

DIRECT FOREIGN INVESTMENT CONTROLS, EXPROPRIATION

Surprisingly, the European Union does not have regionalized foreign investment controls over direct, meaning "greenfields", investments. National laws prevail, and most EU jurisdictions have direct foreign investment control regimes. Smaller, capital hungry EU member states, such as those in Eastern Europe, are generally quite welcoming as are Spain, the United Kingdom and Ireland.

Germany and France, on the other hand, typically undertake close scrutiny of direct foreign investments and may impose conditions thereon. Germany, for example, has "co-determination" laws that require worker (normally union) representatives on corporate Boards of Directors of sizeable companies. Germany tried hard to persuade its EU partners to enact similar rules that would have applied throughout the Union.

Germany failed, but the EU did adopt a "Works Council" law (revised and codified as Directive 2009/38) that will seem quite foreign to U.S. investors. Basically, this legislation mandates extensive sharing of information with employee representatives on a firm's economic and financial status, employment data, work methods, and prospective mergers and lay-offs. The Court of Justice has held that this Directive applies to parent companies located outside the EU.

Thousands of "works councils" operate throughout the European Union.

The European Human Rights Convention of 1950, to which all EU nations plus Russia and others subscribe, protects foreign investors from arbitrary or uncompensated expropriations. This protection has been construed by the European Court of Human Rights to also apply to domestic investors.

FRANCHISING AND TECHNOLOGY TRANSFERS IN EUROPE

Franchising and technology transfer terms associated with foreign investment in the European Union must conform the rules contained in what are called "group exemptions" from EU business competition law (antitrust). Group exemption regulations are largely self-enforced, meaning lawyers drafting franchising and technology transfer provisions typically adhere to them in order to be sure of their validity and secure an exemption from EU competition law fines and penalties.

Franchising. The EU Commission, following leading European Court of Justice decisions, adopted a "group exemption" (Regulation 4087/88) from EU business competition (antitrust) law for franchise agreements. This 1988 regulation required each franchisee to identify itself as an independent enterprise apart from the trademark/service mark/trade name owner. Disclosure could avoid joint and several franchisor liability for the provision by franchisees of defective goods or services. Regulation 4087/88 defined a "franchise" as a package of industrial or intellectual property rights relating to trademarks, trade names, signs, utility models, designs, copyrights, know-how or patents exploited for the resale of goods or the provision of services to customers. "Franchise agreements" were defined as those in which the franchisor grants the franchisee, in exchange for direct or indirect financial consideration, the right to exploit a franchise so as to market specified types of goods and/or services. A "master franchise agreement" involves the right to exploit a franchise by concluding franchising agreements with third parties. Starting with these basics, Regulation 4087/88 proceeded to detail permitted, permissible and prohibited clauses in EU franchise agreements.

This approach remained in force until 2000, when the European Union "group exemptions" for exclusive dealing, exclusive purchasing and franchise agreements were replaced by Regulation 2790/99, known as the Vertical Restraints Regulation, accompanied by lengthy vertical restraints Guidelines. This regulation and its guidelines are more economic and less formalistic than the predecessors. The efficiency enhancing qualities of intra-brand vertical restraints are recognized. Supply, distribution (including selective distribution) and franchise agreements of firms with less than 30 percent market shares are generally exempt; this is known as a "safe harbor."

Companies whose market shares exceed 30 percent may or may not be exempt, depending upon the results of individual competition law reviews.

Since 2004, these may be undertaken by the Commission, national competition authorities and national courts. In either case, no vertical agreements containing so-called "hard core restraints" are exempt. These restraints concern primarily resale price maintenance, territorial and customer protection leading to market allocation, and in most instances exclusive dealing covenants that last more than five years.

In 2010, a new Vertical Restraints Regulation 330/10 (with accompanying Guidelines) was issued. Its content is similar to that of 1999. Restrictions on the use of the Internet by distributors or franchisees with at least one "brick-and-mortar" store are treated as hard core restraints. For example, distributors and franchisees cannot be required to reroute Internet customers outside their territories to local dealers. Nor can they be forced to pay higher prices for online sales ("dual pricing"), or be limited in the amount sales made via the Internet, although a minimum amount of offline sales can be stipulated. Generally speaking, distributors and franchisees may sell anywhere in the EU in response to customer demand ("passive sales"). Restraints on "actively" soliciting sales outside designated distributor or franchise territories, including by email or banner web advertising, are permissible. *Both* supplier and distributor, and franchisor and franchisee, must have less than 30% market shares to qualify for the 2010 "safe harbor."

Patent, Know-How and Software Licensing. In 1996 the Commission enacted Regulation 240/96 on the application of Article 101(3) to transfer technology agreements. The intention of this Regulation was to combine the existing patent and knowhow block exemptions into a single regulation covering technology transfer agreements, and to simplify and harmonize the rules for patent and knowhow licensing. It contained detailed lists of permitted, permissible and prohibited clauses.

The detailed regulation of technology transfer agreement clauses contained in Regulation 240/96 was replaced by Regulation 772/2004, which applies to patent, know-how and software copyright licensing. The new Regulation distinguishes agreements between those of "competing" and "noncompeting" parties, the latter being treated less strictly than the former. Parties are deemed "competing" if they compete (without infringing each other's IP rights) in either the relevant technology or product market, determined in each instance by what buyers regard as substitutes.

If the competing parties have a *combined* market share of 20 percent or less, their licensing agreements are covered by the group exemption. Noncompeting parties, on the other hand, benefit from the group exemption so long as their *individual* market shares do not exceed 30 percent. Agreements initially covered by Regulation 772/2004 that subsequently exceed the "safe harbor" thresholds noted above lose their exemption subject to a two-year grace period. Outside these exemptions, a "rule of reason" approach applies.

Inclusion of certain "hardcore restraints" causes license agreement to lose their group exemption. For competing parties, such restraints include price fixing, output limitations on both parties, limits on the licensee's ability to exploit its own technology, and allocation of markets or competitors (subject to exceptions). Specifically, restraints on active and passive selling by the licensee in a territory reserved for the licensor are allowed, as are active (but not passive) selling restraints by licensees in territories of other licensees. Licensing agreements between noncompeting parties may not contain the "hardcore" restraint of maximum price fixing. Active selling restrictions on licensees can be utilized, along with passive selling restraints in territories reserved to the licensor or (for two years) another licensee. For these purposes, the competitive status of the parties is decided at the outset of the agreement.

Other license terms deemed "excluded restrictions" also cause a loss of exemption. Such clauses include: (1) mandatory grant-backs or assignments of severable improvements by licensees, excepting nonexclusive license-backs; (2) no-challenges by the licensee of the licensor's intellectual property rights, subject to the licensor's right to terminate upon challenge; and (3) for noncompeting parties, restraints on the licensee's ability to exploit its own technology or either party's ability to carry out research and development (unless indispensable to prevent disclosure of the licensed Know-how). In all cases, exemption under Regulation 772/2004 may be withdrawn where in any particular case an agreement has effects that are incompatible with EU business competition law.

MERGERS AND ACQUISITIONS

One alternative to direct investment in Europe is to purchase an existing business. Traditionally, the law governing such acquisitions was almost exclusively national. Since 1990, the EU actively regulates sizeable mergers and acquisitions as part of its competition policy. European law in this area is summarized below. Special attention should also be paid to the United States-European Community Antitrust Cooperation Agreement (1991) under which coordinated exchanges of information and review of transnational mergers frequently occur.

COMMISSION REGULATION OF MERGERS AND ACQUISITIONS

In December of 1989, the Council of Ministers unanimously adopted Regulation 4064/89 on the Control of Concentrations between Undertakings ("Mergers Regulation"). This regulation became effective Sept. 21, 1990 and was expanded in scope by amendment in 1997 (Regulation 1310/97). It vests in the Commission the exclusive power to oppose large-scale mergers and acquisitions of competitive consequence to the Common Market and the European Economic Area. For these purposes, a "concentration" includes almost any means by which control over another firm is acquired. This could be by a merger agreement, stock or asset purchases, contractual relationships or other actions. Most full function joint ventures creating autonomous economic entities are caught by this test. Thus "control" triggering review can be achieved by minority shareholders, such as when they exercise decisive influence over strategic planning and investment decisions. "Cooperative joint ventures" between independent competitors may also be subject to from the Mergers Regulation.

The control process established by the Mergers Regulation commences when a concentration must be notified to the Commission on Form CO in one of the official languages. This language becomes the language of the proceeding. Form CO is somewhat similar to second request Hart-Scott-Rodino pre-merger notification filings under U.S. antitrust law. However, the extensive need for detailed product and geographic market descriptions, competitive analyses, and information about the parties in Form CO suggests a more demanding submission. Form CO defines a product market as follows:

> A relevant product market comprises all those products and/or services which are regarded as interchangeable or substitutable by the consumer, by reason of the products' characteristics, their prices and their intended use.

Meeting in advance of notification with members of the Commission on an informal basis in order to ascertain whether the "concentration" has a regional dimension and is compatible with the Common Market has become widely accepted. Such meetings provide an opportunity to seek waivers from the various requests for information contained in Form CO. Since the Commission is bound by rules of professional secrecy, the substance of the discussions is confidential.

The duty to notify applies within one week of the signing of a merger agreement, the acquisition of a controlling interest or the announcement of a takeover bid. The Commission can fine any company failing to notify it as required. The duty to notify is triggered only when the concentration involves enterprises with a combined worldwide sales turnover of at least 5 billion Euros (approximately $6 billion) *and* two of them have an aggregate regional turnover of 250 million Euros (approximately $300 million). Additionally, since 1997, mergers with a combined aggregate worldwide turnover of more than 2.5 billion Euros and significant member state and regional turnovers must be notified.

As a general rule, concentrations meeting these criteria cannot be put into effect and fall exclusively within the Commission's domain. The effort here is to create a "one-stop" regulatory system. However, certain exceptions apply so as to allow national authorities to challenge some mergers. For example, this may occur under national law when two-thirds of the activities of each of the companies involved take place in the *same* member state. The member states can also oppose mergers by appealing Commission decisions when their public security is at stake, to preserve plurality in media ownership, when financial institutions are involved or other legitimate interests are at risk.

If the threshold criteria of the Mergers Regulation are not met, member states can ask the Commission to investigate mergers that create or strengthen a dominant position in that state. States that lack national mergers' controls seem likely to do this. Similarly, if the merger only affects a particular market sector or region in one member state, that state may request referral of the merger to it. This is known as the "German clause" reflecting Germany's insistence upon it. It has been sparingly used by the Commission.

Once a concentration is notified to the Commission, it has one month to decide to investigate the merger. If a formal investigation is commenced, the Commission ordinarily then has four months to challenge or approve the merger. During these months, in most cases, the concentration cannot be put into effect. It is on hold.

Effective May 1, 2004, the test for EU merger compatibility was changed to the following: Does the merger "significantly impede effective competition" by creating or strengthening dominant positions? Thus the new test focuses on effects, not dominance. A set of Guidelines on Horizontal Mergers was issued by the Commission in 2004 that elaborate on this approach. It is thought that this change will bring EU and U.S. mergers law closer together (the U.S. test is "substantial lessening of competition"). During a mergers investigation, the Commission can obtain information and records from the parties, and request member states to help with the investigation. Fines and penalties back up the Commission's powers to obtain records and information from the parties.

If the concentration has already taken effect, the Commission can issue a "hold-separate" order. This requires the corporations or assets acquired to be separated and not, operationally speaking, merged. Approval of the merger may involve modifications of its terms or promises by the parties aimed at diminishing its anticompetitive potential. Negotiations with the Commission to obtain such approvals follow. If the Commission ultimately decides to oppose the merger in a timely manner, it can order its termination by whatever means are appropriate to restore conditions of effective competition (including divestiture, fines or penalties). Such decisions can be appealed to the General Court. The Court has confirmed that mergers resulting in collective (oligopolistic) dominance of a market fall within European mergers regulation.

MERGERS: CASE EXAMPLES

The first merger actually blocked by the Commission on competition law grounds was the attempted acquisition of a Canadian aircraft manufacturer (DeHaviland—owned by Boeing) by two European companies (Aerospatiale SNI of France and Alenia e Selenia Spa of Italy). Prior to this rejection in late 1991, the Commission had approved over 50 mergers, obtaining modifications in a few instances. The Commission, in the DeHaviland case, took the position that the merger would have created an unassailable dominant position in the world and the European market for turbo prop or commuter aircraft. If completed, the merged entity would have had 50 percent of the world and 67 percent of the European market for such aircraft.

In contrast, the Commission approved (subject to certain sell-off requirements) the acquisition of Perrier by Nestlé. Prior to the merger, Nestlé, Perrier and BSN controlled about 82 percent of the French bottled water market. Afterwards, Nestlé and BSN each had about 41 percent of the market. The sell-off requirements were thought sufficient by the Commission to maintain effective competition. The case also presents interesting arguments that the Commission, in granting approval, disregarded fundamental workers' social rights. This issue was unsuccessfully taken up on appeal by Perrier's trade union representative.

In 1997, the Commission dramatically demonstrated its extraterritorial jurisdiction over the Boeing-McDonnell Douglas merger. This merger had already been cleared by the U.S. Federal Trade commission. The European Commission, however, demanded and (at the risk of a trade war) got important concessions from Boeing. These included abandonment of exclusive supply contracts with three U.S. airlines and licensing of technology derived from McDonnell Douglas' military programs at reasonable royalty rates. The Commission's success in this case was widely perceived in the United States as pro-Airbus.

The Commission blocked the MCI Worldcom/Sprint merger in 2001, as did the U.S. Dept. of Justice. For the Commission, this was the first block of a merger taking place outside the EU between two firms established outside the EU. The AOL/Time Warner merger was approved by the Commission after AOL promised to sever links with a German media group, thereby reducing its music publishing rights for delivery online via the Internet.

Much more controversy arose when in 2001 the Commission blocked the GE/Honeywell merger after it had been approved by U.S. authorities. The Commission was particularly concerned about the potential for bundling engines with avionics and non-avionics to the disadvantage of rivals. This bundling theory was rejected in 2005 by the European General Court. Nevertheless, the merger never took place. The United States and the EU, in the wake of GE/Honeywell, have agreed to follow a set of "Best Practices" on coordinated timing, evidence gathering, communication and consistency of remedies in the mergers field.

The EU General Court (GC) overturned a 1999 decision of the European Commission blocking the $1.2 billion merger of Airtours plc and First Choice Holidays plc. The June 2002 GC decision was the first reversal of an EU merger prohibition since the inception of the EU merger review process in 1990. The GC judgment confirmed that transactions can be blocked on collective dominance grounds, but found that the Commission had failed to meet the three conditions for proving collective dominance: (1) each member of the dominant group is able to determine readily how the others are behaving, (2) there is an effective mechanism to prevent group members from departing from the agreed-upon policy, and (3) smaller competitors are unable to undercut that policy.

In 2002, acting under "fast track" review procedures, the General Court overturned two additional mergers decisions of the Commission. The Court found serious errors, omissions and inconsistencies. Credible evidence, not assumptions or "abstract and detached analysis," must be tendered to prove the strengthening or creation of a dominant position, and the likelihood that the merger will significantly impede competition.

The Commission may be found liable in damages for intervening unlawfully against mergers, notably when making manifest procedural errors. Commission decisions to clear joint ventures or mergers can, in rare cases, be annulled.

HOSTILE TAKEOVERS AND NATIONAL CHAMPIONS

In June of 2002 the European Court of Justice issued three decisions on the use by member states of so-called "golden shares." Such shares allow governments to retain veto rights with respect to acquisitions of or other significant accumulations in privatized businesses. The Court outlawed a golden share decree allowing France to block a foreign takeover of a privatized oil company. The golden share decree created a barrier to the free movement of capital. The Court also outlawed a law giving Portugal the ability to block the acquisition of controlling stakes in privatized state companies, but determined as a matter of public interest that Belgium could retain its golden share in recently privatized canal and gas distribution companies.

In 2004, the EU adopted a directive on hostile takeover bids. Its two most controversial rules are optional. First, boards of directors are required to obtain shareholder approval before taking defensive measures other than seeking alternative offers. Second, once a bid has been made public, restrictions on share transfers, voting restrictions, and special voting rights are unenforceable. Hence member state law on hostile takeovers is not uniform. The French, for example, allow use of any defense permitted by the home country of the bidder, and have published a list of strategic sectors that are off-limits to foreign takeovers. In 2007, the ECJ overturned the decades-old "Volkswagen Law." This law had prevented anyone except the government of Lower Saxony from owning more than 20% of the voting rights to Volkswagen. Its invalidation permitted Porsche to complete its hostile takeover of VW.

EU countries often pursue policies to prevent "national champions" from falling into the hands of foreign investors, particularly those from outside the Union. If, for example, a U.S. firm seeks to acquire a "national champion", state controls and incentives are likely to prevent that outcome, often by arranging a friendly takeover by a national or at least an EU company. Fear of acquisition of major companies has led to novel ideas. France famously indicated that foreign acquisition of Danone, its national champion yogurt maker, would not be tolerated. Austria discussed the establishment of an Austro-fund to buy controlling interests of major Austrian firms, such as Böhler-Uddeholm (steel), Wienerberger (clay bricks), OMV (oil and gas), Voest (steel), and Lenzing (cellulose fiber). Austria has generally been hostile to major takeovers by foreign forms, while Austrian banks and companies have invested heavily abroad.

Spain has long protested major takeovers, sometimes encouraging instead alternative joint ventures. Spanish politicians, fearing a German takeover of Endesa, Spain's largest electricity company, pushed for an acquisition by Spanish-shareholder owned Gas Natural. Then it pushed for Italy's state-owned energy company Enel, to join with the Spanish firm Acciona, which had already acquired some 20% of Endesa, to make an offer.

Since 2005, France requires government approval of foreign takeovers in 11 key sectors of the economy. But failing "national champions" may present opportunities, which proved to be the case in 2015 when GE, not Germany's Siemens, was finally allowed by the European Commission to purchase the French industrial "crown jewel" Alstom.

CHAPTER 6
INVESTING IN NORTH AMERICA

Canada	Mexico	United States
NAFTA		U.S. Securities
Exon-Florio/FINSA/China in U.S.		Franchising
Employment Law		EB-5 Investor Visas

There are two schemes of foreign investments rules which must be addressed in North America. The first are the foreign investment laws and regulations of the individual NAFTA Parties. The foreign investment laws of Canada, Mexico and the United States are not only very different, but have reached their current status by means of quite separate histories. The second scheme is that of the NAFTA, covered in Chapter 8, which establishes common laws in some areas and seeks to extend that harmonization to nearly all foreign investment, with minimum exceptions.

In some respects, Canada and Mexico held similar views toward foreign investment, based on their experience with U.S. investment. Both nations were concerned with dominance by U.S. investment. Both were concerned that they would become the source of foreign (mainly U.S.) investment to extract natural resources for shipment abroad for manufacture. Both were concerned with the impact on their nation's balance of payments from the return of dividends to parent corporate owners. And finally, both were concerned that having so many foreign centers of decision-making would lead to few professional and managerial positions in Canada and Mexico for host-nation citizens, where the best jobs would be the supervision of the extraction of natural resources. This parallel concern is partly why Canada's and Mexico's foreign-investment laws, outlined below, have been quite restrictive. But the Canadian laws have often been more sophisticated, addressing more closely acquisitions than investments commenced from scratch ("greenfields").

Nations have not always welcomed *all* foreign investment. Investment that offers the nation something it lacks, such as technology or a sufficient numbers of jobs, may be so welcome that it is encouraged by incentives. But foreign investment that competes with domestic investment may face very complex obstacles or absolute prohibitions. Thus each nation has its own history of foreign investment rules. The respective histories of Canada, Mexico and the United States in developing each nation's current laws illustrate the struggle with balancing restrictions and incentives.

FOREIGN INVESTMENT IN CANADA

Although U.S. persons often view Canada in a mirror and see themselves, thus assuming that the Canadian government will be very receptive to foreign investment, the policies of Canada over the years reflect ambivalence toward investment. Canada has long regulated foreign investment by both federal and provincial laws. Soon after its creation as a federation in 1867, Canada established high tariffs to protect infant industries from imports from the United States. This caused U.S. manufacturers to invest in Canada to surmount the tariff wall, principally through small "branch plants." Soon the United States was the principal source of foreign investment, and for many U.S. companies Canada was a natural location for their first foreign investments.

Most Canadian investment laws have focused on specific sectors, such as financial institutions, transportation, natural resources and, quite importantly, publishing. Oil and gas acquisitions were prohibited until the *Masse Policy*, adopted in 1992, was rescinded. This repeal left regulation to the Investment Canada Act, which allowed greenfields investments but required approval of some oil and gas acquisitions. However, the threshold before approval was required was quite high, making the law less restrictive than it otherwise appeared. Canada considers publishing to be a cultural industry. Until restrictions in the Canadian *Baie Comeau Policy* on ownership of publishing were relaxed, foreign investment in publishing was very difficult.

Canada was always a natural target for investment from the United States, especially since so much of the industrial development of the United States occurred relatively near the Canadian border. Canada's attitude toward foreign investment remained quite receptive until nationalistic forces in the 1960s began to challenge an open investment policy. The first measure of significance was the creation of the Foreign Investment Review Agency (FIRA) in 1974, which allowed the federal government to review proposed foreign investment, especially acquisitions of Canadian companies, and in some cases deny their development or impose performance requirements. In 1984, a GATT panel notably upheld Canada's right to impose export commitments in order to obtain foreign investment approvals.

The National Energy Program in 1980 was intended to *reduce* foreign ownership in the oil and gas industry. Most of that foreign ownership was by U.S. companies. A Conservative government replaced the FIRA with the Investment Canada Act (ICA) (1985). This Act continues to govern foreign investment in Canada—especially acquisitions. Canada's system, like that of Mexico and the U.S. when national security is involved (below), is a pre-investment clearance system. The foreign investment review is examined under a "national interest" (including national security) standard. For example, when Burger King bought the iconic Canadian food chain, Tim Hortons, this merger was deemed not a threat to Canadian interests or security.

When Canada and the U.S signed a bilateral free trade agreement in 1989, and again when NAFTA was adopted in 1994, decisions by Canada following a foreign investment review under the ICA were excluded from NAFTA's dispute settlement provisions. Hence Canada insisted on retaining some domestic pre-investment control over foreign investment by U.S. and Mexican firms, especially the acquisition of Canadian owned industries, and most especially "cultural" industries.

CANADIAN TRADE AND INVESTMENT RESTRAINTS ON CULTURAL INDUSTRIES

Canada has a long history of supporting cultural industries through investment, financial, tax and other governmental acts. The 1989 free trade agreement between Canada and the United States excluded "cultural industries" from its scope, and this exclusion has been retained under NAFTA. Without doubt it was English-speaking Canada's number one objective in negotiating these agreements.

The argument for this exclusion is not to keep American culture out of the market, but instead to assure a Canadian presence as well. Indeed, Canada maintains that it has neither attempted nor succeeded in keeping out American cultural products. That certainly seems right. Over 90 percent of Canada's movie screens and more than 80 percent of its news and TV broadcasts are U.S. controlled. Books of U.S. origin occupy 60 percent of all Canadian shelf space and U.S. magazines take 80 percent of the English-language market.

Cultural industries are defined as those engaged in publishing, distributing or selling:

- Books, periodicals and newspapers (except their printing or typesetting);

- Films or videos; audio or video music recordings; or printed or machine readable music;

- Public radio communications;

- Radio, television and cable TV broadcasting; and

- Satellite programming and broadcasting network services.

One practical effect of securing the cultural industries exclusion was to insulate Canada's broadcasting regulations from regional scrutiny. In Canada, content requirements and airtime rules are an important means by which the Canadian Radio-Television and Telecommunications Commission (CRTC) restricts the amount of foreign broadcast material. Current broadcasting regulations employ a quota system mandating Canadian content for a minimum of 60 percent of all programming and 50 percent of prime time. Comparable quotas apply to films, broadcast TV, cable TV and satellite transmissions. "Canadian content" is calculated under a points system traditionally requiring that the producer be Canadian and that at least 6 of 10 key creative positions be filled by Canadians. In addition, most production and distribution expenses must be paid to Canadians.

The requirements for radio are similar and focus on the nationality of the composer and performer, and the location and performance of the selection. The government also provides subsidies and tax incentives for national broadcasting enterprises which have financial difficulty in complying with content quotas. Furthermore, investment regulations effectively limit U.S. ownership or control of Canadian cultural enterprises. For example, in 1996 Canada refused to permit Borders to open a super-bookstore in Toronto even after securing a Canadian partner as a majority owner. Ironically, although these economically driven rules ensure a national presence in broadcasting, they do not guarantee Canadian cultural content. Moreover, there is a thriving gray market for dishes aimed at U.S. satellites. More broadly, Internet streaming and Virtual Private Network (VPN) addresses have undermined Canada's cultural industry trade and investment restraints in ways that avoid even the most determined regulator. This is how, for example, Canadians access the full retinue of Netflix films, about only half of which are available via Canadian servers.

In contrast, there is no cultural industry exclusion under NAFTA applicable to Mexico-United States free trade. Integration of U.S.-Mexican cultural industries is occurring. In 1996, for example, the United States and Mexico reached agreement allowing companies in either country to compete for provision of satellite services, including direct-to-home and direct broadcast services. Each country retains the right to impose "reasonable" ownership, content and advertising regulations, but Mexico (unlike Canada) will not impose local content requirements. Media goods and investment have flowed freely across Mexican-U.S. border in both directions.

There are exceptions and qualifications to the general exclusion of Canadian cultural industries from US and NAFTA free trade. Tariff reductions were specified under US for film, cassettes, records, cameras, musical instruments and the like. Additional tariff reductions were agreed to in NAFTA. Responding to a United States complaint about Canadian cable TV "pirates," copyright royalties must be paid when U.S.-sourced free transmissions are retransmitted to the Canadian public by cable. In addition, no alteration or non-simultaneous retransmission of such broadcasts is permitted without the permission of the copyright holder. Likewise, no retransmission of cable or pay TV can occur without such authorization. Occasionally, United States investors may incidentally acquire a Canadian cultural industry company by merger or acquisition. If ordered to divest, the U.S. investor must be paid open market value by Canada. Apart from these exceptions, the Canadian cultural industry exclusion covers the entire gamut of the NAFTA agreement. It applies goods, services, investment, intellectual property, and dispute settlement.

Canada's cultural industry exception comes with a price. The United States can unilaterally implement retaliation for cultural industry protection. The U.S. can undertake "measures of equivalent commercial effect" against acts that would have been "inconsistent" with US but for the cultural industries exclusion. There is no need to utilize US dispute settlement procedures prior to retaliation, which can be anything except a violation of the free trade agreement. The United States could, for example, pursue "Section 301" investigations and unilateral retaliation under the Trade Act of 1974. Each year the United States Trade Representative must identify new Canadian acts, policies and practices affecting cultural industries.

Both Canada and the United States have sought to minimize the potential for cultural industry disputes through negotiations. The "successful" resolution of the Country Music Television (CMT) dispute in 1995 is often cited as an example. CMT of Nashville had, in the absence of a Canadian competitor, been licensed as a Canadian cable TV distributor. When a competitor emerged, CMT's license was revoked by the CRTC. CMT then petitioned the USTR for Section 301 relief, and an investigation was commenced. Intergovernmental negotiations resulted in the creation of a partnership of the two competitors, which was then licensed by the CRTC.

Cultural industry disputes have also been diverted by using the World Trade Organization as an alternative forum. This is permitted under the NAFTA agreement. In 1997, a WTO Dispute Settlement Panel initiated by the U.S. ruled that Canada's taxes, import regulations and postal subsidies concerning magazines (and advertising) violated the GATT 1994 agreement. This longstanding dispute centered on *Sports Illustrated*. Canada was seeking to protect and ensure "Canadian issues" of periodicals and prevent the export of its advertising revenues. Thus the United States overcame culturally-based Canadian policies by electing to pursue WTO remedies, although Canada's compliance was disputed. In May of 1999, a settlement was reached. United States publishers may now wholly-own Canadian magazines. In addition, Canada will permit U.S. split-run editions without Canadian editorial content. Such editions may contain Canadian advertisements not in excess of 12 percent by lineage (rising to 18 percent in several years).

This author's bottom line: Canada's hard won cultural industries exclusion has been almost completely over-run by technology and the use of WTO remedies. One wonders what truly "cultural" concessions Canada might obtain from the U.S. if it offered to entirely abandon the exclusion.

FOREIGN INVESTMENT IN MEXICO

The United States has never viewed Mexico with the same mirror as it does Canada, seeing itself in the reflection. Canada usually has been viewed an equal by the United States. Not so with Mexico. The United States has viewed Mexico as something less than a partner, a rather distant neighbor. The United States views Mexico as needing the United States, but the United States has not seen itself as needing Mexico. Mexico has responded accordingly, with suspicion and deliberation. Canada never really flirted with socialism, as Mexico did in the 1970s by substantially increasing national ownership of the means of production and distribution.

Mexico opened to foreign investment with few restrictions during the *Porfiriato*, the 1876–1911 reign of Porfirio Díaz. But the state assumed a more restrictive role under the 1917 Constitution following revolutionary turmoil begun in 1910. It soon became apparent that the state would begin to intervene in many areas of established foreign investment. After an unsuccessful attempt by Mexico to participate in the foreign owned petroleum industry in 1925, a labor dispute led to the total nationalization of the industry in 1938. This reduced in the minds of many Mexicans the apparent conflict with Article 27 of the Mexican Constitution, which decreed that all natural resources were owned by the nation. Two years later, the government severely limited foreign participation in the communications sector.

A 1944 Emergency Decree was the first broad attempt to regulate foreign investment, and limited certain investments to joint ventures. The joint venture concept was extended by a Mixed Ministerial Commission established in 1947, although it was of limited effectiveness. The 1950s saw the introduction of some limited control of specific industries, and electric power distribution was nationalized in 1960. Foreign investment in mining was subjected to a restrictive 1961 Act.

The Mexican investment law, the transfer of technology, and the trade names and inventions law, all enacted in the 1970s, were models of restrictive laws of developing nations adopted during the tense, often bitter North-South dialogue. Developing nations argued they were poor because the developed nations were rich, and that there had to be a transfer of wealth from the latter to the former. A strict 1972 Law for the Registration of the Transfer of Technology and the Use and Exploitation of Patents and Marks, forewarned the coming restrictiveness towards foreign investment. The 1973 Mexican investment law was a product of such thinking.

The 1973 Law to Promote Mexican Investment and Regulate Foreign Investment to some degree pulled together the policies of encouraging but limiting foreign investment that had been introduced during past decades, and were clearly part of the Echeverrían administration policy, which began in 1970. The 1973 law classified investments, limiting some to state ownership, some to private ownership exclusively by Mexican nations, and some where minority foreign participation would be allowed. The law did not apply retroactively, but if a company expanded into new lines of products or new locations, it was expected to Mexicanize, meaning to sell majority ownership to Mexicans. But escape provisions and the operational code in Mexico (the way things really work), resulting in few existing companies converting to Mexican majority ownership. What the laws did accomplish was to significantly curtail foreign investment. A new institution, the National Commission on Foreign Investment, assumed substantial discretionary power to carry out the 1973 rules.

What President Echeverría started, his successor, José Lopez Portillo, continued when he entered office in 1976. His final year in office, 1982, saw first the amendment of the 1972 Transfer of Technology Law, retaining its restrictiveness and extending its scope, and second, the nationalization of the banking industry. His successor, Miguel de la Madrid, assumed control of a nation with a defaulted national debt, a plunging currency, and diminished interest of foreign investors. Realizing that Mexico must change its policies, de la Madrid issued investment regulations in 1984 that partly relaxed the restrictiveness of the 1970s. Further regulations were issued in the following years, and in 1989, the first year of Carlos Salinas de Gortari's presidency, new regulations were issued that were so inconsistent with the clear philosophy of the restrictive 1973 law that their constitutionality was questioned.

The direction was turned: Mexico's ascension into the stratosphere of developing-nation restrictiveness toward foreign investment had reached its apogee in 1982 and was coming back to earth. Foreign investment was returning. It was further encouraged by Mexico's admission into the GATT in 1986, after years of internal debate. The replacement of the 1973 Investment Law twenty years after its introduction ended an unsettling era of Mexican foreign-investment policy.

This 1993 Investment Act was a highlight of the Salinas administration, an encouragement to the many investors who had made commitments to Mexico during his administration, and a stepping stone to participation in the NAFTA the following year. The 1993 law improved access to investment in Mexico, containing investment-attracting provisions absent from the earlier law. But some significant restrictions remained, including state control over natural resources, reservation of some areas of investment for Mexican nationals, emphasis on joint ventures in the areas of the economy open to foreign investors, and retention of the Calvo doctrine that attempted to limit foreign investors to Mexican remedies in the event of an investment dispute.

The 1993 law nevertheless was a huge reversal of the policies of the 1970s, and it both established a more efficient National Registry of Foreign Investment and allowed proposals to be assumed to have been approved if they were not acted upon within an established time-frame. Regulations adopted in 1999 are consistent with both the 1993 law and its investment-encouraging philosophy. Mexico was not yet as open to foreign investment as Canada and the United States, but it had established a sufficiently respectful base from which to participate in the NAFTA foreign-investment framework. It was quite a remarkable transformation and a credit to several of Mexico's leaders.

When NAFTA arrived in 1994, it reduced the some of the restraints on investment remaining in the 1993 law. But only for U.S. and Canadian investors, though foreign-owned companies incorporated in NAFTA nations generally qualify for NAFTA's favorable and preferential investment regime. This regime is detailed in Chapter 8.

ASSEMBLY PLANTS (MAQUILADORAS)

The United States Tariff Code, various Mexican Decrees, and the economics of assembly plant operations established a growth industry: Maquiladoras. Sometimes called "in-bond" or "border" plants, Mexican maquiladoras enjoyed phenomenal popularity in the 1980s and early 1990s. Maquiladoras provide Mexico with over a million jobs, many of which are filled by women. They are also a major source of foreign currency earnings, second only to oil exports and ahead of tourism. For the investor, the devaluation and depreciation of the peso in 1982 and again in 1994–5 rendered Mexican labor costs lower than those of Taiwan, Hong Kong, Singapore and South Korea (the "Four Dragons"), traditional low-cost assembly plant centers.

As a result, thousands of maquiladoras have been established in Tijuana, Ciudad Juarez, Nuevo Laredo and other border cities. Electronics, apparel, toys, medical supplies, transport equipment, furniture, and sporting goods are examples of the types of industries that have been attracted south of the border. Maquiladoras are being imitated throughout the Caribbean Basin and Central America. Much to the frustration of organized labor, such offshore assembly operations exemplify the internationalization of the United States manufacturing sector.

Complex legal frameworks facilitate maquiladoras. On the United States side, Section 9802.00.80 of the Harmonized Tariff Schedule ("HTS") [formerly Section 807 of the TSUS] allows fabricated United States components to be shipped abroad and returned to the U.S. subject to a customs duty limited to the amount of the value added by foreign assembly operations. This section was first utilized with great success by the Four Dragons, and is the same law which facilitates Caribbean and Central American assembly plants. Mexico initiated its Border Industrialization Program in 1965, which permits wholly-owned foreign subsidiaries not subject to Mexico's traditional mandatory joint venture rules, partly to compete with East Asian countries taking advantage of Section 9802.00.80 through labor-intensive assembly operations.

The net result of Section 9802.00.80 and the law of an increasing number of developing nations is an interdependent legal framework mutually supportive of assembly plant operations. This can be viewed as a "co-production" or "production-sharing" arrangement between the two countries, an arrangement in which others can participate. Japanese corporations and their U.S. subsidiaries have, for example, become significant investors in such industries. Korean firms are also setting up assembly plant operations targeted at the U.S. market, and other Asian investors are expected. These companies appear to find assembly plants attractive even when they use components that are not from the United States, e.g., Taiwanese electronic parts.

If at least 35 percent of the value of an assembly plant product is of local origin, it may qualify for *duty free* tariff status under the U.S. Generalized System of Tariff Preferences (GSP). Most Caribbean and Central American nations (save those with U.S. free trade agreements) are beneficiary countries under the GSP program, whereas the Four Dragons and Malaysia are not. As a matter of business planning, then, development and use of local components in an assembly plant is a strategy that is now being aggressively pursued. Local suppliers, like their East Asian competitors some years ago, are being pressed to improve the quality and utility of their components. The Four Dragons, by comparative example, suggest that if these suppliers meet this challenge, then fabrication of products of completely local origin may follow.

There is an evolutionary cycle in assembly plants—from cheap raw labor to more skill-oriented operations to capital-intensive manufacturing. One of the most interesting comparative questions is whether there is also an evolutionary process in the applicable laws of these countries. In other words, what legal regimes do developing nations have to adopt in order to first attract assembly operations and do they evolve from extremely accommodating to more demanding as the cycle reaches completion? Or, does the manufacturer's ability to go elsewhere to even cheaper labor markets (e.g., from Mexico to Guatemala to Haiti, or from Hong Kong to the People's Republic of China to Vietnam) constantly temper the legal regimes regulating assembly plants?

Many export-driven Mexican maquiladoras historically relied on tariff refunds and waivers on inputs. Under NAFTA, starting in 2001, Mexico stopped the beneficial application of tariff refunds and waivers to assembly plants. Full Mexican tariffs apply to imported components, which makes it more difficult for goods assembled with components from outside NAFTA to qualify for NAFTA free trade. However, Mexico subsequently reduced tariffs on some components, notably electronics, as an incentive to continued maquiladora production.

Many Asian manufacturers using Mexican assembly plants were impacted. As the drafters of NAFTA intended, there should be no preferentially tariffed "export platforms" into Canada or the United States. Some such manufacturers switched to North American suppliers for their assembly plant inputs. Others, notably from Japan and Korea, arranged for their home country suppliers to join them in production in Mexico. Components from these loyal affiliates generally avoided the origin problems created under NAFTA when Mexican customs refunds and waivers were eliminated in 2001. They also add to the North American content of the assembled goods. . . the key to accessing NAFTA duty free status.

As the North American content of Asian and other maquiladora operations rose to meet NAFTA's rules of origin governing free trade, greater access to the Mexican market became available. Traditionally, sales of maquiladora products in Mexico had been limited. Starting in 1994, amendments to Mexico's Maquiladora Decree permitted such sales to increase based upon percentages of prior year individual maquiladora exports from Mexico. In 1994, for example, this percentage was 55%, rising 5% annually to 75% in 1998 and 85% in the year 2000. Since 2001, maquiladoras may sell their entire production in Mexico if they choose. This schedule was coordinated with Mexico's phase-out of customs duty drawback and waivers on imported components.

The year 2001 also brought China into the World Trade Organization, effectively guaranteeing its exports MFN "normal" tariff status. Mexico's labor rates were and are low by American standards, but China's wages at the millennium were incredibly low. Labor intensive, portable assembly plants, notably clothing, furniture and the like, moved almost en masse to China and more generally Asia. Their product prices easily absorbed higher transport and tariff costs compared to Mexican maquiladoras. NAFTA's investment and tariff preferences were just not enough to retain these investments.

By 2016, a few assembly plants withdrawn from Mexico were actually returning due to rising Chinese wages and higher fuel/transport costs. Mexico took a hit, but of late has been bouncing back, particularly as a producer of auto parts and vehicles, a less mobile investment. There is hardly any American, European or Japanese producer of autos not presently invested in Mexico, many with plans for expansion. Can China be far behind?

MEXICAN FREE TRADE TREATIES AS AN INVESTMENT INCENTIVE

Many foreign investors from the United States, Japan, Korea and Europe have established assembly plants (maquiladoras) in Mexico. Increasingly, these investors are using Mexico as an export platform, particularly to those markets covered by Mexican free trade agreements (FTA). A list of these agreements is reproduced below. It is expected that European Union and Japanese investors, following in the wake of the EU-Mexico FTA (2000) and the Japan-Mexico FTA (2004), will likewise take advantage of Mexico's free trade treaties, as well as NAFTA.

United States and Asian producers in Mexico are especially interested in the possibility of shipping their goods to the European Union on a duty free basis, something they cannot do by exporting from their home countries, though Canada has a recent FTA with the EU. Mexico's free trade treaties include:

- The U.S. and Canada (NAFTA, 1994);

- Columbia and Venezuela (G–3 FTA, 1995); (Venezuela terminated, 2006);

- Costa Rica (FTA, 1995);

- Bolivia (FTA, 1995);

- Nicaragua (FTA, 1998);

- Chile (FTA 1999);

- Israel (FTA, 2000);

- EFTA (FTA, 2000);

- The EU (FTA, 2000);

- Guatemala, Honduras and El Salvador (FTA, Northern Triangle, 2001);

- Peru (2002);

- Uruguay (2002);

- Japan (2004); and

- Panama (2006).

FOREIGN INVESTMENT IN THE UNITED STATES

The United States has proven to be one of the most desirable locations for direct and indirect (portfolio) investment by foreign persons. Under U.S. law, "foreign direct investment" means ownership or control, directly or indirectly, by one person, of ten percent or more of the voting securities of an incorporated, business enterprise or an equivalent interest in an unincorporated business enterprise. "Portfolio investment" means any international investment that is not direct.

The United States is viewed as a relatively risk-free environment which welcomes foreign as well as domestic investment and imposes relatively few controls on foreign investment that are not also imposed on domestic investment. The view is merited, but foreign investors under many laws and regulations do not have the same standing as domestic U.S. investors.

As is the case in any nation, these restrictions may constitute obstacles to the entry and formation of an investment, or they may constitute restrictions during the operation of the investment. An example of the former is a limitation on the percentage of permissible foreign ownership, while an example of the latter is taxation. The termination of a foreign investment in the United States through bankruptcy may present some additional concerns. Furthermore, the federal government may choose to block or even divest a foreign investment for vague national-security reasons. Free trade agreements such as NAFTA tend to reduce restrictions on foreign investment, but have no effect on restrictions based on national-security grounds.

Despite a general policy of openness, the United States has maintained a variety of restrictions on foreign investment that tend to reflect three themes: National security, foreign control, and reciprocity. The main deviation from the policies of national treatment and an open-door investment policy is based on grounds of national security. For example, certificates of public convenience and necessity to engage in air transportation may be held only by U.S. citizens because Congress wanted to safeguard national security by assuring U.S. air carriers would provide aircraft to the armed forces in times of war or national emergency. The theme of control is also reflected in the aviation regulations. For example, although the law requires the president and two-thirds of the board of directors of an air carrier to be U.S. citizens, and at least 75 percent ownership of voting equity be held by U.S. citizens, the agencies charged with enforcing that mandate have interpreted the law broadly to require the carrier actually to be controlled by U.S. citizens.

The concept of reciprocity is a continually recurring theme in attitudes toward regulating foreign investment. A foreign firm in the United States is accorded the same treatment as U.S. firms receive in that firm's home country. For example, the government will not allow foreign companies to acquire federal lands for rights-of-way gas pipelines or leases for mining certain minerals and fuels on those lands, if the foreign investor's home-country denies similar rights to U.S. corporations.

CONTRASTING U.S. FEDERAL GOALS AFFECTING FOREIGN INVESTMENT

Foreign direct investment is often subject to U.S. legislative enactments based as much on political as economic goals. These goals may be general or country-specific. How the political goals are expressed within the federal government depends on the perspectives of the sector of the government attempting to achieve such goals. The President and the Congress may have different goals, or they may have similar goals but different views on where the power to control ought to be. Even within the same branch of the federal government there may be different goals. The House may have a view quite different from the Senate, and the various parts of the Executive Branch may disagree over policy.

But the general attitude in both the Legislative and Executive branches has for the most part been receptive of foreign investment, or it at least is viewed from abroad as being receptive when contrasted with other potential host nations. Where differences begin to arise is often related to the nature of technology to which foreign companies may gain access. This is particularly true when a foreign company wishes to acquire a U.S. company that owns advanced technology, notably technology used or adaptable for military purposes.

Attitudes change as political alignments change. For example, the Department of Defense (DOD) approved production of F-16 military aircraft by an offspring of the same Japanese company that built the Zeros which bombed Hawaii in World War II. Furthermore, the DOD eased restrictions on foreign-controlled firms gaining DOD contracts, reversing a historic pattern of opposition to such contractors because of access to key technology.

The Department of Commerce presents the most inconsistent policies on foreign investment, advocating a mix of open investment and industrial protection which does not always appear to have a rational basis. At one time Commerce may oppose any new legal restrictions on direct investment for fear of chilling foreign-investment inflows, suggesting that U.S. industries' expressions of concern regarding national security are merely cries for unmerited government protection, but at another time Commerce may step in and block a planned acquisition of a U.S. firm by foreign interests. Congressional hearings on proposed legislation, such as Exon-Florio discussed below, often expose the lack of cohesion within the Department of Commerce.

The Department of Treasury has historically promoted an open-door investment policy and has been the chief advocate within the cabinet of foreign investors' interests, to the dismay of Treasury's critics, who believe its view too solicitous of foreign investment. Those fears increased when, in 1988, Treasury was designated the chair of the interdepartmental Committee on Foreign Investment in the United States (CFIUS), playing a central role under the Exon-Florio law.

MERGERS AND ACQUISITIONS

The acquisition of or merger with a U.S. company by a foreign entity may raise antitrust issues and attract the interest of the Department of Justice (DOJ) and the Federal Trade Commission (FTC). The legal standard under the Clayton Act of 1914 is whether the merger or acquisition "may tend to substantially lessen competition". The Antitrust Improvements Act (Hart-Scott-Rodino Act) of 1976 requires pre-merger notification of acquisitions of voting securities or assets. It applies if either party is engaged in commerce, if the foreign party will end up holding either 15 percent or more of the U.S. party's assets or voting securities, or more than $15 million worth of assets and voting securities. There are several exemptions based on the location of the acquired assets, whether certain control is conferred, the value of assets in the United States, and when the acquired entity is also foreign.

A waiting period after filing notification of the planned acquisition or merger allows the U.S. agencies time to investigate for possible antitrust implications, sometimes in cooperation with merger authorities elsewhere (the EU for example, see Chapter 5), thus avoiding the later dismemberment of a completed transaction. A decision to challenge the transaction by either the DOJ or FTC typically kills the deal. For example, in 2015 the DOJ rejected on anticompetitive grounds the acquisition of GE's appliance business by Sweden's Electrolux. GE quickly sold that business to Haier of China.

THE UNITED STATES AS A HOST NATION

The 1980s saw a major shift in the United States from an exporter of investment to becoming a host to foreign investment. Yet the relative value of foreign investment in the United States remains low when compared to other industrialized countries, with the exception of Japan. Two general theories seek to explain why multinationals invest in foreign countries: The cost-of-capital theory, which is based on responses to real interest rate differentials, and the industrial-organization theory, which focuses on the internal advantages of firms within certain countries and industries and includes strategies to avoid import restrictions and tariffs. For example, Japanese firms invest in electronics because of advantages their organizations possess in that industry.

Despite the political conflicts at various levels of U.S. government over the value and problems associated with foreign direct investment, the trend in the early 1990s nullified much of the concern about foreign acquisitions of U.S. companies. Foreign direct investment in the United States decreased 47 percent in 1992, including substantial decreases in investment from France and Japan. This decrease contributed to a shift in capital flows from a net inward flow during 1990 to a net outflow from the United States in 1992.

When foreign firms invest, the overwhelming method of establishing new operations in the United States is by acquiring existing firms. This pattern has led to a variety of concerns reflected in policy debates in the United States about whether or how to further regulate foreign investment. Perhaps the greatest concern is that foreign parents may reduce or curtail research and development by their newly acquired U.S. affiliates and transfer "American" technology abroad. A second concern is that foreign-owned investments in the United States use imported rather than domestic components in their production process. That appears less the case with European-owned investments in the United States, many of which have been in the United States for decades, than with Japanese-owned and Chinese-owned investments, nearly all of which are relatively recent arrivals in the U.S. market. This fear did not stop, however, Lenovo of China's acquisition of IBM's personal computer business.

A third concern regarding foreign investment in the United States is that foreign governments may provide support in targeting the acquisition of U.S. companies. Although there is little evidence of any "plan" to bring foreign-government control to U.S. companies, such fears remain, especially regarding China, which has attempted or made a number of U.S. acquisitions in recent years. That said, China's acquisitions in America are rapidly rising, e.g. Smithfield Ham. When Chinese investments are greenfields, for example development of a high speed rail system between Southern California and Las Vegas, state ownership of the Chinese party seems less of a concern.

These concerns have led to new attempts to regulate foreign investment. Many proponents of a free trade and investment policy concluded that the government should intervene as the trade balance deteriorated and inbound foreign investment increased. A popular solution proposed by some federal policymakers supported a broad interpretation of regulations based on national security to include economic security. But this approach failed to become law. It is perhaps noteworthy that Chinese national security regulations include protection of its economic security.

U.S. SECURITIES REGISTRATION AND DISCLOSURE REQUIREMENTS FOR FOREIGN ISSUERS

The general rule is that any public offering by foreign issuers in the United States is subject to the Securities Exchange Act of 1933 Act registration requirements. That means registration and full disclosure or being exempt. Such a rule appears logical when the foreign issuer wishes to come to the U. S. and issue all its securities to United States citizens, or even when it remains abroad in its home nation but addresses the issuance to U. S. citizens. But such regulation becomes increasingly extraterritorial and subject to foreign challenge when the links with the United States further diminish.

Acknowledging the problem, the United States has developed some special rules to address foreign issuers selling to United States citizens or residents. Schedule B to the 1933 Act includes requirements for the registration of securities issued by foreign *governments.* There are special forms for registration and disclosure applicable to foreign issuers. Foreign issuers generally enjoy the same exemptions as domestic issuers. An offering by a foreign issuer is considered in its entirety, not only that part which affects United States purchasers.

The private offering exemption has not been very useful to foreign issuers. A private offering exemption is not generally available to a foreign issuer when all the issuance is made abroad, except for that to a single United States purchaser who falls within the statutory qualifications. But these relatively minor variants affecting foreign issuers do not address the real issue, the extent to which a foreign issuer must register when there is some offering in the United States. Several approaches adopted by the SEC have attempted to address this issue.

Regulations for foreign issuers. The Securities and Exchange Commission has issued regulations which attempt to reach some compromise where foreign issuances reach more than a few United States purchasers. Rule 12g3–2(b) and its regulations essentially allow foreign issuers to satisfy United States disclosure requirements by reliance on home nation disclosure. The biggest problem with these regulations for the foreign issuer is how to limit the number of United States residents to below 300. If a foreign issuer sells its shares exclusively through a national securities market and has tens of thousands of shareholders, it may not believe that the incidental share ownership by 300 United States owners should bring the company within the United States requirements. If it does not comply with United States securities laws, the next step is the extent to which the United States courts will apply the law extraterritorially.

Rule 144A was enacted as recognition of the increasing globalization of the securities market, and to address both the private placement market and purchases by institutional investors. The rule was intended to encourage foreign issuers to raise capital in the United States. Some issuers did use the reporting exemption provisions of Rule 12g3–2(b), but it was not viewed as helpful in certain markets. Rule 144A was designed to create a new market (for secondary trading only) with limited disclosure to attract foreign issuers, and to liberalize the privately placed securities market.

Rule 144A has been used with American Depositary Receipts (ADRs). It has also been used with Regulation S, which limits registration requirements where the offers and sales are outside the United States. The result appears to be the use of two-stage transactions by foreign issuers. First is a listing on a foreign exchange, and second a sale in the United States. The ADRs are denominated in United States dollars rather than the issuer's nation's currency. Dividends are paid in dollars. Changes in the exchange rate of the dollar and the issuer nation's currency obviously affect the value of the security, but the United States investor is not burdened by having to constantly make exchange calculations.

EXON-FLORIO/FINSA NATIONAL SECURITY REGULATION OF FOREIGN INVESTMENTS

Before the enactment of Exon-Florio, when the concern for widespread Arab buyouts of American businesses in the 1970s was perceived as a threat to national security, the U.S. executive, seeking a compromise with the Congress, agreed to create the Committee on Foreign Investment in the United States (CFIUS) as an interagency, interdepartmental group to investigate inward foreign direct investment and recommend policy. CFIUS, which would have no real screening or review power, would serve at the President's discretion. For example, President Carter's administration investigated only one transaction.

During President Reagan's second term, the concern turned more toward the increasing trade deficit and the "Japanese threat." There were large inflows of foreign investment in the 1980s, although they were not limited to Japanese investors. The administration began to intervene in these inflows more frequently, especially when they constituted planned acquisitions of U.S. companies. The policy of open versus controlled investment seemed most confused when the Japanese electronics conglomerate Fujitsu sought to acquire an 80 percent share in Fairchild Semiconductor. Fairchild had openly solicited the bid. Even though the French concern Schlumberger already owned Fairchild, the Commerce, Defense and Justice Departments all joined to oppose the proposed acquisition. The Department of Justice was concerned with antitrust implications, while the departments of Commerce and Defense appeared to object primarily in order to force Japanese markets to open more. Because of the extensive concern, Fujitsu withdrew its proposed acquisition even though CFIUS at the time lacked the power to block the sale.

By 1988, Congress seemed intent on creating some mechanism to review proposed foreign investment in the United States. The determination was increased when the proposed foreign purchase of Phoenix Steel was announced. Phoenix Steel was a producer of many items procured by the Department of Defense. The purchaser, represented by a Hong Kong agent, was to obtain financing for the acquisition from the People's Republic of China. CFIUS had no authority to block the sale, but it nevertheless began an investigation because many of Phoenix's products were subject to U.S. export controls.

Representative Florio of New Jersey proposed foreign-investment control legislation which would allow the President to block the sale of a U.S.-owned company to any entity with financing by a potential enemy, to ensure that the U.S. firm's controlled technology would not be acquired by the foreign nation. The administration accepted the Exon-Florio proposal as a compromise because competing proposals would have imposed even greater reporting and disclosure requirements on foreign investors, which the administration opposed. For example, one proposal required any foreign investor acquiring a five percent or greater interest to report to the Department of Commerce certain information which would become available to the public.

The Exon-Florio amendment to the Defense Production Act of 1950 passed as part of the

Omnibus Trade and Competitiveness Act of 1988. It grants the President the authority to investigate and suspend or prohibit mergers, acquisitions or other transactions leading to the "control" of existing American firms by foreign persons, based on national-security, critical infrastructure (virtual or physical), or critical technology concerns. The main point of contact in the United States for inquiries about the Exon-Florio law is the Committee on Foreign Investment in the United States (CFIUS), located in the Office of International Investment, Department of the Treasury. CFIUS is comprised of nine U.S. departments or agencies (e.g., State, DOD, Justice, Homeland Security) along with other ex officio members. Exon-Florio is the only U.S. law that broadly regulates foreign investment.

There are two basic problems that Exon-Florio presents to foreign investors. The first is that Exon-Florio issues may arise throughout the investment process. Foreign acquisitions that could affect national security must be reported to CFIUS at the outset to allow the government to make a determination. Otherwise, the government may be prompted to investigate on its own initiative and possibly order divestment. The result could be that foreign investors have acquired property that lacks clear title.

The second problem is the uncertainty about the definition of national security under Exon-Florio. The Exon-Florio Regulations offer few bright-line tests. That confirms CFIUS, the President's designated center of investigation, as the omnipotent reviewer of foreign acquisitions. Exon-Florio initially earned the nickname "Lawyers Full Employment Act" because of the potentially broad scope of national security. CFIUS has interpreted national security on a case-by-case basis, leaving other companies, even in similar industries, somewhat baffled about the criteria used to evaluate the transaction. But Exon-Florio does include a list of factors to be considered in the evaluation of a transaction's national-security implications. There nevertheless remains concern about the potential abuse of the broad language and consequent wide scope of Exon-Florio's national-security language.

CFIUS REVIEWS OF PROPOSED FOREIGN INVESTMENTS, PRESIDENTIAL POWERS

Exon-Florio/FINSA authorizes the President or President's designee to investigate the national-security impact of "mergers, acquisitions, and takeovers" by or with foreign persons that could result in control by foreign persons. Since 1992, CFIUS investigations are mandatory when the entity seeking control over a U.S. firm is itself controlled or acting on behalf of a foreign government. This requirement was part of the 1992 Byrd Amendment resulting from the Thomson/LTV case discussed below.

Most investigations are at the discretion of CFIUS after receipt of written notification by the parties. Notice may be submitted and CFIUS review commenced at any time while the transaction is pending or after it is completed. But there is a three-year limitation after the transaction is completed, unless the CFIUS chairman, consulting with other members, requests an investigation. To avoid the possibility of having a completed transaction questioned, companies frequently submit a voluntary notice to commence review before completing the transaction. Any transaction which has been the subject of CFIUS review or investigation is not subject to later Presidential action. Thus, even when there seems to be little apparent impact on national security, a review request might be useful.

CFIUS has 30 days after notification to decide whether or not to investigate, and 45 days after that to investigate and make a recommendation to the President. The President has 15 days to either suspend or prohibit the acquisition, merger, or takeover, or seek divestiture for an already completed transaction. The President may direct the Attorney General to seek appropriate relief in U.S. district courts to enforce his decision.

The President must make two findings in order to exercise his authority. First, he must believe that there is "credible evidence" that the foreign interest would exercise "control" which might threaten "national security." Second, he must believe that other provisions of law, aside from the International Emergency Economic Powers Act, provide inadequate authority to safeguard national security. Although these two findings remain prerequisites to presidential action, they are not subject to judicial review.

Although considerable debate occurred, "national security" remains undefined in either the law or regulations. But the Exon-Florio/FINSA provisions suggest that the President consider several factors in evaluating national security concerns. These are mainly directed to the capacity of domestic industry to meet national-defense requirements in view of the proposed takeover. Amendments to Exon-Florio have added as factors for presidential consideration both the potential for proliferation of missiles and nuclear and biological weapons, as well as the potential effect of the transaction on U.S. leadership in technology that affects national security.

Any information filed with CFIUS is largely confidential, although some releases of information may be made to authorized members of Congress. Critics have charged that CFIUS has abused the confidentiality provisions in some cases, and also has left important players out of the investigation process until after CFIUS has made its decisions. The confidentiality provision has made official reports of cases impossible, but has protected both the interests of foreign investors and national security. The manner in which CFIUS and the President have applied the law, and the criticism generated from such application, have focused on the proper meaning of three terms—"mergers, acquisitions, and takeovers," "control", and "national security."

The regulations take into account devices created to avoid Exon-Florio review, such as foreign-controlled corporations seeking to purchase U.S. businesses using American agents supposedly acting independently. As Treasury drafted the regulations, Rep. Florio and other commentators wondered about the applicability of the law toward other types of transactions, such as proxy solicitations which might lead to foreign control, foreign bank financing which might lead to control by default, joint ventures, and "greenfield" investments. The regulations address most of those issues, although they include few "bright-line" tests.

Exon-Florio/FINSA does not apply to portfolio investments, such as investments where the foreigner obtains ten percent or less of voting securities solely for investment purposes, investments where the foreign buyer has the same parent as the target, or other investments where the foreign investor does not acquire managerial control of a U.S. business. Joint ventures, originally thought to be exempt from Exon-Florio review, are included. Foreign persons soliciting proxies in order to obtain control are also covered. The regulations do not subject lending transactions by foreign persons to Exon-Florio review unless the lender assumes some degree of control, at either the time that the loan is made or when default appears imminent.

As these comments suggest, what *control* would be exercised by the foreign person is the key to determining whether a transaction is within the scope of Exon-Florio/FINSA. The regulations define "control" without limitation on voting percentages or majority ownership, but as "the power, direct or indirect, whether or not exercised . . . to determine, direct, take, reach or cause decisions" in a series of key areas. These areas include the transfer (sale, lease, mortgage or pledge) of assets, the dissolution of the business, the closing or relocation of research and development facilities, terminating or not fulfilling the business contracts, and amending the Articles of Incorporation of the business with regard to any of the aforementioned matters. In addition, when examining control, if more than one foreign person is involved, CFIUS may consider the possibility of their acting in concert. However, an *unrelated* group of foreign investors holding a majority of shares in a U.S. company will not be assumed to control that company.

In contrast with the attempt to define "control," Exon-Florio/FINSA and its associated regulations do not define "national security." Many of the public comments during Treasury's drafting of the regulations urged a specific definition, but the statute and regulations consciously leave the determination of a national-security concern to the President's discretion. Few involved in regulating foreign investment outside the administration were satisfied with that result. Some in Congress thought that the White House interpreted "national security" too narrowly, equating it only with military security. The General Accounting Office (GAO) criticized CFIUS for not determining if anti-competitive behavior by foreign firms might jeopardize national security. A former Attorney General and Secretary of Defense, speaking for a segment of the foreign-investment regulatory community, criticized the rules lack of national-security criteria because more mergers and acquisitions may fall under review than Congress intended. Nevertheless, administration officials stressed the need for "national security" to have a broad scope and not be confined to particular industries, and be particularly applicable should the target company provide products or technologies essential to the U.S. defense industrial base.

EXON-FLORIO/FINSA CASES

The application of Exon-Florio/FINSA in real situations resolves some of the apparent ambiguity with regard to the meaning of "national security" and the other important statutory and regulatory terms. CFIUS has reviewed thousands of proposed acquisitions. Some detailed investigations lead to withdrawals, but rarely a presidential order of divestment. Because of CFIUS' confidentiality requirements, no official reports or summaries of its investigations exist for lawyers or investors to consult. Instead, secondary sources must be used to draw meanings given to the statute and regulations. The cases when the President chose not to act, when the parties themselves withdrew, and the few cases when the President actually ordered divestment present some general patterns of what foreign investors may expect from a CFIUS investigation. Here are some case examples:

Huels AG of Germany/Monsanto. The Department of Defense prompted one of the first investigations under Exon-Florio/FINSA because the U.S. semiconductor research consortium that the DOD sponsors, SEMATECH, wanted guaranteed access to silicon wafers manufactured by Monsanto Electronic Materials Co., which was about to be sold to Huels AG, a German company. Although CFIUS recommended that the President allow the transaction to go forward, notwithstanding the objections of 29 congressmen, CFIUS obtained as part of its approval written assurances that SEMATECH would retain access and no technology would transfer for five years. There appeared to be a quid pro quo that CFIUS would not disapprove the takeover in return for Huels' assurances, creating a performance requirement for foreign investment.

Matra SA of France/Fairchild. CFIUS apparently imposed a similar requirement on Matra SA of France when it sought to purchase Fairchild industries, requiring a restructured export-control system as a condition for CFIUS approval. Foreign investors therefore may have to agree to government-imposed conditions on their transactions, with CFIUS approval received only after an Exon-Florio/FINSA investigation is conducted as a bargaining tool.

British Tire & Rubber (UK)/Norton. The administration is not alone in using Exon-Florio/FINSA as a bargaining tool. United States companies which are targets of hostile takeovers by foreign investors have used Exon-Florio/FINSA as one method to oppose proposed takeovers. Within two months of passage of the law, companies began to invoke Exon-Florio to delay or discourage takeovers.

A good example of an American firm using political pressure on a foreign buyer through Exon-Florio/FINSA and other mechanisms is the attempted purchase of the Norton Company of Worcester, Mass., by British Tire and Rubber, PLC (BTR). Norton manufactured ceramic ball bearings used in the space shuttle. More than 200 congressmen urged an investigation, including Senator Kerry of Massachusetts, who noted Norton's role in the Massachusetts economy as justification for an investigation in addition to national-security reasons. The Massachusetts state legislature soon enacted a law depriving BTR of control should the purchase succeed, leading BTR to pull out, and a French buyer to make a friendly offer at a much higher price.

No security concerns were raised when the friendly French buyer appeared offering a better price, even though Norton had earlier argued that BTR planned to dismember Norton and reduce its research and development budgets to the detriment of national security. This led many to conclude that the Exon-Florio process was easily abused. Critics argued that existing DOD regulations could handle true national-security concerns, and that Exon-Florio only added a political element to the ability of foreign investors to acquire U.S. companies.

China Nat'l Aero Tech./NAMCO. While some firms use a CFIUS investigation to scare away hostile foreign investors, one transaction that the President decided to reject had already been finalized at the time of the order. The order forced the foreign entity to divest. The target was MAMCO Manufacturing, Inc., a U.S. company in Seattle that manufactured metal parts for commercial aircraft made by Boeing. MAMCO mainly supplied Boeing, and although some of its products were subject to export controls, MAMCO had no contracts involving classified information. The buyer was China National Aero-Technology Import and Export Corp. (CATIC), owned by the People's Republic of China.

During the investigation, it appeared that CATIC had previously violated export-control laws concerning aircraft engines purchased from General Electric. But concerns about CATIC went beyond export-control problems with China. Administration sources revealed that CATIC had been trying to obtain technology to build jet fighters capable of refueling during flight. In addition, there were concerns by the administration and Congress that the Chinese government used CATIC as a base for covert operations in the United States.

The Executive Order directing CATIC to divest itself of MAMCO contained none of the above concerns or information, but simply stated that the two requirements of Exon-Florio had been satisfied: Credible evidence existed of a threat to national security, and no other provision of law could protect the national-security interest. Considering the relatively low level of technology involved, however, the President's action on CFIUS' unanimous recommendation to terminate the investment surprised many observers, leading some to believe that the national-security concern was a pretext for other political motives. Foreign-investor lobbying organizations agreed with this perception, fearing that Exon-Florio/FINSA would become a foreign-policy tool. But the administration stressed that the order did not constitute a change in America's general policy of openness toward investment from foreigners or reflect upon the PRC in particular. That said, the order seemed to indicate that investment owned or supported by foreign governments would receive particular scrutiny under Exon-Florio.

Nakamichi/Applied Magnetics. MOST, a United States incorporated subsidiary of Nakamichi Corp. of Japan, agreed to purchase the Optical Products Division of United States Applied Magnetics Corporation. Although about 98 percent of OPD's sales were optical heads for computers, the products have application in some weapons systems. CFIUS reviewed the application and approved the sale one day before the inauguration of President Clinton. Congress was unaware of the ongoing review until the announced approval. But some members quickly intervened and produced evidence allegedly showing that the CFIUS review was based on misleading and incomplete information. That would allow reopening of the review process. Although much publicity followed there was no further review, but a clear warning sounded that a clearance by CFIUS may lead to public outcry if the process remains silent until the CFIUS decision.

Thomson/LTV   and   1992   Exon-Florio Amendments.   By   1992,   Congressional dissatisfaction with how the President and CFIUS had interpreted Exon-Florio led to proposals for new and stricter controls. The circumstances that led to the first substantive amendments to the Exon-Florio law involved foreign-government participation in a proposed acquisition, the attempted purchase of the missile division of LTV Corp. by Thomson-CSF, a conglomerate partially owned (58 percent) and financed by the French government.

LTV, a defense contractor, had been operating under bankruptcy protection since 1986. Thomson made a bid for $450 million in association with an American investment bank and Northrop, the U.S. aircraft company, to buy LTV's aircraft and missile business. The bankruptcy court approved the sale. Thomson outbid the U.S. defense contractor Martin Marietta by nearly $100 million. Martin Marietta was the buyer LTV favored because of the prospective problems Thomson would have with CFIUS. Thomson filed the notice for review under Exon-Florio. To diminish concerns regarding national security, Thomson initially proposed to the DOD to structure its purchase of LTV through an agreement that would allow some control over LTV. As pressure increased, Thomson withdrew that proposal and stated that a proxy agreement would suffice, with the proxies being U.S. citizens who had no prior connection to the parties. But Thomson was unable to satisfy DOD demands to protect classified information. The DOD has separate authority under the Industrial Security Regulations to protect classified information, including the ability to block an acquisition.

There was immediate adverse Congressional reaction, acknowledging that the United States and France were allies, but noting that French interests have not always been the same as America's. The Senate even passed a non-binding resolution (vote of 93–4) finding the proposed acquisition to be harmful to national security. Administration officials were reluctant to discuss even the general policy of allowing a foreign government-owned or-controlled company to purchase a U.S. defense contractor while the investigation was in process. Because the DOD apparently did not at first intend to object to the sale, it was criticized for failing to consider the questionable record of Thomson and the French government in exporting weapons to countries with which the United States did not have good relations, such as Iran, Libya and Iraq, and also for ignoring a Defense Intelligence Agency warning of extensive technology leakage. The lesson is that even "friendly" nations may have skeletons in the closet which the DOD and other critics of a proposed investment will quickly make public. France's military policy, which is made independently of NATO, did not help.

Other commentators remained equally critical of Thomson's proposal suggesting that although an open-door policy makes sense for *private* foreign investors, that policy should be reexamined where foreign *governments* are involved, especially in this case, where LTV's products could not be replaced by another domestic firm. Exon-Florio (as it then existed) did not seem an appropriate vehicle to carry out a policy intended to prevent foreign-government ownership of defense contractors.

It became apparent during the controversy over LTV that the CFIUS was almost certain to recommend that the President block the transaction. Consequently, Thomson first withdrew its bid to restructure the deal and ultimately withdrew completely, leading to a suit by LTV for breach of contract. Martin Marietta soon submitted a higher bid, justified because it would not have to compete with the inexhaustible resources of a government-assisted competitor.

During and following the Thomson-LTV attempted merger, Congress, not the President and CFIUS, assumed the lead role. Congress led the effort to gain more information on Thomson, and as a result of its hearings to reconsider the policy of open direct investment involving foreign governments, Thomson's bid was withdrawn. Because of the perception that the administration took up the case only with prompting by Congress, amendments to Exon-Florio soon appeared on Capitol Hill.

The committee working on what would become the Byrd Amendment to Exon-Florio identified three factors of greatest concern in the attempted merger. First, LTV was a substantial contractor with the

DOD and NASA, and was the largest contractor ever for sale to a foreign firm. Second, as much as 75 percent of the work LTV did for the DOD required access to highly classified information that is generally prohibited for foreign nationals or representatives of foreign interests. Third, the French government owned 58 percent of Thomson's stock. Of considerable concern to the committee was that government ownership would introduce into the company's decision-making process the foreign government's political and diplomatic interests, which may contrast with those of the United States.

Two major amendments to Exon-Florio are directly attributable to the experience of the failed Thomson purchase of LTV. When Congress assumed the lead in that investigation, the President appeared to be slow to react to the attempted takeover involving a foreign government. The first change sought by Congress was to remove any presidential and CFIUS reticence in carrying out their responsibilities under Exon-Florio. The Byrd Amendment *requires* the President or his designee to investigate if the purchasing foreigner is "controlled by or acting on behalf of a foreign government." The "acting on behalf" language is not without some ambiguity. It remains unclear whether this would include a lesser form of control as defined in the regulations (issued before the Byrd Amendment), consequently increasing Exon-Florio's coverage when a foreign government is involved. But the Byrd Amendment does add a new concept of "effective control" by a foreign government, which may increase the ambiguity of the meaning of "control by a foreign government."

The second important amendment forbids the sale of some U.S. companies to certain foreign investors, principally those involved with foreign governments. In a separate section of Exon-Florio/FINSA, entities controlled by a foreign government are prohibited from acquiring certain Department of Energy or Defense contractors. Such contractors may not be acquired by entities controlled by or acting on behalf of foreign governments if they work under a national-security program that cannot be done without access to a "proscribed category of information." Furthermore, any firm awarded at least $500 million in prime DOD contracts or at least $500 million in prime Department of Energy contracts under national-security programs may not be acquired. There may be an escape clause, however. Section 2170a(b) suggests that if foreign investors are patient and go through an investigation that ends without suspension or prohibition, the acquisition restraints may not apply.

There was an additional 1992 amendment which requires the President to report to Congress his Exon-Florio decision, including a detailed explanation of how the decision was reached. These reports are not disclosed to the public under an exemption to the Freedom of Information Act.

FOREIGN INVESTMENT AND NATIONAL SECURITY ACT OF 2007 (FINSA)

In 2005, CNOOC, a state-owned Chinese oil company, sought to buy Unocal Corp. Congressional opposition was so fierce this proposed acquisition was withdrawn. In 2006, responding to the proposed purchase by Dubai Ports World of a British operator of six American ports, a concerned Congress amended the Exon-Florio provisions by the Foreign Investment and National Security Act of 2007 (FINSA). Well before Congress acted, Dubai Ports World removed the controversy by selling its U.S. ports to an American company.

The FINSA amendments: (1) allow the President to intervene in transactions perceived to be a national security risk; (2) establish a mandatory 45-day investigation period for acquiring companies owned by foreign governments; (3) require high level U.S. agency approvals; (4) reinforce the role of the National Intelligence Director in CFIUS reviews; (5) mandate tracking of withdrawn transactions; and (6) create a flexible definition of national security that includes foreign acquisition of "critical infrastructure" and "critical technology", both broadly defined.

FINSA tightened national security review of foreign investment, notably by clarifying examination of less than 10 percent shareholdings, by treating sovereign wealth funds as state-owned enterprises subject to strict scrutiny, and by detailing when U.S. investments are "controlled" by foreigners. It also mandates monitoring of CFIUS mitigation agreements undertaken by foreign investors.

In general, a pattern exists that if a foreign government plays a role in a foreign investment, CFIUS, or perhaps its apparent watchdog, the Congress, will examine the proposal very carefully. Exon-Florio/FINSA has proven to be a law the operation of which Congress follows closely, ready to enter into the review of a proposed acquisition with the threat of amendments that would undo any CFIUS or presidential approval. Subsequent to the Thomson-CSF attempted merger, other sensitive cases have been heard by CFIUS. When China or Mid-East countries are involved there seems to be immediate suspicion of the intention of the proposed acquisition. In 2010, for example, Huawei Technologies of China, was "asked" by CFIUS to apply for approval of the acquisition of 3Leaf Systems, a U.S. cloud computing tech firm. Huawei applied, but when informed that CFIUS intended to recommend divestiture to the President, threatened to go through with the transaction before quickly backing out of it.

CHINA INVESTS IN THE USA

Since FINSA was enacted in 2007, the CFIUS has reviewed numerous transactions, investigating roughly half of them. Eight foreign buyers of U.S. companies agreed to CFIUS mitigation measures related to U.S. national security. For example, China's state-owned CNOOC was notably cleared to acquire Canada's Nexen subject to alterations in Nexen's control over U.S. oil and gas drilling leases.

Moreover, some 98 percent of proposed acquisitions since 1988 that have been notified under the law have been approved without a full investigation under "no action" letters. Chinese, British and Canadian firms have filed the largest number of notices for CFIUS review. The President prohibited the acquisition of just one set of companies owning and operating wind farms near Naval Weapons restricted air space in Oregon. Chinese nationals were the intended buyers. They successfully challenged the President's order as violating U.S. due process principles for want of an adequate opportunity to review and rebut the evidence upon which CFIUS relied. See *Ralls Corp. v. CFIUS,* 758 F.3d 296 (D.C. Cir. 2014).

China's investments in the United States continue to grow, by and large through mergers and acquisitions: AMC Entertainment Holdings in 2012, Smithfield Foods in 2013, Motorola Mobility in 2014, and Legendary Entertainment, Carmike Cinemas and GE's appliance business in 2016. All of these investments have survived CFIUS review.

However, there was a notable "extraterritorial" CFIUS rejection in 2016 of an attempt by a Chinese venture capital company to buy Lumaleds from Royal Philips NV of The Netherlands. CFIUS was concerned that Lumaleds has extensive U.S. assets and patent holdings in the LED lighting field. Similarly, a Chinese investor withdrew from a multi-billion dollar deal to acquire a stake in Western Digital, a California disk-drive maker, when CFIUS commenced an investigation. At this writing, a wave of Chinese acquisitions are pending CFIUS review: The HNA Group of China seeks technology distributor Ingram Micro, a Chinese company has bought the Chicago Stock Exchange, and China National Chemical has agreed to buy Syngenta AG of Switzerland, which has substantial U.S. agricultural chemical and seed interests. The latter is part of a pattern of Chinese goals to achieve "food security".

SPECIFIC FEDERAL PROHIBITIONS OR LIMITATIONS ON FOREIGN INVESTMENT

Federal law includes few absolute prohibitions on foreign ownership of U.S. means of production and distribution. Some industries are more strictly regulated with regard to permissible levels of foreign ownership than others.

Atomic Energy. Foreign ownership or control is not permitted for commercial licensees of atomic energy. The Nuclear Regulatory Commission is prohibited from issuing a license to any person "for activities which are not under or within the jurisdiction of the United States" or to an alien or any corporation or other entity "if the Commission knows or has reason to believe it is owned, controlled, or dominated, by an alien, a foreign corporation, or a foreign government." The broad concluding phrase discloses the intent of the statute, that in any event, "no license may be issued to any person within the United States if, in the opinion of the Commission, the issuance of a license to such person would be inimical to the common defense and security, or to the health and safety of the public."

Merchant Marine. A similar policy justification is in the Jones Act statutes governing the merchant marine. Stating that it is "necessary for the national defense and for the proper growth of its foreign and domestic commerce," the merchant marine must serve as a naval or military auxiliary in time of war or national emergency. Thus, merchant marine vessels are "ultimately to be owned and operated privately by citizens of the United States." To enforce that policy, no merchandise may be transported by water, or by land and water, between points in the United States, in any other vessel than one built in and documented under the laws of the United States and owned by U.S. citizens. Control extends to the transfer of ownership of U.S.-owned vessels. A U.S. owner is prohibited from selling any interest in a vessel (other than certain pleasure and fishing vessels) to a non-citizen of the United States without approval of the Department of Transportation.

Airlines. The airlines rules were developed in the 1920s and 1930s, when airlines were subsidized and U.S. airspace was rigidly protected. The industry has changed, but the foreign investment rules have not. Concerns now seem focused on reciprocity: Access to foreign routes in exchange for domestic routes, with airline ownership of necessary determination to understand who has what rights. Thus the current laws follow outmoded justifications, but with new considerations of a "managed" balance in access apparently being the reason for limiting foreign ownership. These limitations may well place U.S. airlines in a disadvantageous position. They are denied foreign equity and must turn to less favorable domestic debt financing, which in turn may cause their demise.

United States citizens must own 75 percent of the voting shares of an air carrier, as well as constitute two-thirds or more of the board of directors and managing officers, and specifically the presidency. Voting equity remains the key focus of Department of Transportation (DOT) investigations concerning control by foreigners. But combined with other factors of control, an extensive foreign total-equity ownership, absent voting powers may result in denial of participation. Under new policies of the DOT, a foreign airline may be allowed up to 49 percent of the total equity, but the limit of 25 percent of the voting equity remains.

For example, the Dutch airline KLM planned to acquire up to 57 percent of the total equity of Northwest, with its ownership of *voting* equity remaining under the limit. The DOT concluded that the high percentage of total foreign equity ownership, along with other relationships between the two airlines, created a potential for control and influence inconsistent with the law. DOT and KLM eventually concluded a consent agreement that reduced KLM's total planned equity stake and limited KLM's participation on Northwest's board of directors. Its participation could only be what was necessary to protect its interest, and its appointed members would have to excuse themselves from discussion of any bilateral issues between the companies. The DOT, subsequent to the KLM case, indicated a desire to balance the benefits of foreign investment without imposing arbitrary obstacles, as successful investments by British Air in US Air and Air Canada in Continental appear to demonstrate.

Banking. Regulation of the foreign participation in banking has changed because in several instances foreign participation was not disclosed until losses were incurred. Subsequent to the Bank of Credit and Commerce International (BCCI) and Banca Nazionale de Lavorro (BNL) scandals involving the operations of foreign banks in the United States, Congress enacted new legislation, particularly the Foreign Bank Supervision Enhancement Act of 1991 (FBSEA). The FBSEA mandated that the Federal Reserve approve establishment of U.S. offices by foreign banks only if the bank is under comprehensive and consolidated regulation by its home country's authorities. The role of foreign direct investment is more significant in banking than most other sectors of the economy. United States affiliates of foreign banks account for roughly 20 percent of the total assets of all banks.

Mineral Leases and Timber Rights. The laws governing interests in mineral leases involve more direct reciprocity. Deposits of natural resources and the lands containing them owned by the United States are available for exploitation by U.S. citizens, but not to foreigners of any country that does not grant comparable rights to Americans. The United

States formerly maintained a list of "reciprocal" nations, but since 1982 administrative procedures have been used to make such determinations.

Current law traces to the 1920 Mineral Lands Leasing Act. The regulations reflect a policy of reciprocity, stating that foreigners may hold mineral leases through their interests in U.S. corporations provided that their home country does not deny similar rights to citizens and corporations of the United States. Under this law, the state-owned Kuwaiti Petroleum Corp. (KPC), which owned Santa Fe Petroleum and other U.S. corporations, was barred from obtaining further oil and gas leases on public lands. Timber rights are also restricted. United States citizens have various rights to use timber on federal lands. Aliens who are bona fide residents may also obtain such access.

Outer-Continental Shelf Activities. Federal law governs foreign ownership of offshore leases on the outer-continental shelf. The federal government has control beyond the three-mile limit which defines the outer reach of state authority. Federal regulations govern both the outer continental shelf and offshore leases. There is no statutory prohibition of foreign access because there is no citizenship requirement. But Department of Interior regulations have limited the access. Aliens are allowed access when admitted for permanent residence. There is no reciprocity requirement.

What is important are the restrictions on aliens working on the outer-continental shelf. U.S. immigration rules apply. The statutory provisions essentially limit the manning of outer-continental shelf rigs, vessels and platforms to U.S. citizens, with some special exceptions.

Communications. The laws governing the communications industry remain a key area of federal foreign investment regulation. The principal law governing electromagnetic media is the Federal Communications Act (FCA) of 1934. Of particular concern is the television industry, part of the "wireless communication" industry. For example, during the 1980s, Australian media owner Rupert Murdoch became a U.S. citizen in order to acquire a U.S. television station. But foreign investment in U.S. communication companies holding licenses issued by the Federal Communications Commission (FCC) is not totally prohibited.

The FCC may not grant a station license to any foreign government or representative, or to an alien or alien corporation, but the law does allow for less than 20 percent of the shares to be foreign owned. The reason for the restrictions is to maintain control by U.S. citizens. The FCC will not grant licenses to "any corporation directly or indirectly controlled" by any corporation where 25 percent or more of the directors and officers are aliens, or where 25 percent or more of the shares are owned of record or voted by aliens, their representatives, or a foreign government or corporation. Cable television is considered to come under this provision because it uses microwave stations.

Wire communications are also governed by the same FCA. There is no citizenship requirement for this industry, but because states retain considerable control over telephone services they may have restrictions. These restrictions are usually applied to all out-of-state, vice truly foreign, persons. A special area, satellite communications, is subject to the Communications Satellite Act of 1962, which prohibits more than 20 percent of the shares of a satellite corporation to be owned by aliens.

Real Estate. There are four principal federal laws of the United States that mandate disclosure when aliens purchase U.S. realty. These are the International Investment and Trade in Services Survey Act of 1976, the Agricultural Foreign Investment Disclosure Act of 1978, the Foreign Investment in Real Property Tax Act of 1980 (reduced taxation was adopted in 2015), and the Tax Equity and Fiscal Responsibility Act of 1982. These laws particularly impact foreign pension funds, which are major investors in U.S. commercial real estate. Restrictions on foreign investment in United States real estate at the federal level concern U.S. government-owned public lands. Most of these public lands are located in Alaska and the Western states. Federal statutes regulating grazing, mining, and energy resources are uniquely relevant to the foreign investor.

STATE REGULATION OF FOREIGN INVESTMENT

Unlike the merchant marine or airline regulations at the federal level, most state regulations governing foreign investment do not have national security as their justification. State laws that seek to review foreign investments are essentially state versions of Exon-Florio/FINSA without the national security justification. These state laws often prove to be unconstitutional. They frequently violate the commerce clause as well as the doctrine of uniformity, meaning that the United States ought to speak with one voice where foreign investment is concerned. But the laws buy time and send a message to the foreign investor that it is unwelcome and likely to be subject to harassment at the state level, notwithstanding federal rejection of successive state attempts to regulate.

One example of the barriers a state may create to block foreign investors was Ohio's attempt to block a foreign corporate raider acting by means of a Canadian corporation and its wholly owned New York subsidiary, CRTF Corporation, in an attempt to acquire Federal Department Stores, Inc. (Federated), a Delaware corporation. Ohio quickly enacted the Ohio Foreign Business Acquisitions Act to regulate control of a "resident business" by a "foreign business." On the same day, the foreign investor filed suit challenging the constitutionality of the Act, which required foreign businesses to file an "application for approval of acquisition" with the state.

The restrictions on establishing businesses in Ohio by foreign persons did not apply to U.S. firms incorporated in the United States, or to foreign businesses that already maintained "substantial interests" in Ohio. The federal district court held the

act to be discriminatory on its face and granted a
motion for a preliminary injunction. The court
concluded that although a state may enact laws
pursuant to its police powers that have the purpose
and effect of encouraging domestic industry, a state
may not enact laws which discriminate against
foreign commerce or which create the risk of
inconsistent state regulation. *See Campeau Corp. v.
Federated Department Stores*, 679 F.Supp. 735
(S.D.Ohio 1988).

Notwithstanding the experience of state statutes
like that in Ohio, many states continue to maintain
statutes governing foreign investment in *real estate.*
States restrict the real property rights of aliens and
alien corporations in a variety of ways. Some states
have onerous restrictions, and others have no
restrictions. Those states whose laws are essentially
restraint-free regarding real estate include
Alabama, Arizona, Colorado, Delaware, the District
of Columbia, Florida, Georgia, Maine, Maryland,
Massachusetts, Michigan, Nevada, New Hampshire,
New Mexico, Rhode Island, Tennessee, Texas, Utah,
Vermont, Washington and West Virginia.

Banking regulation also has a state level that
foreign investors must consider. For example, New
York has considered adopting banking regulations
similar to those at the federal level requiring home-
country supervision and cooperation. The state
regulatory board has also suggested that foreign
banks without offices incorporated in New York
should obtain approval for changes in control of 25
percent or more.

FRANCHISING IN THE UNITED STATES

Franchising is an important sector in the United States economy. Thousands of franchisors have created and administer franchise systems throughout the nation. United States franchisees number in the hundreds of thousands. These franchisees are typically independent business persons, and their local franchise outlets employ millions of people. It has been estimated that approximately one-third of all retail sales in the United States take place through franchised outlets. Just as United States franchisors have found franchising particularly effective for market penetration abroad, Canadian, European and Japanese companies are increasingly penetrating the United States market through franchising.

Franchising is a business technique that permits rapid and flexible penetration of markets, growth and capital development. In the United States, there are traditional distinctions between product franchises and business format franchises. Product franchises involve manufacturers who actually produce the goods that are distributed through franchise agreements. For example, ice cream stores, soft drink bottling companies and gasoline retailers are often the subject of product franchises. Business format franchises are more common. These do not involve the manufacture by the franchisor of the product being sold by the franchisee. More typically, the franchisor licenses intellectual property rights in conjunction with a particular "formula for success" of the business.

Fast food establishments, hotels, and a variety of service franchises are examples of business format franchising.

United States regulation of franchise relationships occurs at both the federal and state levels of government. Such regulation can be as specific as the Federal Trade Commission Franchising Rule or as amorphous as the ever present dangers of state and federal antitrust law. The latter can particularly impact the drafting of United States franchise agreements so as to avoid potential liabilities for *per se* unlawful resale price maintenance, unreasonable market division or customer restraints, Robinson-Patman Act price discrimination violations, and heavily litigated "tying arrangements" (coercive purchasing requirements).

State Franchise Disclosure Requirements and Regulations. The most obvious form of governmental regulation of franchising occurs through disclosure statutes enacted by a number of the states. These disclosure statutes resemble those commonly found when securities are offered for sale. At least fifteen states have such franchise disclosure laws. The typical franchise disclosure statute adopted at the state level in the United States, and also through the Franchises Act of Alberta Canada, creates criminal penalties for material misrepresentations or omissions in the franchise circular. It also ordinarily permits withdrawal from any franchise agreement if the franchisee did not receive a copy of the prospectus. Moreover, if there has been a misstatement or omission of material facts, the franchisees may rescind the agreement.

Most franchise disclosure laws require the franchisor to register with a state agency by filing a proposed prospectus for the franchise offering. Such a prospectus is often called a franchise offering circular. The state agency then reviews the circular to insure that it meets the necessary disclosure requirements. Once the franchise offering is registered with the state, the franchisor is effectively licensed to sell franchises in that state. One issue in connection with these disclosure statutes is what constitutes a "franchise." A franchise normally exists when one person grants another the right to distribute goods or services using the trademark of the grantor under a marketing plan created substantially by that person and in return the franchisee pays a fee in order to maintain the franchise relationship.

In some jurisdictions franchises are said to exist whenever there is a community of interest between the franchisor and the franchisee in the distribution of goods or services. Such a community of interest would typically be found when the franchisor controls the site or territory of the franchisee, tells the franchisee what hours to operate or in what manner to operate the local premises, or generally controls the manner in which the franchisee's business or marketing is conducted.

Practically speaking, many state registration agencies also review the capitalization of franchisors before permitting the sale of franchises. This is done notwithstanding the fact that few state laws or regulations specify what constitutes adequate capitalization for a franchisor. A general review of the franchisor's financial statements is typically undertaken. This scrutiny may call into question the solvency of the franchisor, as for example where loans to officers are on the books as an asset. As a general rule, a franchisor's net worth should exceed the initial capital investment that is being requested of a franchisee.

States that actively regulate the sale of franchises have developed a "coordinated review" process working through a lead state. This "one-stop" regulatory process is expected to significantly reduce inconsistent results as well as costs and expenses.

The authority of state agencies to regulate franchises is not unlimited. In one decision, for example, a manufacturer of photo processing machinery (KIS) was ordered ex parte to stop selling its equipment in Wisconsin. The Commissioner of Securities claimed that the manufacturer was a franchisor because it offered suggestions and advice to equipment purchasers. In a lengthy decision, an administrative law judge held that mere suggestions do not amount to a prescribed marketing plan or system constituting a franchise. KIS was therefore not required to register as a franchisor under the Wisconsin disclosure statutes. If the suggestions made by KIS had been combined with penalties or sanctions for failing to follow them, or it could have been otherwise shown that as a practical reality the purchaser did not have unrestricted autonomy in operating the photo finishing business, then KIS would have been a franchisor subject to Wisconsin registration requirements.

States may require disclosure if there is a community of (financial) interest between the parties. The basic question is whether there is a manufacturer/distributor relationship or a franchise. In this area, Wisconsin law is again prominent. A Wisconsin Supreme Court decision (*Ziegler Co. v. Rexnord, Inc.*, 139 Wis.2d 593, 407 N.W.2d 873 (1987)) emphasizes that the test is not merely percentages of business time or revenues devoted to the products in question. Rather, the finder of fact must also review a range of factors in making community of interest determinations: (1) length of dealing; (2) extent of obligations; (3) territorial scope; (4) use of trademarks; (5) financial investments; (6) personnel commitments; (7) advertising and promotions; and (8) supplementary services. Under these criteria, a community of interest amounting to a franchise existed where a sales representative had been the manufacturer's sole Midwest stocking inventory dealer for five years, devoted 70 percent of his time to that effort and derived 60 percent of his income there from, and had invested $15,000 in developing the business.

Another variety of state regulation of franchising is more intrusive than disclosure requirements. Approximately half of the states regulate the franchise relationship over its life. In particular, states have enacted legislation which deals with the termination of franchisees. These laws ordinarily prohibit a franchisor from undertaking termination before the ordinary end of the franchise contract unless there is "good cause." Good cause is frequently defined to mean a breach by the franchisee of a material provision of the franchise agreement that has not been cured. Good cause typically does not include the relevant business needs of the franchisor. Some of these laws also require renewal of the franchise agreement unless there is "good cause" for nonrenewal. In some jurisdictions, this provision may not apply to a franchise which has a fixed term as opposed to a franchise which creates by contract a right of renewal or option for a successor.

There is relatively little case law elaborating upon what constitutes good cause to terminate franchisees. However, the following have been recognized as good cause for such terminations: (1) failure to meet sales goals; (2) health and safety violations by the franchisee; (3) breach of implied covenants; and (4) verbal customer abuse. If there is good cause for franchisee termination, the fact of economic hardship to the franchisee may not override the franchisor's right of termination. Ending franchise relationships can sometimes be tumultuous. Texas franchisees who set up a directly competing business one month before the termination of their muffler franchise even using the same phone number were ultimately held liable for actual and punitive damages of $10,000 plus

$560,000 in attorneys' fees on breach of contract and civil conspiracy claims. The general trend in the courts is against finding any fiduciary duties as between franchisor and franchisee. But the duty to act in good faith in connection with termination of franchisees has been affirmed in a number of leading opinions.

FTC Franchising Rule. Federal law may also concurrently regulate franchising in the United States. In particular, the U.S. Federal Trade Commission has issued a Trade Regulation Rule on Franchising and Business Opportunity Ventures (16 C.F.R. Part 436). This rule applies to continuing business relationships such as package franchises (business format), product franchises (distribution systems) and business opportunity ventures involving significant financial risks for the franchisee and subject to significant assistance or control by the franchisor. In addition, the franchise must involve the distribution of goods or services associated with the franchisor's trademark. Employer-employee, retail cooperative, single license and general partnership relationships are excluded from coverage under the FTC rule. Individuals and groups may petition for exemption from the FTC rule on the grounds that unfairness and deceptive practices are not issues requiring its applicability, for example when the franchisees are sophisticated business persons.

The FTC rule requires disclosure in advance to prospective franchisees. However, unlike state law, the FTC rule does not require a filing of an offering circular with the Federal Trade Commission. If the necessary disclosures are not undertaken, the Commission may enforce the rule through cease and desist order proceedings. The FTC franchising rule can also be enforced through civil penalty actions in the federal district courts. In such actions, the FTC may seek up to $10,000 per violation of the rule as well as a permanent injunction against future violations. There is no private right of action in connection with the FTC Trade Regulation Rule on Franchising and Business Opportunity Ventures.

The FTC Disclosure Rule mandates a thorough description of the franchise system, and detailed biographies of the persons who are principally responsible for that system. Any civil or criminal litigation involving the franchise or any officers of the franchisor must be revealed. The rule also requires disclosure of costs at the front end to the franchisee, royalties that must be paid over time, any advertising or promotional payments by the franchisee, and inventory purchasing requirements. The net effect of these duties is to give the franchisee a reasonably clear picture of the financial commitments that flow from the franchise agreement. If the franchisor wishes to represent the likely success or earnings schedule of the franchise, a separate earnings document must be released. The disclosure notice must also clearly indicate what are the terms and conditions of termination or non-renewal.

A common way in which states enforce the Federal Trade Commission Rule on franchising and business opportunities is through what are known as Little FTC Acts. Under these statutes, many states have held that a violation of the Federal Trade Commission Rule constitutes an unfair or deceptive act or practice for purposes of state law. Any such holding typically results in injunctive or public civil penalty relief through actions by local prosecutors. Unlike federal law, state Little FTC Acts sometimes permit private parties to obtain relief, including in some cases damages relief. Thus the FTC Disclosure Rule in the franchising area has a broader remedial scope than that which is provided in the Federal Trade Commission Act.

The Federal Trade Commission has undertaken evaluative studies of its franchise rule. These studies were conducted by independent research organizations. The first study examined the utility of disclosure to purchasers and those who did not purchase a franchise. The second study examined the costs and benefits to franchisors in complying with the FTC rule. Some broad conclusions were reached as a result of these studies. Roughly two-thirds of all franchisees indicated that they used the FTC disclosure document in making their purchasing decision. A significant number of franchisees found that the disclosure document was helpful in obtaining financing. As a result of reading the disclosure document, roughly three-quarters of all prospective franchisees contacted other existing franchisees. About half of all the prospective franchisees also sought professional advice. The franchisees indicated that the disclosure document was most useful because it created an awareness of the information necessary to make an intelligent purchasing decision. Many indicated that it revealed information that they had not previously known and that it saved them time in their information search.

Among the franchisors contacted in the second study, the most important disclosures were the necessary initial investment to be made by franchisees, the franchisor's obligations, earnings claims and renewal and termination details. Many franchisors believed that the disclosure document contained information that franchisees otherwise would not have had and that it added credibility to their franchise proposal. They not only thought that disclosure protected franchisees from fraudulent sales practices, but they recognized that franchisors were less likely to be subject to claims of misrepresentation by franchisees. Franchisors also felt that the disclosure statement helped them qualify prospective franchisees.

A variety of other uses for the disclosure information was found. Franchisors often used the same documents in reporting to their banks, in assisting franchisees to obtain financing, in reporting to stockholders or potential investors and in federal or state tax returns or securities filings. On the negative side, franchisors noted the administrative time and expense in complying with disclosure laws, including legal and accounting fees. Some objected to the difficulty in making earnings claims under existing disclosure criteria.

LABOR LAW RULES FOR FOREIGN INVESTORS IN THE UNITED STATES

Businesses operated in the United States by foreign investors remain subject to the same laws regarding the operation of a business as those owned by domestic investors. This is true generally with regard to taxation of foreign controlled companies operating within the United States. However, such companies may retain more flexibility to employ and dismiss employees than companies controlled by U.S. investors.

Generally, foreign companies with operations in the United States remain subject to U.S. civil rights laws affecting the employment relationship. But a possible exception may exist, even for subsidiaries incorporated in the United States, under commercial treaty protections, provided that the particular employment decisions were directed or controlled by the foreign parent. Two cases suggest an exception: *Sumitomo Shoji America, Inc. v. Avagliano*, 457 U.S. 176 (1982) and *Fortino v. Quasar Co.*, 950 F.2d 389 (7th Cir.1991).

In *Sumitomo*, Avigliano and other female secretarial employees brought a class-action suit against Sumitomo, a New York corporation and wholly owned subsidiary of a Japanese trading company. They alleged violation of 42 U.S.C.A. § 1981 and Title VII of the Civil Rights Act because of the company's practice of hiring only male Japanese citizens to fill executive, managerial, and sales positions. Sumitomo moved to dismiss the suit because first, any discrimination based on Japanese citizenship does not violate those provisions, and second, Sumitomo's practices were protected under the Treaty of Friendship, Commerce, and Navigation between Japan and the United States.

The trial court agreed with Sumitomo on the § 1981 claim and dismissed it because neither sex nor national-origin discrimination were covered by the provision. The court refused to dismiss the Title VII claim because, although Sumitomo was a wholly owned Japanese subsidiary, it was incorporated in the United States and not covered by the treaty. The Second Circuit Court of Appeals reversed in part, stating that the treaty did cover locally incorporated subsidiaries, although that would not end the Title VII analysis.

The Supreme Court agreed with the trial court and vacated the Circuit Court's decision. It held that the intent of the United States and Japan in concluding the FCN treaty was not to include subsidiaries regardless of their place of incorporation. The Court stated that the treaty's provision giving companies of each country the right to hire, within the other country, certain managerial and support staff of their choice, applied only to companies from the other country itself. Rejecting Sumitomo's claim that the U.S. entity was a Japanese company, the Court held that the treaty's definition looked to the place of incorporation, in Sumitomo's case, New York—an interpretation that both the U.S. and Japanese governments supported.

While Sumitomo failed in its attempt to assert FCN privileges, Quasar succeeded. Quasar is an unincorporated division of a U.S. company wholly owned by the Japanese firm Matsushita Electric Industrial Company Ltd. Matsushita assigned several financial and marketing executives to Quasar, who remained under Quasar's day-to-day control, but they retained their status as Matsushita employees. The executives' temporary work visas pursuant to the FCA treaty offered further evidence of the employees' temporary status at Quasar. The meaning of temporary or expatriate employment is not fully settled, since some such employees remain as managers of the foreign plant for many years.

When Quasar lost $20 million in 1985, Matsushita assigned one of these expatriate executives to reorganize the company. He reduced the managing employees by half, discharging Fortino and the others who sued Quasar. None of the "temporary" executives were among those discharged, and though two were rotated back to Japan, those who remained received pay increases, while the remaining American management staff did not. Fortino's suit charged that Quasar's behavior violated the Age Discrimination in Employment Act and also Title VII of the Civil Rights Act because of discrimination based on national origin. The suit succeeded at the trial court level because of the different treatment of the remaining Japanese and U.S. executives.

On appeal, Quasar argued that the national origin discrimination claim was not supportable because the discrimination was in favor of foreigners employed temporarily in the United States in accordance with the FCN treaty that permits Japanese firms to employ executives of their own choice. Fortino argued that by failing to bring the treaty to the attention of the trial court, Quasar had waived the defense. The Seventh Circuit decided that it would hear the appeal, not only because of interests in international comity, amity, and commerce, but also because the issue was not so much a defense, but part of the background argument for why Title VII should not apply at all. To the court the essence of the case was the distinction between discrimination based on national origin, which Title VII forbids, and discrimination based on citizenship, which the treaty allows.

The court found that the better treatment Quasar afforded the remaining foreign executives constituted favoritism, and although it might have appeared to be discrimination based on national origin because of the apparent homogeneity of the Japanese people involved, it was actually discrimination based upon citizenship allowed by the treaty. The court saw Quasar's firing of some Japanese-Americans as evidence of citizenship discrimination rather than Title VII national origin discrimination. In dismissing the Title VII claim it stated that the "exercise of a treaty right may not be made the basis for inferring a violation of Title VII."

One difference between *Quasar* and *Sumitomo* pertains to who directed the allegedly discriminatory behavior. In *Sumitomo* there was no

contention that the parent dictated the
discriminatory behavior of the subsidiary, as
Matsushita did with Quasar. But a subsidiary ought
to have the capacity to assert the parent's FCN
rights if the parent could have been sued.

The Quasar court concluded with one final
reciprocity policy rationale. Observing that the
United States, not Japan, had wanted the inclusion
of a treaty provision allowing each nation's
companies to select their employees, the court
stated that American jobs in Japan would be
jeopardized by reciprocal decisions of Japan's courts,
should Fortino's argument have won. This
reciprocity argument may be used by counsel
attempting to argue the non-application of the U.S.
laws governing employment discrimination. But
such an argument weakens when the decision is
made by a U.S. incorporated but foreign owned
company.

U.S. IMMIGRANT INVESTOR EB-5 VISAS

A popular United States employment based
immigrant visa is the Fifth Preference Employment
Based (EB-5) category, renewed in 2015. While it is
referred to as an employment category in actuality
it is an *investment* based classification. This
category, commonly referred to as the "Million
Dollar Green Card," offers the only option to aliens
who wish to petition for an immigrant visa based on
an investment made in the United States. A
maximum of 10,000 EB-5 visas may be issued
annually to alien investors. A petition for

classification as an EB-5 "alien entrepreneur" may only be filed by the alien on the alien's own behalf.

In order to qualify for an EB-5 visa the alien must establish and engage in a new commercial enterprise by investing $1,000,000 in that enterprise, and create ten *new* full-time jobs for United States workers. In certain circumstances the required investment may be increased to as much as $3,000,000, or in "high unemployment areas" (sometimes gerrymandered by local officials to achieve this status) decreased to as little as $500,000.

Only active investments will qualify an alien in the EB-5 category. Passive investments such as ownership of real estate or stocks would not qualify even if the job creation criteria are somehow satisfied. Not only must the investment be active but it also must be invested in a *new business;* and it must create ten new full-time jobs for United States workers. The purpose of this requirement is to ensure that an alien is not just "buying" lawful permanent resident status, but is actually creating something that will benefit the country.

In most cases purchasing an existing enterprise will not fulfill the "new business" requirement. However, the regulations have defined when this is permissible. The establishment of a new commercial enterprise may consist of:

1. The creation of an original business;

2. The purchase of an existing business and simultaneous or subsequent restructuring or

reorganization such that a new organization results; or

3. The expansion of an existing business through the investment of the required amount, so that a substantial change in the net worth or number of employees results from the investment of capital. Substantial change means a 40 percent increase either in the net worth, or in the number of employees, so that the new net worth, or number of employees amounts to at least 140 percent of the pre-expansion net worth or number of employees. Establishment of a new commercial enterprise in this manner does not exempt the petitioner from the required amount of capital investment and the creation of full-time employment for ten qualifying employees. In the case of a capital investment in a troubled business, employment creation may meet separate criteria.

The EB-5 visa is issued on a two year conditional basis. Ninety days prior to the end of the two years the alien investor must apply to have the condition lifted. To qualify for removal of the condition the investor must establish that the business is still operating according to the stipulated guidelines and is still employing at least ten full-time United States workers. If these criteria are met the condition will be lifted and the alien and the alien's family will become *lawful permanent residents, unconditionally*. However, if the business is no longer in operation the alien and accompanying family members will lose their immigrant status— no waiver is permitted.

In 2014, almost 11,000 foreign nationals applied for EB-5 visas, up from just 470 in 2006. A majority of the applicants were from China, with many Chinese parents hoping to help their children stay in the U.S.A. after college. Wealthy Indians from Dubai, not entitled to citizenship there, are also active pursuers of EB-5 visas. Construction and the film industry account for the lion's share of EB-5 investments. Marriot, Sony and the Barclays Center developers have tapped hundreds of EB-5 investors to fund huge projects. On a more modest scale, U.S. franchisors are also obtaining EB-5 franchisees, including McDonald's, Subway and Burger King. All of them benefit from inexpensive financing under the EB-5 program, whose foreign investors are ready to take well below market returns. The S.E.C. monitors EB-5 programs and has terminated several fraudulent operations.

My thanks to San Diego Attorney and Adjunct USD Professor of Law, Geoffrey Leibl Esq., for his contribution to this coverage of EB-5 investor visas.

CHAPTER 7

FOREIGN INVESTMENT TREATIES
AND ARBITRATIONS

Bilateral Investment Treaties (BITs)

Foreign Investor Rights and Arbitrations

ICSID   Energy Charter

Given the absence of a cohesive body of widely accepted foreign investment law, and notably the failure of the Multilateral Agreement of Investment (MAI) discussed in Chapter 1, many nations have turned to negotiation of foreign investment treaties. From the perspective of capital exporting countries, such treaties offer protection from host state actions that violate the foreign investor rights contained therein. From the perspective of capital importing countries, investment treaties create incentives to invest in what may be perceived as high-risk markets.

There is a long history of foreign investors' purchasing political-risk insurance against expropriation, civil unrest and the like, sometimes from their home governments. See Chapter 3. In Latin America, the spread of "Calvo Doctrine" rules designed to limit foreign investors to host nations' judicial and administrative remedies increased the desire for protection. Investor-state dispute settlement (ISDS) by arbitration, discussed below, first appeared in a 1959 treaty between Germany and Pakistan. Since the 1990s the signing of bilateral investment treaties (BITs) has proliferated.

The principal focus of BITs is the protection and promotion of foreign investment. It is not only the United States which has emphasized these treaties. They are common features of most developed nations in their relations with developing host nations. Tracking its rise as a capital exporter, China has investment protection agreements with such nations as Australia, Austria, Belgium/ Luxembourg, Denmark, France, Germany, Japan, the Netherlands, and the United Kingdom. A benefit of such an agreement is that its provisions prevail over domestic law and remedies, although the agreements usually allow for exceptions to investment protection when in the interests of national security.

Approximately 3,000 bilateral investment treaties (BITs) lattice the globe. China and Germany have well over 100 BITs, France, Britain and the Netherlands about 100, India, Romania, Italy, The Czech Republic, Belgium/Luxembourg 75 to 85, Russia, Sweden, Poland 65, while Brazil has none and South Africa has said it will withdraw from any ISDS treaty obligations. Singapore has a number of BITs that seem to be designed to attract foreign investors to incorporate there so as to take advantage of Singaporean subsidiaries as foreign investment vehicles in the likes of Jordan and

Egypt. Investment arbitrations administered by the Singapore International Arbitration Center have skyrocketed.

The Netherlands is known for allowing "mailbox" companies to utilize their network of BITs by making foreign investments through them. Critics assert that this lattice allows foreign investors to engage in "treaty shopping", the making of investments in order to raise arbitral challenges to national laws. A prominent example is the Phillip Morris (Asia) acquisition of a Hong Kong firm to facilitate challenge of Australia's 2011 plain packaging (no brand) cigarette law under the 1993 Hong Kong-Australia Bilateral Investment Treaty. This arbitration was dismissed by the arbitrators in 2015 on jurisdictional grounds.

FOREIGN INVESTOR RIGHTS

BITs provide foreign investors with designated rights, and establish mandatory investor-state arbitration procedures to resolve alleged violations of those rights. The United States, for example, has nearly 50 BITs, mostly with developing nations, in addition to comparable coverage of foreign investment under its free trade agreements (NAFTA, CAFTA, etc.). Unlike the latter, U.S. BITs are ratified only by the Senate and do not require implementing legislation. In 2012, the United States issued a revised Model BIT, usually employed as a starting point in its BIT negotiations. This Model BIT includes a definition of "foreign investment" that reaches broadly to sovereign obligations and intellectual property rights, expressly covers indirect expropriations, and omits any balance of payments safeguard escape clause. The United States is presently negotiating a BIT with China, which inked a BIT with Canada in 2012 that does not cover regulatory controls over permissions to invest ("pre-investment" rules). In other words, the Canada-China BIT only concerns operational and disposal aspects of foreign investment law. This approach is common in European-based BITs, which are the most prevalent around the globe.

A highlight of all U.S. BITs is the consent in advance of host sovereign states to arbitration of foreign investor disputes; no separate consent is required. BIT arbitrations are subject to review in the place of arbitration *and* wherever enforcement is sought. Bilateral investment treaties traditionally provide foreign investors with certain core rights: (1) "national treatment"; (2) "most-favored-nation treatment"; (3) "fair and equitable treatment"; (4) "full protection and security"; and (5) expropriation rules.

Some BITs also require host governments to comply with obligations undertaken with foreign investors, often via foreign investment agreements, including for example "stabilization clauses" intended to stabilize or even freeze the law of the host country at the time of the signing of the agreement. If the investor-state agreement contains a "stabilization" clause, promising no significant change in the host state's law will adversely affect the investment, such clauses may give rise to breach of contract claims which become BIT violations subject to arbitration. Veolia, a French utility, for example commenced BIT arbitration proceedings against Egypt for raising the minimum wage. Such BIT provisions are typically called "umbrella clauses". NAFTA Chapter 11 notably does not contain such a provision, but the Energy Charter Treaty does. Article 2(2)(c) of the U.S. Model BIT (2012) similarly provides: "Each Party shall observe any obligation it may have entered into with regard to investments."

National treatment promises nondiscriminatory, equal treatment with domestic investors. Most-favored-nation treatment means foreign investors from different nations will be treated equally, thus sometimes allowing investors to claim more generous benefits provided in other BITs. In one such dispute, an Argentinian investor in Spain obtained the benefit of a Chile-Spain BIT dispute resolution provision not requiring prior exhaustion of local judicial remedies. General exception clauses in some BITs, notably the Canada-EU Comprehensive Economic and Trade Agreement (CETA), tend to mirror Article XX of the GATT and Article XIV of the GATS. Such clauses create state immunities for permissible policy objectives and acts, such as for the protection of human, animal or plant life or health, and the conservation of natural resources.

Fair and equitable treatment, and full protection and security, are notably open-ended "minimum standards" derived from customary international law. In determining fair and equitable treatment, the investor's legitimate expectations and the transparency, predictability, consistency and denial of justice under state rules have been evaluated as appropriate criteria. In addition, the duty of fair and equitable treatment has frequently been construed by arbitrators as protecting the stability of the legal and business framework under which the foreign investor operates... an interpretation that can resemble "umbrella clause" protection. For example, ICSID arbitrators found Argentine tariff changes unfair and inequitable under this approach.

Unfair and inequitable treatment have become the primary violations found by BIT and other foreign investment arbitration tribunals. For an informative review of "unfair and inequitable" conduct by Argentina in connection with emergency financial measures and judicial access to remedies, see the U.S. Supreme Court case *BG Group PLC v. Argentina,* 134 S.Ct. 1198 (2014) (litigate first requirement in UK-Argentina BIT excused in New York Convention recognition and enforcement proceedings).

Beyond core foreign investor rights, some BITs broadly allow arbitration of "other claims" related to the investment. Most BIT rules on expropriation require valid public purposes and prompt, adequate and effective compensation. NAFTA rules protect foreign investors from governmental acts "tantamount to expropriation", an ambiguous term (see below). Acts of sub-central government authorities or state-owned companies may be attributed to the state for BIT liability purposes. In addition, BITs may also protect capital movement and limit performance requirements. All of these rights may extend beyond the life of a BIT, which cannot be retroactively revoked, allowing for investor claims against states under "tails."

If the investor obtained investment rights by unlawful means, for example corruption, dismissal of its claims is appropriate as a matter of international public policy.

BIT FOREIGN INVESTOR-HOST STATE ARBITRATIONS

BITs almost always establish mandatory, binding dispute settlement procedures allowing foreign investors to invoke arbitration procedures by filing claims for damages against host nations. The formulae for these provisions differ. Many channel investor-state disputes to the World Bank's International Centre for Settlement of Investment Disputes (ICSID) in Washington, D.C, discussed below. Some BIT arbitrations have gone to the Stockholm Chamber of Commerce, the Permanent Court of Arbitration in The Hague, the U.N. Commission on International Trade Law (UNCITRAL), and the International Chamber of Commerce (ICC) in Paris.

Hundreds of investor-state disputes have been filed, the largest number against Argentina (many arising out of its sovereign debt repudiations and emergency economic measures affecting utilities).

The mere filing of such claims facilitates leverage in renegotiation of investment contracts as well as compensation.

Claims have been lodged against the United States, while U.S. investors abroad have very actively pursued claims against U.S. BIT and free trade partners, notably Argentina. Exxon Mobil obtained a $1.6 billion expropriation award in ICSID proceedings under the U.S.-Venezuela BIT. Dow Chemical received a $2.2 billion award in ICC proceedings against Kuwait. Under the U.S.-Ecuador BIT, in ICSID proceedings, Occidental Petroleum won a $2.3 billion award against Ecuador for termination of an oil-concession contract.

Some investor-state claims are settled, others dismissed on technical grounds. UNCTAD data indicates that arbitrated investment disputes reaching final awards favor the state by close to two to one. That said, it is clear that investors from the developed world (notably the United States, the Netherlands, the United Kingdom and Germany) comprise a large majority of the claimants against developing nations (notably Argentina, Venezuela, Ecuador and Mexico). As a general rule, BIT arbitration awards can be recognized and enforced in foreign courts under the 1958 New York Convention on the Recognition and Enforcement of Arbitral Awards.

The growth of arbitration under BITs has in many instances overrun contract-based choice of forum clauses, including alternative arbitral proceedings. When "parallel proceedings" exist, BIT arbitrators have often declined to defer to party autonomy. For example, U.S. investors in an Argentine port terminal agreed "for all purposes" in their concession contract to the jurisdiction of Argentinian courts. They invoked instead the U.S.-Argentina BIT arbitration procedures under ICSID. The arbitrators upheld their "jurisdiction" to hear the dispute.

Critics of BIT provisions focus on the fair and equitable treatment obligation, which has been increasingly construed by arbitrators to create "legitimate expectations" (future profits), and "specific commitments" that host governments will compensate foreign investors for changes in law, notably regulatory law. This has created a degree of foreign investment "regulatory chill." Investors have also been arguing that they are entitled to the legitimate expectation that governments will adhere to their international treaty obligations, notably under TRIPs concerning intellectual property rights. Investors have also used BIT and NAFTA provisions to influence and challenge proposed host state regulations.

Additional criticisms assert there is something of a "good old boy" network of inherently biased ISDS arbitrators drawn significantly from corporate legal worlds operating with relatively little transparency. Arbitrators who simultaneously act as counsel in other ongoing BIT arbitrations have been particularly critiqued. Most NAFTA and ICSID awards and related documents are published, and greater transparency should be forthcoming under the UNCITRAL Mauritius Convention (2015).

"Treaty shopping" to access investor-state arbitration remedies is said to occur, notably in connection with the formation of "mailbox companies" for that purpose. Philip Morris is thought to have made a strategic investment in Hong Kong so as to be able to challenge Australia's no-brand, plain packaging cigarette rules under a Hong Kong-Australia BIT dating from the British era. Philip Morris fears losing Marlboro Man and other trademarked brand names. In 2015, the arbitrators dismissed this proceeding on jurisdictional grounds.

At Australia's insistence, the United States-Australia free trade agreement does NOT contain investor-state arbitration procedures, though the Trans-Pacific Partnership (TPP) may alter that result generally. However, arbitration claims regarding the regulation of tobacco are specifically excluded under the TPP. Philip Morris is also utilizing the Swiss-Uruguay BIT to challenge Uruguay's comparable plain packaging cigarette rules. In the first "jurisdictional" round of this ICSID dispute, Philip Morris persuaded the arbitrators that an "investment" had indeed been made in Uruguay on the basis of its economic contribution to development, despite smoking's adverse effects on the people and economy of that country.

Reacting negatively to investor-state arbitrations, some developing world BITs, for example the Indian

Model BIT and the Southern African Development Community (SADC) Model BIT, require foreign investors to first exhaust local remedies. South Africa is actively terminating its BITs in favor of national investment code rules. Australia, Indonesia, South Africa, Japan and Brazil have started moving away from investor-state arbitrations, replacing them with state-to-state dispute settlement, including the World Court and Permanent Court of Arbitration in The Hague, Ombudsmen, conciliation, and diplomatic remedies. State-to-state remedies force foreign investors to seek remedies via their home governments, very different from investor-state arbitration mechanisms.

UNITED STATES BITs

To promote national treatment and protect U.S. investors abroad, the United States embarked on a BIT program in the early 1980s. The BIT program followed earlier extensive use of Friendship, Commerce, and Navigation (FCNs) treaties, some of which provided for diplomatic state-to-state protection for U.S. foreign investors. Some U.S. FCNs remain in effect, e.g. the U.S.-Japan FCN. Unlike the FCNs, the Model U.S. BIT distinguishes treatment of foreign-owned, domestically incorporated subsidiaries and branches of foreign firms for some provisions, particularly employment. As a result of *Sumitomo Shoji America v. Avagliano,* 457 U.S. 176 (1982), the Japan-U.S. FCN treaty afforded no protection to a foreign company using its nationals in hiring inside the United States. See

Chapter 6. Under the typical U.S. BIT, explicit freedom to hire nationals exists in a narrow range of management provisions.

The United States has entered into approximately 50 bilateral investment treaties (BITs), as well as about 20 free trade agreements that contain comparable foreign investment coverage. A compilation of these treaties and agreements can be found at http://www.ustr.gov. Most of the BITs were negotiated with small developing countries, though the United States has signed a BIT with Argentina, Egypt, Turkey and a number of Eastern European countries. These agreements generally repeat the foreign investor rights and investor-state claims procedures found in NAFTA. See Chapter 8. The United States is actively negotiating a BIT with China.

Numerous U.S. investors have filed and frequently won arbitration awards for damages against Argentina. Under U.S. law, ICSID awards (below) are given full faith and credit in federal courts. The Federal Arbitration Act does not apply, and reliance on the New York Convention is not needed. Hence the enforcement rate of ICSID awards in U.S. courts is high. Argentina has as a rule unsuccessfully defended itself on foreign sovereign immunity grounds. One court held that Argentina waived its immunity by becoming a party to ICSID, and further noted that the U.S. Foreign Sovereign Immunities Act exempts arbitration awards. See *Blue Ridge Investments v. Argentina*,

902 F.Supp.2d 367 (S.D.N.Y 2012), affirmed 735 F.3d 72 (2d Cir. 2013).

United States BITs do not prohibit nations from enacting foreign investment control laws. Such laws are common in developing nations, notably in Latin America. For coverage of the Mexican foreign investment law, see Chapter 8. But some developed nations, such as Canada, also screen foreign investments, particularly mergers and acquisitions, see Chapter 8. Most U.S. BITs provide that such laws should not interfere with any rights in the treaty, but since no rights to avoid national foreign investment controls are created, challenges to foreign investment control laws are generally not possible under U.S. BITs.

One important provision the United States seeks to include in its BITs is the "prompt, adequate and effective" concept of compensation subsequent to expropriation. For example, the Argentina-United States BIT uses language referring to compensation for the "fair market value . . . immediately before the expropriatory action." Many of the nations which have recently agreed to this language disputed its appropriateness during the nationalistic North-South dialogue of the 1960s and 1970s. But as they began to promote rather than restrict investment, the nations had to accept the idea that expropriated investment had to be compensated reasonably soon after the taking ("prompt"), based on a fair valuation ("adequate"), and in a realistic form ("effective").

Most BITs do not include provisions for consultations when differences arise in the interpretation of the treaty. The Argentina-United States and Sri Lanka-United States BITs are exceptions. U.S. BITs often provide for investor-state arbitration, sometimes with no necessary recourse to prior exhaustion of local remedies. The 2012 Model U.S. BIT is thought to have reduced the scope of foreign investor protections, but they remain very controversial in the U.S Trans-Pacific Partnership (TPP) and Transatlantic Trade and Investment (TTIP) negotiations. Ratification of the Canada-EU Comprehensive Economic and Trade Agreement of 2014 (CETA) has been delayed primarily due foreign investor-host state issues. It appears these may be resolved by creating a new foreign investment court comprised of Canadian, European and other jurists. A comparable approach may be adopted in the TTIP.

Regarding CETA and the TTIP, a fundamental question is whether ISDS is really needed when both parties have sophisticated judicial systems capable of handling foreign investor disputes.

FOREIGN INVESTMENT ARBITRATION: ICSID

Arbitration rules were adopted under the 1966 Convention on the Settlement of Investment Disputes between States and Nationals of Other States (ICSID). Over 150 countries are parties to this Convention, but Brazil, Canada (until 2013), Mexico, Russia, Thailand and Vietnam have notably

not joined the ICSID Convention. In recent years, Bolivia, Ecuador and Venezuela have withdrawn from ICSID, asserting it is biased toward investors and undermines national sovereignty.

The Convention was implemented in the United States by 22 U.S.C. § 1650 and § 1650a. An arbitral money award, rendered pursuant to the Convention, is entitled to the same full faith and credit in the United States as a final judgment of a court of general jurisdiction in a State of the United States.

The 1966 Convention provided for the establishment of an International Center for the Settlement of Investment Disputes (ICSID), as a non-financial organ of the World Bank (the International Bank for Reconstruction and Development). ICSID is designed to serve as a forum for both conciliation and arbitration of disputes between private investors and host governments. It provides an institutional framework within which arbitrators, selected by the disputing parties from an ICSID Panel of Arbitrators or from elsewhere, conduct arbitration in accordance with ICSID Rules of Procedure for Arbitration Proceedings. Arbitrations are held in Washington D.C. unless agreed otherwise.

Under the 1966 Convention (Article 25), ICSID's jurisdiction extends only "to any legal dispute arising directly out of an investment, between a Contracting State or . . . any subdivision . . . and a national of another Contracting State, which the parties to the dispute consent in writing to submit to the Centre. Where the parties have given their

consent, either in respect of future disputes or in respect of existing disputes, no party may withdraw its consent unilaterally." Consent by signatory states cannot unilaterally be withdrawn so long as that state is still a member of ICSID. Thus, ICSID is an attempt to institutionalize dispute resolution between States and non-State foreign investors. The disputes often arise under contracts between foreign investors and member states. Many sovereign consents to ICSID arbitrations are found in bilateral investment treaties (BITs, see above) and free trade agreements (see NAFTA in Chapter 8).

Unlike international commercial arbitrations, the law of the place of arbitration generally has no influence over ICSID arbitrations, which are therefore said to be "delocalized." If one party questions such jurisdiction (predicated upon disputes arising "directly out of" an investment, between a Contracting Party and the national of another, and written consent to submission), the issue may be decided by the arbitration tribunal (Rule 41). A party may seek annulment of any award only by an appeal to an ad hoc committee of persons drawn by the Administrative Council of ICSID from the Panel of Arbitrators under the Convention (Article 52). An ICSID award cannot be set aside by national courts or in any other way. Annulment is available only if the ICSID Tribunal was not properly constituted, exceeded its powers, seriously departed from a fundamental procedural rule, failed to state the reasons for its award, or included a member who practiced corruption.

Divergent ad hoc Annulment Committee decisions, particularly those known as the "Argentine Gas Sector Cases", have cast doubt on the legitimacy of ICSID annulment proceedings. Those cases concern challenges by foreign investors to emergency measures converting U. S. dollar bank deposits to pesos after Argentina's sovereign default in 2001. Depending on the Committee, with nearly identical facts, some investors have prevailed and others have lost arguments centered on whether Argentina was entitled to invoke public order and/or customary law of necessity defenses.

Enforcement of the award (with attachment of assets if needed) is automatically possible within ICSID signatory state courts, including those of the host state, without further review or consideration of setting aside the award. All member states must enforce ICSID awards as if they were final, binding judgments of their national courts. There is no need to go through the New York Convention procedures associated with international commercial arbitration awards.

ICSID ADDITIONAL FACILITY ARBITRATIONS

The Convention's 1966 jurisdictional limitations have prompted the ICSID Administrative Counsel to establish an Additional Facility for conducting conciliations and arbitrations for disputes which do not arise directly out of an investment and for investment disputes in which one party is not a Contracting State to the Convention or the national of a Contracting State. The Additional Facility is intended for use by parties having long-term relationships of special economic importance to the State party to the dispute and which involve the commitment of substantial resources on the part of either party. The Facility is not designed to service disputes which fall within the 1966 Convention or which are "ordinary commercial transaction" disputes. ICSID's Secretary General must give advance approval of an agreement contemplating use of the Additional Facility.

Because the Additional Facility operates outside the scope of the 1966 Convention, the Facility has its own Arbitration Rules. Under them, ICSID Convention rules regarding exclusion of other remedies, denial of provisional relief in national courts, internal annulment review, and recognition and enforcement do not apply. Additional Facility awards are subject to the set aside rules of the arbitral seat, and enforceable under the New York Convention.

The ICSID Convention has been used under numerous bilateral investment treaties (BITs). Because neither Canada (until December 2013) nor Mexico are ICSID signatories, the Additional Facility Rules have been employed in most NAFTA Chapter 11 investor-state arbitrations (see Chapter 8), and, more recently, in CAFTA-DR Chapter 10 investor-state arbitrations.

ENERGY CHARTER TREATY ARBITRATIONS

Some 60 nations have signed the Energy Charter Treaty of 1991. Article 26 permits foreign investors to take to arbitration disputes with signatory states concerning investment treatment rights contained in the Charter. These rights focus on national treatment, protection from direct or indirect expropriation, and contract adherence duties of the host state. Such arbitrations can be conducted under ICSID, UNCITRAL or Stockholm Chamber of Commerce rules.

In 2009, the Permanent Court of Arbitration in The Hague held that Russia's signing of the Charter, without subsequent ratification, was sufficient to confer jurisdiction. In 2014, that body ordered Russia to pay billions to the shareholders of Yukos for what it described as Russia's "devious and calculated expropriation" of assets designed to bankrupt Yukos, which happened. Because Yukos had unclean hands as a result of tax abuses, the arbitrators reduced the award by 25% to roughly $50 billion. Collection efforts are expected to center on Russian state assets and Rosneft, the Russian company that gained control of most of these assets in a series of politically driven bankruptcy proceedings. As of 2016, some success has been had in the Dutch, French and Belgian courts.

Another controversial invocation of ISDS before the Permanent Court of Arbitration occurred in 2011 when Germany, following the Fukushima disaster, decided to close its nuclear power industry.

Vattenfall, a Swedish operator of two nuclear power plants in Germany, is currently demanding billions in expropriation compensation under the Energy Charter Treaty.

CHAPTER 8

NAFTA FOREIGN INVESTMENT LAW AND ARBITRATIONS

Foreign Investor Rights   **Expropriation**

Arbitration of Investor-State Disputes

Case Examples

The North American Free Trade Agreement of 1994 (NAFTA) broke new ground on foreign investment law and dispute settlement. Drawing from bilateral investment treaty precedents (BITs, see Chapter 6), NAFTA expanded the scope of foreign investor rights and the use of arbitration to resolve investor-state disputes. It is presented here as a richly revealing and controversial case study, one which has had a substantial impact on subsequent BITs and trade and investment agreements. For more extensive coverage, see R. Folsom, *NAFTA, Free Trade and Foreign Investment in the Americas* (West Academic Publishing).

NAFTA AND MEXICAN FOREIGN INVESTMENT LAW

NAFTA places special emphasis on relaxation of Mexico's foreign investment controls. As outlined in Chapter 6, these controls find their roots in the revolutionary 1917 Mexican Constitution and the nationalization of foreign oil and gas interests in 1937, as well as the widespread adoption of foreign investment control commissions throughout Latin America during the 1970s. Under Mexican regulation of foreign investment since the 1940s, some industries were reserved for state ownership while others could only be owned by Mexicans. Foreigners were ordinarily allowed to invest in less sensitive industries, but often subject to mandatory joint venture requirements with majority Mexican ownership and "Calvo Clause" rules limiting foreign investor dispute remedies to those available under Mexican law.

In 1973, Mexico promulgated an Investment Law that mandated more use of joint ventures if approved by the National Foreign Investment Commission. This Law was the most restrictive of its kind in Mexican history. By the 1980s, after years of mismanagement and corruption while awash in petroleum dollars, Mexico had a massive national debt problem. Foreign investment regulations issued by Presidential decree in 1989 shifted significantly towards allowance of wholly-owned subsidiaries. However, these regulations conflicted with the 1973 Investment Law. These uncertainties were finally resolved in 1993 as a direct consequence of NAFTA when Mexico adopted a new Law on Foreign Investment.

The 1993 Law is much more permissive of foreign investment without prior approval of by the Mexican Investment Commission. Although adopted on the eve of NAFTA, the 1993 Law opens many of the same doors to all investors, not just those from NAFTA. Investment opportunities based upon the NAFTA agreement that are not generally available include the suspension of many performance requirements, the phased removal of market share caps on financial services, and reduced thresholds triggering Investment Commission review. In addition, NAFTA investors are not subject to Mexico's mandatory joint venture rule, nor its "Calvo Clause." Removal of these restrictions represents a major concession on the part of Mexico.

Acquisitions or sales of existing Mexican companies are generally subject to Commission review if exceeding $25 million U.S. This threshold increased to $150 million U.S. for NAFTA investors in 2003. For NAFTA investors, no permission from the National Commission is required to invest on a wholly-owned basis or acquire or sell Mexican companies whose values fall below this threshold.

NAFTA FOREIGN INVESTOR RIGHTS

In an unusual provision, Article 1112 subordinates all of Chapter 11 on investment to the rest of the NAFTA agreement. In other words, if there are inconsistencies between Chapter 11 and other parts of the NAFTA agreement, those other parts are supreme. That said, NAFTA provides investors and their investments with a number of important rights.

Canadian, Mexican and United States citizens, permanently resident aliens, and other designated persons are eligible to benefit from NAFTA's investment rules. In addition, most private and public, profit and nonprofit businesses "constituted or organized" under Canadian, Mexican or United States law also qualify. This coverage specifically includes businesses operating as corporations, partnerships, trusts, sole proprietorships, joint ventures and business associations.

Furthermore, in a notable change from CUSFTA, it is not necessary for such businesses to be owned or controlled by Canadian, Mexican or U.S. nationals or enterprises. As with services, this means that businesses owned by anyone which are "constituted or organized" inside NAFTA benefit from the agreement *provided* they carry on substantial business activities in North America. Thus Asians, Europeans and Latin Americans (for example) can invest in North America and benefit from NAFTA. See *Corn Syrup Sweeteners* below. Exceptions are made for NAFTA businesses owned or controlled by third parties from countries lacking diplomatic relations with or economically embargoed by Canada, Mexico or the United States.

Beneficiaries of NAFTA rights enjoy a broad definition of "investment." This definition includes most stocks, bonds, loans, and income, profit or asset interests. Real estate, tangible or intangible (intellectual) business property, turnkey or construction contracts, concessions, and licensing and franchising contracts are also generally included. However, under Annex III, each member state reserves certain economic activities to its state or domestic investors. Mexico has done so under its

1993 Foreign Investment Law. For purposes of Chapter 11, investment is defined so as to exclude claims to money arising solely from commercial contracts for the sale of goods or services, or trade financing, and claims for money that do not involve the interests noted above.

TREATMENT OF FOREIGN INVESTORS AND INVESTMENTS

The NAFTA agreement establishes a so-called "minimum standard of treatment" for NAFTA investors and investments which is "treatment in accordance with international law," including "fair and equitable treatment and full protection and security" (Article 1105.) For example, if losses occur due to armed conflict or civil strife, NAFTA investors and investments must be accorded nondiscriminatory treatment in response.

An official 2001 NAFTA interpretative ruling indicates that Article 1105 embraces treatment in accordance with "customary" international law, a ruling intended to limit the scope of protection afforded to foreign investors. Subsequent NAFTA arbitral bodies have consequently limited claims of unfair and inequitable treatment to state conduct that is arbitrary, grossly unfair, unjust or idiosyncratic, discriminatory, or lacking in due process offending judicial or administrative propriety. Refinements of the customary international law standard under NAFTA Chapter 11 refer to "sufficiently egregious and shocking" state acts that amount to gross denials of justice, manifest arbitrariness, blatant unfairness, a complete lack of due process, evident discrimination or a manifest lack of reasons. In addition, limiting definitions of "fair and equitable treatment" and "full protection and security" have been established in subsequent U.S free trade agreements (see below).

Beyond this minimum, NAFTA investors and their investments are entitled to the better of national or most-favored-nation treatment from federal governments. Such treatment rights extend to establishing, acquiring, expanding, managing, conducting, operating, and selling or disposing of investments. From state or provincial governments, NAFTA investors and their investments are entitled to receive the most-favored treatment those governments grant their own investors and investments. Along these lines, United Parcel Service found Mexico lacking when it was initially limited to using smaller vans than Mexican competitors. UPS persuaded the United States to lodge a complaint under Chapter 20 which led to intergovernmental consultations followed by NAFTA Commission mediation. These efforts lasted many months but eventually UPS got permission to use larger vans.

Article 1102 of NAFTA prohibits requiring minimum levels of equity holdings by nationals of the host government. Hence the historic bias in Mexican law towards mandatory joint ventures is overcome by NAFTA. No investor can be forced on grounds of nationality to sell or dispose of a qualified investment. Mandatory appointment of senior managers on the basis of nationality is also contrary to NAFTA. However, it is permissible to require boards of directors and corporate committees with majorities from one nationality or residence, provided this does not materially impair the investor's ability to exercise control. Canadian law often makes such stipulations. Residency requirements are generally authorized if there is no impairment of the treaty rights of NAFTA investors.

Article 1106 of NAFTA prohibits various investment performance obligations, including tax-related measures, in a scope that surpasses the WTO Agreement on Trade-Related Investment Measures (TRIMs, see Chapter 1). Requirements relating to exports, domestic content, domestic purchases, trade balancing of foreign exchange inflows or earnings, import/export ratios, technology transfers, and regional or global sales exclusivity ("product mandates") are broadly prohibited. All other types of investment-related performance requirements, such as employment and research and development obligations, are not prohibited and therefore presumably lawful.

Article 1106.3 of NAFTA further prohibits conditioning the receipt or continued receipt of "an advantage" (e.g., a government subsidy or tax benefit) on compliance with requirements relating to domestic content, domestic purchases, domestic sales restraints or trade balancing. But "advantages" can be given when the requirements concern production location, provision of services, training or employing workers, constructing or expanding facilities, or carrying out research and development locally. By way of exception, domestic content or purchase requirements *and* advantages can be linked to investor compliance with: (1) Laws and regulations that are consistent with NAFTA; (2) laws necessary to protect human, animal or plant life or health; or (3) laws needed to conserve living or non-living exhaustible natural resources. However, such requirements cannot be applied arbitrarily or unjustifiably, and may not constitute a disguised restraint on trade or investment.

All monetary transfers relating to NAFTA investments are to be allowed "freely and without delay." (Article 1109) Such transfers must be possible in a "freely usable currency" at the market rate of exchange prevailing in spot transactions on the transfer date. For these purposes, monetary transfers specifically include profits, dividends, interest, capital gains, royalties, management, technical assistance and other fees, returns in kind, and funds derived from the investment. Sale or liquidation proceeds, contract payments, compensatory payments for expropriation and NAFTA dispute settlement payments are also encompassed.

Requiring investment-related monetary transfers or penalizing them is prohibited. However, such transfers can be controlled in an equitable, nondiscriminatory and good faith application of bankruptcy, insolvency, creditors' rights, securities, criminal, currency reporting and satisfaction of judgment laws. Whereas tax withholding was a justifiable basis for restricting monetary transfers under CUSFTA, this is not the case under NAFTA. Special restraints may arise in connection with balance of payments problems and taxation laws.

EXPROPRIATION

Article 1110 of NAFTA generally prohibits direct or indirect nationalization or expropriation of NAFTA investments. Measures "tantamount to" nationalization or expropriation, such as creeping expropriation or confiscatory taxation, are also prohibited. Expropriation, nationalization or tantamount measures may occur for public purposes on a nondiscriminatory basis in accordance with due process of law and NAFTA's "minimum level of treatment" (above). Post-NAFTA U.S. free trade agreements have expressly limited the possibility of succeeding with "indirect" regulatory taking expropriation claims (see below).

Any authorized expropriation must result in payment of compensation without delay. The amount of payment must be equivalent to the fair market value of the investment immediately prior to expropriation. In valuing the investment, going concern value, asset value (including declared tax values of tangible property) and other appropriate factors must be considered. Payment must be made in a manner that is fully realizable, such as in a "G7" currency (U.S. dollars, Canadian dollars, EUROS, British pounds sterling, Japanese yen). Interest at a commercially reasonable rate must also be included. If payment is made in Mexican pesos, this amount must be calculated as of the expropriation date in a G7 currency plus interest.

Certain governmental acts are not treated as expropriations. For example, NAFTA specifies that nondiscriminatory measures of general application that impose costs on defaulting debtors are not tantamount to expropriation of a bond or loan *solely* for that reason. Compulsory licensing of intellectual property rights is not an expropriation. Revocation, limitation or creation of such rights as allowed by Chapter 17 of NAFTA is also deemed not an expropriation. In one Chapter 11 proceeding, lawful, court-approved annulment of a Mexican concession contract with a U.S. firm was determined by NAFTA arbitrators not to amount to an act of expropriation. No denial of justice in the Mexican courts was alleged (*Azinian v. Mexico*, 1999).

The NAFTA provisions embody an historic change in Mexico's position on expropriation law. Without explicitly saying so, Mexico has essentially embraced the U.S. position that under "international law" expropriation of foreign investments requires "prompt, adequate and effective" compensation. Mexico had specifically rejected this standard in negotiating a settlement of its oil and gas (and land) expropriations in the 1930s. Down through the years Mexico adamantly clung to its view that compensation would only be paid according to Mexican law. For investors protected under NAFTA (which are not just

Canadian and U.S. investors), Chapter 11 represents the dawn of a new era.

EXCEPTIONS AND RESERVATIONS, THE ENVIRONMENT

Annexes I–IV of the NAFTA agreement reveal a host of investment-related reservations and exceptions. Many pre-existing, non-conforming regulations were grandfathered though most (not including basic telecommunications, social services and maritime services) are subject to a standstill agreement intended to avoid relapses into greater protection. In contrast, regulations promoting investment "sensitive to environmental concerns" are expressly authorized. Mexico's tradition of assessing the environmental impact of foreign investments will therefore continue. There is also a formal recognition that creating exceptions to environmental laws to encourage NAFTA investors to establish, acquire, expand or retain their investments is inappropriate. However, NAFTA's Chapter 20 dispute settlement mechanism cannot be invoked concerning this "commitment." Only intergovernmental consultations are mandatory.

Other investment-related exceptions concern government procurement, subsidies, export promotion, foreign aid and preferential trade arrangements. These exceptions apply mostly to the rules on nondiscriminatory treatment and performance requirements. Most general exceptions to NAFTA, such as for Canadian cultural industries, also apply to its investment rules. The general national security exception, for example, allows the United States to block the acquisition of U.S. companies by foreigners (including Canadians and Mexicans) under FINSA ("Exon-Florio") regulations (see Chapter 5).

ARBITRATION OF FOREIGN INVESTOR-HOST STATE DISPUTES UNDER NAFTA

NAFTA has created a highly innovative and increasingly controversial investment dispute settlement system. This system provides a way for foreign investors to challenge governmental and state enterprise acts and recover damages for violation of rights established in Chapter 11. Remarkably, investors may not only assert claims as individuals, but also on behalf of NAFTA enterprises they own or control directly or indirectly (Article 1117). This authorization avoids one of international law's most famous problems. . . "standing to sue" when the investor's only loss or damage is injury to its investment abroad.

Chapter 20 NAFTA dispute settlement does not apply to "investor-state disputes." Such disputes are instead subject to binding arbitration, another major concession on the part of Mexico which has always adhered to the "Calvo Doctrine." That doctrine (widely followed in Latin America) requires foreign investors to forego protection by their home governments, be treated as Mexican nationals, and pursue legal remedies exclusively in Mexico. For an example, *see* Article 27 of the Mexican Constitution.

Individual investors claiming that a government has breached NAFTA investment or state enterprise obligations, or that one of its monopolies has done so, commence the dispute resolution process. All claims are filed against the federal government even when it is state, provincial or local government action that is being challenged. This can place Canada, Mexico and the United States in the awkward position of defending sub-central governmental acts. *See Metalclad* and *Loewen* below.

The investor must allege that the breach of NAFTA caused loss or damage. Such claims must be asserted no later than three years after the date when knowledge of the alleged breach and knowledge of the loss or damage was first acquired or should have been first acquired. However, decisions by the Canadian or Mexican foreign investment control commissions, national security actions, and Canadian cultural industry reservations cannot be the basis for such a claim. Moreover, a host of reservations and exceptions contained in Chapter 11B deny access to NAFTA's investor-state arbitration remedy. Even so, as outlined below, the number of claims being filed is rising, some claims are producing unexpected results, and the process itself, though now quite transparent, is under dispute.

Before submitting a claim to arbitration, individual investors must give 90 days' advance notice to the host country. Such notice must include an explanation of the issues, their factual basis and remedies sought. Claimants must also consent in writing to arbitrate under the procedures established in the NAFTA agreement. They *must waive* in writing their rights to initiate or continue any other damages proceedings. Individual investors need not, however, waive their rights to injunctive, declaratory or other extraordinary relief (not involving damages). These remedies may not be awarded through NAFTA arbitration of investor-state disputes.

ARBITRATION PROCEDURES, APPEALS AND REMEDIES

The NAFTA nations consented unconditionally in advance to the submission of investor claims to arbitration under NAFTA procedures. Furthermore, they agreed not to assert insurance payments or other investor indemnification rights as a defense, counterclaim, right of setoff or otherwise.

The investor submitting a claim to arbitration against a NAFTA state ordinarily can elect between the following arbitration rules:

(1)   The ICSID Convention (see Chapter 2) if both member states adhere. (At present the United States and Canada have ratified ICSID);

(2)   The Additional Facility Rules of ICSID provided one member state adheres to the ICSID Convention; or

(3)   The U.N.-derived UNCITRAL Arbitration Rules.

Until Canada's ratification of ICSID in 2013, joining the United States but not Mexico, opens the door to investor-state claims under ICSID or the UNCITRAL Rules. The key difference between them is that ICSID has its own annulment procedures (see Chapter 7), which exclude use of the New York Convention on enforcement of arbitral awards (below). NAFTA investor-state tribunals have three panelists. The investor and the state each choose one arbitrator. If possible, the third presiding panelist is chosen by agreement. The ICSID Secretary-General selects the presiding arbitrator if agreement is not reached within 90 days. That person is chosen from a consensus roster of acceptable names, but may not be a national from either side of the dispute.

Investor-state tribunals must decide the dispute in accordance with the NAFTA agreement and "applicable rules of international law." The responding state may raise defenses based upon reservations or exceptions contained in Annexes I–IV to the NAFTA agreement. In such instances, the NAFTA Commission (not the arbitration panel) will generally issue a binding ruling on the validity of such a defense. Defenses based upon permissible regulation of monetary transfers by financial institutions are generally decided by the NAFTA Financial Services Committee.

By agreement of the parties, the investor-state arbitration tribunal can obtain expert reports on factual issues concerning environmental, health, safety or other scientific matters. The tribunal may also order temporary relief measures to preserve rights or the full effectiveness of its jurisdiction. It may, for example, order the preservation of evidence. The tribunal cannot, however, order attachment or enjoin governmental regulations that are being challenged.

NAFTA investor-state tribunals are authorized to award investors or NAFTA enterprises actual *damages* and interest, or restitution of property, or both. At this writing, damages have been awarded against and paid by Canada and Mexico, but not the United States. See *Metalclad* and *S.D. Myers* below. If the award is to an enterprise, any person may *also* pursue relief under "applicable domestic law." If restitution is ordered, the responsible member state may provide monetary damages and interest instead. NAFTA tribunals can apportion legal fees between the parties at their discretion. Such fees routinely run into hundreds of thousands, if not millions, of dollars. The costs of administering Chapter 11 tribunals, including generous fees for the arbitrators, often exceed $500,000. The losing party is typically required to pay these costs.

The award of the tribunal is binding on the parties, but subject to revision or annulment in the courts of the arbitration's *situs*. See *Metalclad* and *S.D. Myers* below. Absent agreement, the arbitrators determine *situs*. Professor Brower and others have argued that a standing appellate body not unlike that of the WTO would provide greater legitimacy and uniformity to Chapter 11 arbitrations. Awards are specifically not "precedent" in future NAFTA arbitrations (Article 1136), yet routinely cited and argued in Chapter 11 proceedings and decisions. NAFTA investor-state arbitration awards are supposed to be honored. Should this not occur, the investor may seek enforcement of the award. NAFTA nations have agreed to provide the means for such enforcement. The NAFTA investor-state dispute settlement system meets the various requirements of the ICSID Convention, its Additional Facility Rules, the New York Convention on Recognition and Enforcement of Foreign Arbitral Awards (1958), and the Inter-American Convention on International Commercial Arbitration (1975).

Should it become necessary to judicially enforce an investor-state arbitration award, the New York Convention provides a likely recourse as all three nations adhere to it. However, U.S. courts have held the grounds for denying enforcement of NAFTA awards under the New York Convention limited strictly to its provisions. Thus, the longstanding U.S. doctrine of denying enforcement when arbitrators "manifestly disregard the law", a doctrine not incorporated in the New York Convention, was not applied in a NAFTA award enforcement proceeding.

If there is no compliance with the award and enforcement proceedings fail, the investor's government may as a last recourse commence intergovernmental dispute settlement under Chapter 20 of NAFTA. This panel rules on whether noncompliance inconsistent with the NAFTA agreement has occurred and can recommend compliance. If compliance still does not follow, benefits granted under NAFTA to the noncomplying nation may be suspended.

FOREIGN INVESTOR CLAIMS AGAINST HOST STATES UNDER NAFTA

Investors have not hesitated to invoke the innovative investor-state arbitration procedures authorized under Section B of Chapter 11 of NAFTA. Since 2001, in an official Interpretation, Chapter 11 has been construed as not imposing a general duty of confidentiality. The NAFTA governments have therefore released all documents submitted to or issued by Chapter 11 arbitration tribunals. A particularly good collection of these materials can be found at http://www.naftaclaims. com/. Moreover, since late 2003 open Chapter 11 hearings have become the rule, as have permissive procedures for non-party submissions (amicus curiae).

Many investors allege state action that is "tantamount to expropriation." This is a claim that Article 1110 authorizes and one which could be construed to fit many fact patterns. National treatment and the NAFTA minimum standard of treatment (see above) are also commonly disputed. Some examples of these disputes follow.

Metalclad. A prominent dispute involved Metalclad Corp. of California, which had acquired a hazardous waste site operated by a Mexican company in Guadalcazar, San Luis Potosi subject to various federal approvals, all of which were obtained. State and local opposition to opening the site after an expensive clean-up resulted in the denial of a building permit in a newly created "ecological zone." Metalclad claimed these acts were tantamount to expropriation, and denial of national and the NAFTA minimum standards of treatment. It sought $90 million in damages from the Mexican federal government, which despite having supported the Metalclad contract was obliged to defend the hostile local and state actions. Metalclad received an award of $16 million under NAFTA Chapter 11 in 2000. The arbitration was conducted under the ICSID Additional Facility rules.

Mexico instituted judicial proceedings to set aside the award in British Columbia, the arbitration's legal *situs*. Canada intervened in support of Mexico. The arbitrators had found the Mexican regulatory action a breach of NAFTA's minimum standard based on a lack of "transparency," and regulatory acts tantamount to expropriation without adequate compensation.

Despite a Canadian brief in support of Mexico, the British Columbia Supreme Court, ruling under the B.C. International Arbitration Act, agreed that the expropriation decision fell within the scope of the dispute submitted and was therefore valid. It rejected, however, the transparency decision as beyond the scope of the submission. The court found no transparency obligations in Chapter 11, and none as a matter of *customary* international law (which traditionally bars only "egregious," "outrageous" or "shocking" conduct). Mexico subsequently paid Metalclad approximately $16 million U.S., the first payment by a state to an investor under Chapter 11.

Ethyl and Methanex. A second prominent dispute involved Ethyl Corp. of the USA, which claimed $250 million U.S. damages against the Canadian government as a consequence of 1997 federal legislation banning importation or interprovincial trade of the gasoline additive, MMT. Canada was the first country to ban MMT as a pollution and health hazard, although California has also done so. MMT is a manganese-based octane enhancer alleged to interfere with the proper functioning of catalytic converters. Ethyl Corp. is the sole producer of MMT in North America. Ethyl claimed that the new law was tantamount to expropriation, violated NAFTA's national treatment standards and constituted an unlawful Canadian-content performance requirement (because the ban would favor Canadian ethanol as a substitute for MMT).

A dispute resolution panel under Canada's Agreement on Internal Trade struck down the interprovincial trade ban. In 1998, Canada withdrew its ban on MMT and paid $13 million to Ethyl Corp. Ethyl then withdrew its $250 million arbitration claim. Canada noted the current lack of scientific evidence documenting MMT harm, an apparent abandonment of the "precautionary principle." Environmentalists decried evidence of NAFTA's negative impact, and Europeans cited *Ethyl* as good reason to reject multilateral investment guarantee agreements in the OECD

(Organization for Economic Cooperation and Development). Both groups believe Chapter 11 has created a privileged class of "super-citizens" who are a threat to state sovereignty.

Methanex Corp. of Canada submitted a claim that was in some ways the reverse of *Ethyl*. Methanex claimed that California's ban of the MTBE gasoline additive (for which it makes feedstock) amounted to an expropriation of its business interests and violated its minimum treatment rights. It sought $970 million in damages and simultaneously filed a petition under the North American Environmental Cooperation Agreement asserting that California failed to enforce its gasoline storage regulations, which Methanex saw as the source of MTBE water pollution. In 2002, the *Methenex* panel working under the UNCITRAL Rules largely rejected the complaint on jurisdictional grounds, allowing a limited re-filing on the question of intentional injury. The *Methanex* panel notably ruled that it would accept NGO amicus briefs, in this instance from the International Institute for Sustainable Development. This position was subsequently ratified for all Chapter 11 arbitrations by the NAFTA Free Trade Commission in 2003.

Loewen. The Loewen Group of Canada was held liable by a jury in 1995 to $500 million in a Mississippi breach of a funeral home contract suit. The case was settled for $150 million after the Mississippi Supreme Court required posting a $625 million bond prior to appealing the jury's verdict, a sum in excess of Loewen's net worth. In 1998,

Loewen filed a claim under NAFTA alleging discrimination, denial of the minimum NAFTA standard of treatment, and uncompensated expropriation. This claim, like that of Ethyl Corp., was destined for controversy. Among other things, it challenged the discretion of American juries in awarding punitive damages. Note that it does so in a forum that does not give the American Trial Lawyers Association an opportunity to respond.

In 2003, the *Loewen* panel, calling the Mississippi decision "a disgrace," nevertheless ruled heavily against the bankrupt funeral home giant because its status as a Canadian (versus U.S.) company entitled to NAFTA foreign investor rights was in doubt. Loewen had consolidated its numerous U.S. funeral home subsidiaries into a Delaware holding company, and hence its "foreign" status was not continuous. In a later clarification, the panel stressed that Loewen's failure to appeal or seek review of the judgment was critical to their denial of its claim. Watch for a re-run challenging American punitive damages in the future.

Pope & Talbot. Pope & Talbot, Inc. of Portland, Oregon claimed that the 1996 Softwood Lumber Agreement (see Chapter 2) violated the national treatment, most-favored-nation treatment, minimum treatment and performance requirements rules of NAFTA. The claim asserted that the company's British Columbia subsidiary was the victim of discrimination in that the Canadian export restraints required under that Agreement applied only to four Canadian provinces. Pope & Talbot sought $20 million in compensation from the Canadian government. Rejecting most of the claims, the *Pope and Talbot* panel found Canada did violate the NAFTA minimum standard of treatment in denying export authorization to the company's B.C. subsidiary.

Although the award was only about $460,000 U.S., the panel's reasoning set off fireworks. In its view, Article 1105 demanded something more than the level of treatment commanded by customary international law. "Fair and equitable treatment" and "full protection and security" were seen as "additive;" new and expansive norms created by NAFTA's novel investor protection regime.

The additive reading of *Pope & Talbot* was subsequently rejected by the British Columbia Supreme Court in *Metalclad* (above), and collectively negated by a binding interpretation of Article 1105 issued by the three NAFTA parties in 2001. This controversial, defensive interpretation "clarifies" that Article 1105 corresponds to and thus does not expand the *customary* international law standard of minimum treatment (see *Metalclad* above), and that a breach of a NAFTA obligation does not ipso facto constitute a breach of that Article.

S.D. Myers. S.D. Myers is an Ohio company specializing in hazardous waste management of PCBs. Its Canadian affiliate imported PCBs from Ontario, to the consternation of the only Canadian PCB remediation company, Chem-Security of Alberta. In 1995, Canada banned PCB exports, intentionally giving Chem-Security a monopoly. S.D. Myers asserted this export ban violated the national treatment, performance requirements, expropriation and fair and equitable treatment provisions of Chapter 11. The arbitrators found in favor of S.D. Myers on the national treatment and fair and equitable treatment claims, awarding over $6,000,000 CDN in damages. Canada appealed to the courts of Ontario, the situs of the arbitration, and lost. In Ontario, at least, considerable deference is given to arbitral decisions. Compare British Columbia in *Metalclad* below. Subsequently, S. D. Myers and Canada settled the dispute.

Mondev. Mondev is a Canadian company engaged in commercial real estate development. It pursued various claims against the City of Boston and the Boston Redevelopment Authority in the Massachusetts courts, which were denied on sovereign immunity grounds. Mondev then filed a Chapter 11 claim arguing primarily unfair and inequitable treatment in the Massachusetts courts.

In its complaint, Mondev directly challenged the 2001 Interpretation of Article 1105, arguing it was de facto an amendment of the NAFTA agreement. Mondev also argued that customary international law should be construed in light of conclusions reached under hundreds of bilateral investment treaties and modern judgments. The tribunal recognized that fair and equitable treatment had evolved by 1994 (NAFTA's effective date) beyond what is "egregious" or "outrageous" (a frequently cited standard derived from *Neer v. Mexico*, 21 Am.

J. Int'l L. 555 (1927) (U.S. and Mexico General Claims Commission), and that bad faith on the part of states need not be shown. It then ruled against Mondev's denial of justice claims.

Waste Management. Waste Management, through its Mexican subsidiary, contracted for waste disposal, street cleaning and landfill services with the city of Acapulco. When Acapulco allegedly failed to honor various contract terms, Waste Management asserted unfair and inequitable treatment in its Chapter 11 claim. Under customary international law, the tribunal held Acapulco would be liable if its conduct was "arbitrary, grossly unfair, unjust or idiosyncratic . . . [or] discriminatory . . . exposing the claimant to sectional or racial prejudice, or involves a lack of due process leading to an outcome that offends judicial propriety." In applying this standard, the tribunal deemed breach of representations by Acapulco reasonably relied upon by Waste Management "relevant" to its denial of unfair and inequitable treatment findings.

Glamis. A Canadian mining company, Glamis, alleged that government regulations limiting the impact of open-pit mining and protecting indigenous peoples' religious sites made its *proposed* California gold mine unprofitable. Under Chapter 11, it asserted violations of the NAFTA rules against government acts tantamount to expropriation, and denial of fair and equitable treatment. In June of 2009, a Chapter 11 tribunal accepted, in principle, that "regulatory taking" measures could amount to "creeping expropriation." That said, the tribunal undertook a detailed accounting of Glamis' alleged losses and found the mine project still had a net positive value of $20 million U.S. Hence it concluded Glamis was not impacted sufficiently to support a NAFTA expropriation claim.

While the outcome once again allowed the United States to avoid paying Chapter 11 damages, the willingness of the tribunal to entertain a regulatory taking claim was controversial (to put it mildly) and once again raised concerns that foreign investors may have greater rights under NAFTA than U.S. investors possess under United States law. *Glamis* continues the trend in NAFTA arbitrations of treating fair and equitable treatment as an evolving customary international law standard, referencing *inter alia* BIT arbitration decisions.

Chemtura. Crompton (Chemtura) Corp. of the USA filed a "tantamount to expropriation" Chapter 11 complaint against Canada after it banned lindane-based pesticides. The arbitral tribunal, in 2010, unanimously noted that this ban had been undertaken in a non-discriminatory manner motivated by human health and environmental concerns. As such, it was a valid exercise of Canada's police powers and did not constitute expropriation.

Corn Syrup Sweeteners. Late in 2009, a third Chapter 11 tribunal ruled against Mexico concerning its 20% tax from 2002 to 2007 on the production and sale of soft drinks using High Fructose Corn Syrup (HFCS). This tax was imposed in the context of a trade dispute between the U.S.

and Mexico over HFCS exports south of the border and Mexican sugar exports headed north. U.S. agribusiness giants Cargill, Corn Products International and Archer Daniels Midlands, along with British Tate and Lyle's U.S. subsidiary, successfully argued that the tax constituted a "performance requirement" in violation of NAFTA Article 1106. The Mexican government was ordered to pay a total of $170 million plus interest.

AbitibiBowater. In August 2010, the Canadian federal government agreed to pay $130 million CDN to settle a Chapter 11 claim by a U.S. pulp and paper multinational, AbitibiBowater (AB). In 2008, AB closed a longstanding mill in Newfoundland via bankruptcy, terminating 800 workers without severance. Newfoundland passed a law returning, without compensation, the company's water and timber rights to the crown, and expropriating with compensation AB lands, buildings and dams in the province. AB asserted NAFTA expropriation violations. This settlement, along with the *Glamis* decision (above), has raised concerns that resource-related NAFTA investor claims may increase. For example, a Brazilian company with a U.S. subsidiary received a $15 million settlement form Canada after alleging permit delays for rock quarrying.

Apotex. Apotex is a Canadian manufacturer of generic pharmaceuticals. It has filed at least three Chapter 11 claims against the United States. These filings challenge U.S. federal court decisions denying its efforts to obtain "patent certainty" for drugs (in order to allow its generic versions to proceed), FDA denial of approval for another Apotex generic drug, and FDA import inspection practices for drugs. All of these complaints were pending as of this writing.

Exxon/Mobil. Exxon/Mobil challenged Canadian Petroleum Board rules mandating fees to support R & D in Newfoundland and Labrador. Nearby, Exxon/Mobil has developed oil fields offshore. A Chapter 11 panel affirmed in 2012 that these fees amounted to NAFTA-prohibited "performance requirements." The amount of damages is as yet undetermined, and may be influenced by increased equity stakes the provinces have obtained in the oil fields.

Bilcon. Bilcon of Delaware sought to develop a quarry and marine terminal in Nova Scotia, subject to environmental review. A joint federal/province review denied approval based upon "incompatibility with community core values". Bilcon alleged NAFTA Chapter 11 violations of the national and minimum treatment standards (the latter claim focused on fair and equitable treatment). By agreement, the UNCITRAL Rules controlled before the Permanent Court of Arbitration. In a split 2015 decision, the arbitrators held in favor of Bilcon, noting particularly an absence of fair notice and treatment in the environmental review process, and a fundamental departure from the "likely significant adverse effects after mitigation" standard of evaluation required by Canadian law.

Other NAFTA/CAFTA Claims of Note. Several U.S. companies have commenced Chapter 11 proceedings against Canada asserting that Ontario's requirement that that a percentage of its green energy program be locally sourced excludes and damages them. Another U.S. firm is seeking damages based on Quebec's moratorium on "fracking", the use of water and chemicals to release sub-surface oil and gas reserves. Eli Lilly has filed a claim for damages because Canadian courts have invalidated the patent on one of its drugs.

One of the largest banks in France, the convoluted owner via a Nevada corporation of a share in Dominican Republic electric utilities, argued expropriation claims against the Dominican Republic after scheduled electricity rates increases were delayed. A parallel claim was filed under the France-DR Bilateral Investment Treaty (BIT). After initial success under the BIT claim, the bank obtained a $26.5 million settlement of both claims from the DR.

The U.S. investor in Guatemala's privatized railroad system collected over $11 million after a CAFTA panel ruled that Guatemala's moves to revoke its contract amounted to "unfair and inequitable treatment." Claims are also pending against Guatemala by privatized owners (mostly Spanish, with a U.S. minority investor) of its electricity distribution system. The U.S. investor challenges governmentally lowered rates.

After President Obama's rejection in 2015 of the Keystone Pipeline from Alberta's tar sands to Texas,

Trans Canada has filed a Chapter 11 claim against the United States alleging discriminatory (non-national) treatment, breach of the duty of most-favored-nation treatment, U.S. governmental acts tantamount to expropriation, and unfair and inequitable treatment. Trans Canada seeks in excess of $15 billion in damages.

POST-NAFTA SUMMARY

These examples of investor-state claims under NAFTA and CAFTA represent only the tip of the iceberg. Lawyers have learned that U.S. FTAs can be used to challenge or threaten to challenge all sorts of existing or proposed government actions, particularly regulatory decisions. There is leverage in the broad investor rights, and in its mandatory arbitral procedures. No wonder Australia refused to allow investor-state arbitrations in its free trade agreement with the United States.

Whether, and if so in what form, they will be replicated in the proposed Free Trade Area of the Americas, Trans-Pacific Partnership and Transatlantic Trade and Investment Partnership agreements is hotly contested. Already, mutations on the law of investor-state claims have appeared in the U.S.-Chile/Singapore/Bahrain/Oman/Morocco/South Korea/CAFTA-DR/Panama/Peru and Colombia free trade agreements. Regarding investor-state claims, for example, post-NAFTA U.S. free trade agreements insert the word "customary" before international law in defining the minimum standard of treatment to which foreign investors are entitled. This insertion tracks the official 2001 Interpretation issued in that regard under NAFTA. Further, the contested terms "fair and equitable treatment" and "full protection and security" do not require treatment in addition to or beyond that customary standard, and do not create additional substantive rights. This language is defined for the first time:

"fair and equitable treatment" includes the obligation not to deny justice in criminal, civil, or administrative adjudicatory proceedings in accordance with the principle of due process embodied in the principal legal systems of the world; and

"full protection and security" requires each Party to provide the level of police protection required under customary international law.

More significantly perhaps, starting with the U.S.-Chile FTA, these agreements contain an Annex restricting the scope of "indirect expropriation" claims:

Except in rare circumstances, nondiscriminatory regulatory actions by a Party that are designed and applied to protect legitimate public welfare objectives, such as public health, safety and the environment, do not constitute indirect expropriations.

Hence the potential for succeeding with "regulatory takings" investor-state claims has been reduced. The CAFTA-DR agreement also anticipates creating an appellate body of some sort for investor-state arbitration decisions.

These mutations are in part a response to Congressional concerns expressed in the Trade Promotion Authority (fast-track) Act of 2002 that Chapter 11 of NAFTA may accord "greater substantive rights" to foreigners with respect to investment protection than enjoyed by U.S. investors in the United States. Similar concerns were raised by Congress in adopting fast track in 2015, targeting U.S. participation in the Trans-Pacific (TPP) and Transatlantic (TTIP) Partnership negotiations.

The Trans-Pacific agreement awaiting ratification by 12 nations contains a number of attempts at ISDS reform. For example, financial stability regulation falls outside indirect expropriation claims, tobacco regulation may not be challenged, mere frustration of profit expectations is insufficient to pursue investor-state arbitrations, the burden of proof falls on investor claimants, no shell companies may be used to access investor-state arbitral remedies, and state-owned enterprises along with authorized government agents are made subject to the Trans-Pacific ISDS regime. In addition, the TPP agreement mandates public access to hearings and documents, allows amicus briefs, facilitates expedited dismissals of frivolous claims, and generally protects existing IP license royalties and durations from alteration.

INDEX

References are to Pages